Spiritwalker

SPIRITWALKER

Messages from the Future

Hank Wesselman

BANTAM BOOKS

New York   Toronto   London   Sydney   Auckland

SPIRITWALKER

A Bantam Book / August 1995

All rights reserved.
Copyright © 1995 by Henry Wesselman.

BOOK DESIGN BY GLEN M. EDELSTEIN.

Library of Congress Cataloging-in-Publication Data

Wesselman, Henry Barnard.
    Spiritwalker : messages from the future / Hank Wesselman.
        p.   cm.
    ISBN 0-553-09976-0
        1. Ecstasy—Case studies.   2. Voyages to the otherworld—Case studies.
3. Shamanism—Case studies.   4. Wesselman, Henry Barnard.
    I. Title.   II. Title: Spiritwalker.
    BL626.W47   1995
    291.4'2'092—dc20
    [B]   94-40469
                                                                            CIP

Published simultaneously in the United States and Canada

Bantam Books are published by Bantam Books, a division of Bantam Doubleday
Dell Publishing Group, Inc. Its trademark, consisting of the words "Bantam
Books" and the portrayal of a rooster, is Registered in U.S. Patent and Trademark
Office and in other countries. Marca Registrada. Bantam Books, 1540 Broadway,
New York, New York 10036.

PRINTED IN THE UNITED STATES OF AMERICA

BVG 10 9 8 7 6 5 4 3 2 1

To the lovely Jill Kuykendall,
the one who knows . . .
with deep gratitude and great affection.

It seems appropriate at the onset to invoke the spirit of François Rabelais, who wrote in 1535,

I will not offer to solve such problems . . .
for it is somewhat ticklish,
and you can hardly handle it without coming off
    scurvily;
but I will tell you what I have heard

Gargantua and Pantagruel
(Translated by Sir Thomas Urquhart)

Gratitude is also offered to Lao-Tsu for these words written two thousand years before:

"Who will prefer the jingle of jade pendants
if he once has heard stone growing in a cliff?"

Tao Te Ching
(Translated by Witter Bynner)

Contents

Introduction

I AM ABOUT TO TELL YOU A MOST UNUSUAL STORY, A
chronicle of something that happened to me while I
was living on the flank of an active volcano on the
island of Hawai'i. I now believe that where I was residing
had something to do with what happened, although during most of my life, I would have scoffed at the very idea
of such a connection.

I'm a scientist, an anthropologist who works as part of
an international team of specialists investigating the ancient eroded landscapes of eastern Africa's Great Rift
Valley in search of answers to the mystery of human
origins. My early academic training was in ecology and
evolutionary biology, so my research involves reconstruct-
ing the environments of prehistoric sites from which the
stone tools and fossilized remains of humanity's earliest
ancestors have been recovered.

Scientists tend to focus on their goals within an exclusively scientific, intellectual view of the world. I am no
exception. I mention this to show that I was in no way

preprogrammed for what was to occur. In fact, my scientific training and prejudices would seem to have preprogrammed me *against* having such an experience.

One morning just before dawn about ten years ago, I experienced a full-fledged, spontaneous altered state of consciousness. During this event, my physical body was largely paralyzed by somatic sensations that could have been very frightening had they not been so exquisitely pleasurable. Quite suddenly, the word *ecstasy* achieved entirely new levels of meaning for me. While I was in this state of expanded awareness, I had a vivid visionary encounter with what a tribal person might call a spirit.

I was considerably shaken by this event, yet reason prevailed, and I chose to write it off as a lucid dream—as one of those odd things that happen in life that we never completely understand. I had almost forgotten about it when I had another—and then one more, just to make sure I was paying attention. My curiosity was roused, and any residual fear overcome. I wanted more direct experience of this extraordinary phenomenon, but the episodes stopped at this point, leaving me baffled about how to proceed.

Several years later, my family and I moved to upcountry Kona, where I taught anthropology at the local branch of the University of Hawai'i. There, between 1985 and 1989, I experienced a series of spontaneous altered states that were quite remarkable. All were accompanied by the same exquisite, paralytic sensations, and all were heralded by curious visual hallucinations—spots and lines of light, zigzags, grids, and vortexes.

In the first of this series, my consciousness was brought dramatically into contact with that of another man. I felt as though I were inside his physical body. I could see what he was seeing and hear what he was hearing. I could "listen" to his thoughts, and as if this were not enough, I could tap into his memory banks and receive information as a multilayered complex of thoughts, emotions, impressions, memories, and judgments. He seemed totally unaware of my presence. It was as if I were "there" as a visitor, an invisible one. To say that this surprised me would be an understatement of vast proportions.

I had heard other people's tales of things such as channeling and shamanic journeying, and they had caused me to wince with embarrassment
more than once. Now here I was, a trained scientist, experiencing the
awesome jolt of the "real thing" myself. My carefully constructed scientific
worldview began to come apart.

I had twelve altered-state episodes over the next four years. They were
largely spontaneous in the sense that I could not deliberately induce them,
yet each time, my conscious awareness merged with the same man's. At first,
our lives seemed intertwined only occasionally, but gradually our lives
moved toward each other more and more—converging. Without any previous knowledge that such a psychic journey was possible, I found myself
involved in quite a different sort of expedition from the scientific field trips
and digs I was used to, one in which my investigations extended far beyond
the ordinary nature of reality into the inner realms of the human mind and
spirit. During these extraordinary experiences, I learned much information,
both disturbing and enlightening.

Sounds fantastic, doesn't it? In my dark moments, I wondered more than
once if I was going crazy, yet the anthropologist in me would calmly
observe what was happening, make mental notes during the altered state,
and then take actual notes when it had subsided. Eventually I created a
journal of the scenes and sensations I had experienced. In my attempts to
understand how and what I was seeing through the other man's eyes, I did
research into many disciplines. Most helpful were my investigations of an
area of anthropology about which I knew almost nothing—shamanism.

In Western society, many people associate the word *shaman* with a
masked and costumed tribal person who dances around a fire in the dark,
accompanied by drumbeats, in a naive, mysterious ritual. In reality, however, the individual shaman—apart from his cultural shell of mask, costume, and ritual—possesses a very real skill, one that distinguishes him
from other kinds of religious practitioners.

All true shamans are able to achieve expanded states of awareness,
visionary perceptions of what tribal people often call the spirit world. They
usually exercise this unusual ability to heal members of their communities

—spiritually, psychologically, and physically. Directed by strong, altruistic motivations, the traditional shaman is a master of trance.

As a biological anthropologist, I was not particularly attracted by shamanic masks, costumes, songs, chants, and charms, although these can be very beautiful and very powerful things in themselves. In seeking to understand my altered-state experiences, however, I became interested in the old time-tested shamanic methods of achieving expanded states of awareness, and I specifically researched those that were non-drug-induced.

At the time I first had these experiences, I would not have described myself as a religious person. As a scientist, I had fairly strong negative feelings about religious dogma and organized religion in general. Yet I must admit, I had had leanings toward Zen. In the 1970s I had visited an old hot-springs resort called Tassajara that had been transformed into a Zen Buddhist practice center in the mountains behind the Big Sur coast of central California. The natural wildness of the locale had been attractive, as had the ordered simplicity with which the Zen students accomplished whatever needed to be done. My scientific nature was impressed, and I began to study Zen Buddhist thought.

It was also during this time that I attended art school in San Francisco one or two afternoons a week. Immersed in writing my dissertation, I needed something different, something separate from my intellectually fatiguing scientific work. I had already studied art for many years, and I knew that painting, drawing, and sculpture engaged my intuitive self and brought a kind of balance into my life. I mention this because I believe my artistic practices had a direct bearing on what was to follow. My art studies have also enabled me to know quite clearly when my creative imagination is engaged and when it is not.

Upon the completion of my doctorate, my wife Jill became pregnant with our first child. And then, that morning just before dawn, I had that first full-fledged, spontaneous altered-state experience.

So, what does one do when one is handed a plate with a slice of something quite different from what one is used to eating? Those with more conserva-

tive tastes or closed minds might send it back to the kitchen. Having always had an interest in the unusual or bizarre, however, I chose to eat it—and to analyze how it was made, and then to try to get into the kitchen for second and third helpings.

In 1989 I returned from Hawai'i to teach for a year at one of the branches of the University of California. There I formally wrote up my "Hawaiian journal," expanding it to include my investigations into shamanic practices of trance and mind travel so that I could look for patterns of meaning and causality behind my experiences. The scientific side of me was still hesitant about communicating these experiences to others, and my first impulse was to write a novel, a fictional narrative within which I could safely reveal what I had learned without jeopardizing my scientific reputation. That way I could spare my academic colleagues the embarrassment of having one of their own publicly go off the deep end.

Yet my story is not science fiction, nor is it imaginative fantasy. It happened as I will tell it to you in this book. I cannot hide or disguise my experiences. I have long ceased to regard these happenings as "lucid dreams," and I have upgraded the phenomenon in my scientific evaluations to the level of "fieldwork," much to my esteemed colleagues' possible dismay.

What follows is an autobiographical account, a chronicle. Some readers already consider it an archetypal, mythic journey or visionary narrative. Some will no doubt discount it as utter horsetweedle. Everything that I recount in this book I experienced as real. It is the story of two individuals on a journey—a physical, mental, and spiritual journey. These two men were initiated into an expanded vision of reality at the hands of "the spirits," and they came face-to-face with these spirits in their quest for knowledge. This is also the account of a hard-headed scientist-realist who found himself involved in an absolutely extraordinary experience—and perhaps stumbled upon another piece of the ongoing puzzle of human evolution.

1
Initial Encounters

THE FIRST ENCOUNTER

IN AUGUST 1983, I WAS LIVING IN BERKELEY, CALIFORNIA. My wife Jill was near the end of her first pregnancy, and it was difficult for her to lie comfortably in any position for very long. One morning, we were both awake in the dark at three o'clock, so I sat up and gently massaged her long back and hips, trying to ease her discomfort, trying to help her get back to sleep. The massage progressed into lovemaking, yet even afterward Jill remained wakeful and finally turned on a light to read.

I felt quite blissful and was just slipping off to sleep —when I felt a peculiar sensation in my body. As my dissolving attention re-formed and turned toward it, the feeling abruptly intensified, paralyzing me where I lay. Startled, I opened my eyes. I saw momentary spots of light interspersed with strange lines and zigzags against the darkened field of the ceiling. A transparent

arc seemed to coalesce out of the lights, and then the bedroom disappeared.

I found myself in a forest in almost total darkness. Around me in all
directions, tall black tree trunks and branches stretched away into the night.
The night was very still, and a faint fragrance floated on the warm air. The
illusion was vividly real, and yet paradoxically, I could still feel myself lying
in bed next to Jill and hear her turning the pages of her book. I felt very
much awake.

As my attention turned toward Jill, the forest dimmed somewhat, as
though it were going slightly out of focus. I continued to lie quietly in bed,
looking at the trees all around me, listening to Jill turn the pages. I
refocused my attention upon the sensations that filled my body, and the
trees came back into focus. My mind made an association with a childhood
memory—my mother pushing me on a swing with very long ropes. As the
swing in my memory rushed down and up, down and up, in its heady arc,
my body in the present surged with this same sensation, again and again
and again.

As my attention shifted back into the "dream" and the forest around me,
these sensations, these rushes of feeling, increased. At this point I discovered that I could move, and I proceeded to walk through the trees, profoundly impressed at how real everything appeared. I wasn't too sure how I
was moving or what I was walking on, but as in a dream, my intention
seemed to be enough to take me here or there. My body in bed, however,
was still immobilized by the sensations.

My scientific mind registered details of the trees—the faint scent hanging in the air was familiar. My memories of Africa suggested the trees were
jacarandas, a tropical species that produces great clouds of lavender flowers.
In spite of the darkness, I found a flowering branch that confirmed this
guess.

The sensations abruptly intensified, and my body swelled and stiffened,
becoming increasingly paralyzed, as though I were wrapped in an invisible
fist that was slowly squeezing me, cutting off my breath. For a moment, I

worried that I might be having a seizure of some sort, and I felt the edge of fear. The fear departed as abruptly as it had appeared, however, when I realized that the sensations were intensely pleasurable. Each increase in pressure was accompanied by a euphoric surge mixed with an indescribable joy.

Something cut through my absorption in this overwhelming rapture and drew me toward the trees to my right. There among the shadowy tree trunks I saw a huge, dark form. It was vaguely manlike, and I could make out what I thought was a distinct head and body, but the body was strangely geometric and . . . doorlike. The head was rounded and small, there seemed to be no arms or legs. It was flat, completely black, and featureless.

My mind struggled, attempting to classify what I was seeing. The dark form was considerably taller than I, and it looked somewhat like a giant, black, elongated keyhole standing upright under the trees. Near its right "shoulder" wafted a spherical light about as big as a basketball, as bright as the humanoid form was dark. The light hovered motionless above the ground.

The sensations continued to flow around and through me, exerting pressure from both within and without. I tried to move but I was now completely paralyzed. I heard Jill turn another page and thought to myself, "I've got to try to tell her what's happening," but my jaw was locked, and my entire body was as rigid as a stick of wood. I couldn't close my hands.

Determination formed within me, and through my clenched teeth I tried to tell Jill about the grove of trees and the dark form, but I could only hiss. I finally managed to hiss a barely intelligible "The trees . . . the trees" and "The shadow . . . the shadow."

I stared at the dark form and its bright companion and wondered if I was dreaming, even though I could hear Jill turning pages. What was going on? Was this dark shadow the source of the sensations? With this thought the feelings of pressure, of force suddenly increased to an intensity almost beyond endurance. They were terrifying and superb at the same time. I was

fully conscious, fully awake—and trying in vain to classify what I was perceiving and feeling while also trying to move my hands. I had never in my life felt what I was experiencing at that moment, a full-blown "ecstasy."

Abruptly, it seemed as if the shadow had increased the sensations so much that I felt myself "lift off." I drifted slowly up through the trees until I was standing above the ground, turning slowly in space among the leaves and flowers. The ecstatic sensations surged through and around me, and my muscles shook, trembling with the force. To fight against the enormous strength that enfolded me seemed absurd. The dark form was obviously immensely strong, and yet it hadn't harmed me.

I heard a roaring sound and waited to see what would happen next. Then as abruptly as the experience began, it stopped. I was gently placed back on the ground, and the dark form changed, shifting its shape to blend into the shadows under the trees. Simultaneously, the sensations that had held me rigid began to flow out of me in slow surges, each one less powerful than the last. Progressively the trees, the shadow, and the bright sphere dissolved, and the darkened bedroom reappeared before my eyes. The paralysis ceased abruptly, and I finally managed to sit bolt upright in bed, heart pounding, muscles shuddering, half in shock. I turned to Jill, but she was now asleep. The residues of sensation faded until they were gone, and the world was ordinary once again. The first light of dawn was illuminating the sky. My mind was reeling.

I sat lost in thought for some time, wondering what I had just been through. The whole thing had seemed much too real to be a dream. I had seemed fully awake and conscious, aware of lying in bed next to Jill the entire time. As my mind raced through the experience, it returned repeatedly to dwell on that mysterious dark form. My personal journal lay next to the bed, and I made hasty notes, recording everything I could recall. When Jill awoke, I related the entire encounter to her. Then I described my enormous effort to tell her what had been happening.

"That's strange," she said. "I started to read when you went to sleep, and after a while, I heard you whispering. You never talk in your sleep, so I tried to hear what you were saying. But you were muttering, and I couldn't make anything out, so I decided not to wake you."

This reassured me somehow. Something *had* really happened.

In the days that followed, I thought it odd that I had automatically categorized the dark form as the "shadow." Carl Jung had conceived of the "shadow" as a mental construct or projection of the "dark" or repressed side of the self. I considered this idea at some length. Could the dark shape have been a creation of my own mind, even though it had seemed quite separate from myself? If it wasn't a mental projection, what was it? It had felt neither hostile nor benevolent, but as I was in its viselike grip, I felt that *it* had been curious about *me.*

In retrospect, the entire event had the quality of a challenge, as if something were saying to me "Here, let me show you something—now, what are you going to do about it?" But who or what had issued the challenge?

THE SECOND ENCOUNTER

About a week later, I had a similar but briefer physical experience. Jill was having another rough night, and we were awakened at three-thirty by the barking of our next-door neighbor's dog. We lay in bed, talking in the dark almost until dawn. Once again, my efforts to help her sleep progressed into lovemaking, after which I began to fall back asleep. Suddenly I was again aware of the "sensations," the sudden tingling of the spine and the sweeping "high" that spread up my back and engulfed my brain. I was instantly, fully awake. As the sensations roared into me, up my back and into my head and extremities, they paralyzed me completely. As before, I was conscious of being simultaneously in the altered state and in my ordinary reality with Jill beside me.

This time, however, I didn't see the jacaranda forest or anything else—

except for immense shadows, which dominated my field of vision. I tried to visualize the jacaranda forest, but it didn't appear. This was actually reassuring somehow, since it suggested that my imagination was not creating the whole experience after all. Again, I tried to speak, and with great effort, I finally managed to croak, "The shadow."

Instead of invoking the shadow and intensifying the experience as before, at these words the "sensations" almost immediately withdrew. Disappointed, I tried to recapture the state but could not. I felt several parting surges, each less than the one before. Then they were gone.

Moments after their disappearance, I recorded the experience in my journal. Over breakfast the next morning, I discussed the incident with Jill, who is a physical therapist. Although she is much more knowledgeable than I about neurophysiology, she had no suggestions about what might have caused such a physical and mental state. As she stared at me thoughtfully through the steam rising from her cup of tea, however, she smiled and suggested brightly, "Maybe you should ask it some questions. Not spoken questions, but questions you form in your mind—like 'Who are you, why are you here, what do you want?' "

With all due respect to Jill, at the time that seemed absurd to me, a scientist. I resolved to put the whole matter out of my mind and went back to work on my fossils. I could not deal with being unable to explain my experience.

THE THIRD ENCOUNTER

Life returned to normal for a few weeks, then changed considerably when our daughter Erica was born in September. We got very little sleep during the next half-year of parenthood. Still, unable to forget my strange encounters with the shadow completely, I did some reading and learned that many traditional tribal peoples use methods of sensory deprivation—which may include intentional sleeplessness—to achieve altered states. I often wondered, during those months of shattered sleep patterns, whether an-

other "event" might be induced—but nothing out of the ordinary occurred.

Then just before dawn on a foggy morning in mid-February 1984, it happened once again.

Jill had risen to nurse our hungry baby, while I drifted in and out of that shallow state between sleep and wakefulness. The next thing I knew, Jill was peering out the window above the bed into the darkness of the backyard below. Alarmed, she whispered that she had heard a loud noise. Our cat had heard it too and was on the sill, staring down at something.

I shook off my sleepiness, wondering uneasily if I was going to have to deal with a prowler. "What did it sound like?" I asked.

"It was a screeching crack—like a board being torn from a fence or a large branch from a tree," she whispered tensely.

We had a Japanese-style bathhouse in the modest garden behind our house. Worried that it was being vandalized, I got out of bed and picked up a Maasai *rungu* that I had acquired one blazing afternoon at a trading post in the Rift Valley. The hardwood cudgel sported a large knob at its business end, and its weight felt reassuring as I slipped down the stairs and out the side door into the darkness.

Very primal stuff—inspecting your territory in the middle of the night. I gripped my club as my eyes adjusted to the darkness, then drifted silently around our property on my bare feet, sticking to the cover of the bushes, pausing in the shadows, trying to psych myself up to bash any intruder, but nothing appeared amiss. The bathhouse and fencing were intact. There were no broken trees. No one was there. I went back up to bed, but could not get back to sleep. Jill and I lay in bed wondering what was in the woods behind the house. Our attempts to reassure and comfort each other led to our making love, and it was close to dawn before I was relaxed enough to sleep again.

I was just dropping off when the doorbell rang, which brought me back to full wakefulness in an instant. The bedroom was filled with the warm yellow light of an early summer dawn, which struck me as curious since it had been pitch-dark only moments before. The light seemed to flicker with a kind of shimmering ripple that disappeared when I looked at it directly, but which I could see with my peripheral vision.

I rose from the bed, wondering who could be at the door at such an hour. As I crossed the room, I became dimly aware of still feeling the bed under my body, and at the doorway I turned and looked back. Jill was asleep, and there next to her was someone stretched out—it was myself! This did not strike me as odd at the time, perhaps because the bell had elicited such a strong response in me. I turned away, continued downstairs, and opened the front door.

No one was there. The warm predawn glow pervaded the familiar neighborhood scene, although the suburban landscape seemed strangely flat, without shadows. I stepped out onto the walk and carefully looked around. I was alone. Was someone playing a prank on me?

Without any warning a tremendous rush of the sensations slammed into me. Gasping, I struggled against them in a brief pulse of fear and surprise. But once again the exquisite nature of the sensations quickly dispelled my fear by overwhelming me with a monumental feeling of exhilaration verging on joy. Was this what traditional tribal people felt in their mystical shamanic visions?

My intellect was fully awake and clicking through different analyses and scenarios. Could these feelings have been caused by the presence or proximity of whatever had made the noise in the backyard? I recalled my meeting with the shadow and how its nearness had enormously increased these sensations. The moment I had that idea, I had a definite sense of the nearness of "another," although I could see nothing.

While still conscious of being in the front yard, my awareness shifted slightly to include my body lying in bed next to Jill. I was definitely there. I could feel the covers of the bed around me. But how was this possible? I tried to speak, but once again, even with enormous effort, I could manage nothing more than a muffled, slurring whisper. Wrapped as I was in the invisible fist, movement was virtually impossible.

Following Jill's suggestion of months before, I formed a tentative question in my mind: "Why are you here?" There was no answer, so I tried again: "What do you want?" Again there was no response, but I felt a sense of urgency, as though I had to go somewhere. This feeling increased, and impulsively I said, "Okay, let's go."

Immediately I was lifted off into the air above the front yard and flew up over the house at great speed. Staggered, I looked down at my familiar neighborhood from this dizzying perspective. I noticed that the roof of my car was dirty. The cat was observing me alertly out of an upstairs window. I rose swiftly until the details of the scene below were lost in the distance and I was traveling up through luminous clouds.

I can only describe what followed as a kind of otherworldly travelogue. I was taken to places and shown things that were vividly real, places to which I had never traveled, places not in my memory banks. Some were mono-chromatic and lunarlike, with gray ashy plains and stony lifeless deserts under starry black skies. Others were brilliantly hued and alive, but their plants and animals were completely unfamiliar to me. My training in biology and paleontology had provided me with a good working knowl-edge of the taxonomy of plants and animals, both fossil and contemporary, but after the trip, I was not very successful in my attempts to draw these life-forms on paper with precision. I simply had no familiar frame of reference with which to compare much of what I saw or how I saw it. During the course of this extraordinary experience, the creatures and land-scapes seemed ever more "alien."

Some of the landscapes were pleasant, while others were frightening or lonely in their immensity. In at least one scene, the sky held two suns of different sizes, which produced interesting double shadows of slightly dif-ferent hues behind the objects they illuminated. A series of vignettes played before me, each scene limited in duration and extent yet complete in some undefinable way. I have no idea how long this trip lasted nor how many places I visited, but it could not have been more than a half hour in ordinary time, although it seemed like hours psychologically.

Throughout the experience I always sensed the presence of another, some sort of invisible companion. The incredible sensations flowed contin-uously through my body.

As suddenly as it had begun, the experience ended, with a feeling of descent and settling. The impression of lying in bed restored itself as primary. The force that had filled me ebbed, and as I tried to catch a glimpse of my unseen companion, I saw one startling last image. Back in my bedroom, I glanced out the window to see the first light of a typical Bay Area foggy winter dawn. Right outside the glass panes, three floors up, a woman was staring in at me. She was slender, with short-cut dark hair and dark eyes. She may have been wearing something, but I don't remember because her eyes held mine intensely. Her stare pinned me as if I were an insect; it excluded all else. She was neither angry nor hostile, not benevolent, happy, or amused. There was just her look: neutral, detached, and emotionless.

With great effort I raised my arm in her direction. I did not know whether Jill was awake, but I pointed at the woman hovering outside the window and managed to hiss, "There she is. . . . There she is."

There was a sense of movement in the dark room, and the woman's full figure appeared between the window and me, silhouetted against the light behind her, her form completely dark and shadowlike but still distinctly human.

Suddenly her left eye became visible within the darkness of her face, as though that eye alone were illuminated by a spotlight. It gazed down at me impassively from beside the bed, like the eye of Osiris. I had seen this unforgettable mystical eye among the Egyptian talismanic ornaments called *udjat* at the British Museum in London. On each talisman a single disembodied eye gazed outward across time and space into the eyes of the beholder.

This woman's eye held me similarly in thrall. Then in an instant she was gone. At once the sensations within me ceased completely, leaving me awake and shivering uncontrollably as my mind filled with questions that my scientific training could not answer.

Having caught my full attention with this extraordinary journey, the experiences ceased—to my utter frustration. After the third taste I wanted more! I wanted to understand the nature of these experiences. What did this most recent event have in common with those of six months before? All three had happened just before dawn; all had been preceded by making love. All had involved exquisite somatic sensations of incredible force that had produced an almost total paralysis as long as they had lasted.

How long had they lasted? I wasn't sure since I hadn't looked at the clock, but the two longest had probably been thirty minutes or less in their entirety. I determined to check the clock the next time, as soon as I felt the sensations coming on.

After making lists of the similarities of the experiences, I tried to determine the physical nature of what had happened to me and why it had happened. I read into medical diagnoses, wondering if I had epilepsy or some other convulsive disorder. The literature on gran mal, petit mal, Jacksonian epilepsy, and other psychomotor seizures left me uncertain. Anyone can have an epileptic seizure, I learned, which is basically a period of disorganized activity in the brain. The only difference between individuals with diagnosed epilepsy and everyone else is that "known epileptics" are more likely to have such neurological disturbances than the undiagnosed. I had never had seizures of any kind, but these three experiences certainly fit the medical description for seizures: abrupt, transient symptoms of a sensory, motor, or psychic nature associated with changes in consciousness believed to be the result of sudden alterations in brain function, associated with rapid electrical discharges in the gray matter of the neocortex. Some seizures occur during sleep, while others are thought to be triggered by sleeplessness, physical stimulation, or emotional disturbances. I had certainly been physically and emotionally stimulated by lovemaking, but what connection did this have to the altered states?

A more likely possibility was that I had experienced a sleep disturbance commonly known as "sleep paralysis," a syndrome of unknown cause often associated with narcolepsy (recurrent episodes of an uncontrollable desire to sleep). Sleep paralysis may occur either during awakening or while falling asleep and is often accompanied by visual and auditory (hypnagogic) hallucinations. I had no symptoms of narcolepsy or any other sleep disorders, but it is known that sleep paralysis occurs alone in about 5 percent of the cases of narcolepsy.

Aside from these isolated, spontaneous experiences, my central nervous system still seemed to function normally. I had no symptoms of organic brain disease, tumors, traumas, infections, or hypoglycemia. I was ingesting no drugs or even alcohol at the time. In short, I was in perfect health. At this early point I was concerned only with the immoderate physical and mental sensations. Later, I would decide that even if the "episodes" had an underlying neurological component, they were not *only* a physical experience. They had, and have, I believe, a significance beyond my individual experience and perceptions. What I really needed, I decided, was to talk with someone knowledgeable about altered states of consciousness.

The previous year, I had come across an interesting book entitled *The Way of the Shaman* in a bookstore.[1] As I leafed through it, I realized that I didn't know much about shamans. Anticipating that I might have to say something intelligent about them in a class someday, I bought the book and put it on the "to be read" stack at home.

A month later, one of my wife's friends called to inform me of an upcoming event she thought might interest me—a weekend workshop on shamanism taught by an anthropologist named Michael Harner. The name seemed vaguely familiar, and in poking around my study, I discovered him to be the author of the book I had bought. A coincidence perhaps, but it got my attention.

I had some reservations about participating in this event. I was in the midst of frenzied last-minute revisions on my doctoral thesis, and the prospect of spending several days with a group of New Age types did not exactly fill me with passionate anticipation. After I hung up the phone, however, something stirred briefly in my mind—and then was gone. My scientific curiosity took note and tried to probe the elusive thought, which re-formed as a memory of something odd that had occurred many years before while I was on expedition in the deserts of southern Ethiopia.

In those months of isolation and silence, I had drifted through sun-drenched days of survey work, excavation, and discovery. At midday the rocks were almost too hot to touch, and dust devils danced through the thorn trees. At night the sky blazed with stars, and the universe revealed itself undimmed by a single man-made watt.

Perhaps it was the sensory deprivation of those stark, arid landscapes. Perhaps it was the heat. One day at midday I had a curiously dreamlike experience, while I was wide awake.

I had been out in the bush for the better part of three months, and at odd moments I had suddenly sensed that I was being watched. Anytime I looked around, though, I hadn't seen anyone. Yet the feeling was strong, and given my vulnerability in the open, I looked carefully around me whenever I felt it. Then one hot August day, I saw something.

It was around noon, the temperature was close to 120 degrees, and I was excavating a site that was yielding remains of an early form of human called *Australopithecus.* I was working with two Africans, and we had finished up the morning's work and were preparing to return to camp for lunch when I suddenly felt something or someone watching me.

I slowly straightened up, brushing the dust from my arms and clothes. I glanced around and saw nothing out of the ordinary, but one of the men was looking at something off to my left.

Peering around in that direction, about ten feet away I saw something big with my peripheral vision. When I looked directly at it, however, it disappeared. One moment it was there, and the next it was as though the "something" had stepped through a tear in the fabric of the air, zipping it closed to leave a momentary wrinkle, a shimmering arch about six feet off the ground, which straightened out and vanished.

Had the Africans seen it? The one called Atiko was watching me with his alert birdlike gaze. He was a Dassenetch tribesman native to that region who worked for the expedition whenever we were "in residence." Atiko spoke six languages, including, Swahili, but unfortunately English was not one of them. My Swahili was minimal, so our communication was limited.

I pointed to my left and shot Atiko an inquisitive glance. The African silently appraised me, then smiled and pointed to the exact spot in the air where "it" had been. He said something in his own language, which he repeated in Swahili. The other African, a Wakamba tribesman from Kenya named Muthoka, also spoke no English but did speak Swahili. After Atiko's words a long dialogue ensued, of which I understood not a word— and that was the end of it, until I found out years later from one of the expedition geologists that the term Atiko had used—*shaitani*—is the Swahili word for "spirit." In those days I worshiped solely at the altar of science, and so I wrote the episode off as some odd hallucination caused by extreme heat and forgot all about it.

Now this unsettling recollection kept me from closing a mental door on Harner's shamanism workshop. I needed a break from my thesis, the workshop was very reasonably priced, and maybe I'd be able to develop a lecture out of it for my own future classes. So despite my fairly strong distaste for New Age mysticism, I found myself sitting on the floor of a high school auditorium in a circle of fifty or so others, listening with interest to Michael Harner.

Harner turned out to be a robust bearded man with intense dark eyes and a sparkling sense of humor. He had a lively style, interspersing blocks of information with outrageous jokes that ranged from corny to hilarious. He didn't say much about his own fieldwork with the Jivaro and Conibo peoples of the Upper Amazon Basin but instead drew on his cross-cultural knowledge, discussing core concepts that are held in common by tribal shamans the world over. The methods shamans use for achieving altered states, he showed, are strikingly similar everywhere. The ability to experience them, he suggested, might be the biological heritage of a substantial portion of the human species. With a minimum of training, even nontribal Westerners like ourselves, he speculated, could achieve the level of expanded awareness he called "the shamanic state of consciousness."

In the experiential work that followed, Harner introduced participants to the classic shamanic journey, a disciplined way of making contact with the "spirits" in "nonordinary reality" and acquiring knowledge from these inner sources of wisdom. The technique was a method of personal divination, a practice that I had seen performed often while I was living in Africa.

As I listened to Harner, I understood for the first time what divination was all about.

Using monotonous and repetitive drumming as an aid to achieving trance, we attempted under Harner's guidance to journey as the traditional shaman does, in a structured state of awareness, to make contact with "helping spirits" and thus obtain information and guidance on matters of personal importance.

I found it all very interesting, and during the drumming sessions I achieved moderate success in perceiving an alternate, spiritual reality. These meditative states, however, were unlike the three vivid altered states that I would have a year later, although I believe the workshop helped me immeasurably in coming to terms with my strange experiences later.

After my third altered-state experience, I wondered if taking Harner's workshop had in some way initiated these experiences or opened me up to the "shamanic state of consciousness." Wanting to know more about the "nonordinary reality" that traditional tribal shamans perceive, I read several anthologies of papers compiled by various authorities on shamanism. But I was much more interested in experiencing these altered states than in reading about them. I knew how strongly the creative imagination can influence a scientist's attempts to be objective. For these reasons I stopped reading the literature. I didn't want to fill up my memory banks with others' experiences and interpretations and thereby risk "polluting" my own.

My preliminary research had turned up some interesting pieces of information, however. Many traditional peoples, for instance, believe that there is a doorway within our minds, a portal or interface that exists between the ordinary reality of everyday experience and "nonordinary reality," often referred to as the spirit world. The Huichol Indians of Mexico call this opening the *nierika*.[2] Most of us are unaware of the existence of this portal, I read, because it also functions as a barrier, blocking access to the unready. We may live out our lives ignorant of it entirely. Some people, however, learn to open it at will, so that they can journey through it across the

interface and into the region of death and visions to accomplish specific tasks. In traditional tribal societies the people who are able to accomplish this curious task are the shamans.

If such a portal existed in my mind, had it opened briefly, giving me a glimpse into what lay beyond? Folklore and myth are filled with stories of individuals who have had such experiences, but I had always considered them to be wholly symbolic. If there was in fact a portal in my mind, though, why had it opened at all? Since I had been unaware of its existence, I could not have opened it myself. But if I hadn't opened it, who had? Or what had? And what were these overwhelming sensations? Were they associated with the opening of the *nierika*? Was that dark figure my own imaginative projection, or was it something with its own identity and agenda? Who was the strange woman who had appeared at the end of my journey? What precisely had been revealed to me, and why? Might these figures be honest-to-god "spirits"?

I had no scientific or any other kind of answers to these questions. My scientific nature was shaken by these speculations about shamans and spirits, and as the impact of the most recent "experience" lessened over time, I went back to work on fossils. The doorway, if such it was, remained closed.

CROSSING THE THRESHOLD

In August 1985, two years after my trio of altered states, Jill and I decided to break our personal and professional ties in California and move out to the Kona coast of the island of Hawai'i for a sabbatical. A decade before, when agricultural real estate was still affordable, we had bought a small farm above Kealakekua Bay from friends. The one-acre property had since become riotously overgrown through lack of care, and the old house was in sore need of restoration. The opportunity to live in Hawai'i for a while and raise a family was simply too inviting to pass up.

Our land was at the twelve-hundred-foot level on the western slope of Mauna Loa, one of the world's most active volcanoes. From our broad lanai, or porch, we could look down and out across lush tropical greenery to the rocky coast far below. To the west lay the vast expanse of the Pacific Ocean, stretching to the vivid blue horizon. To the north stretched the blue curve of Kealakekua Bay, encircled by the towering cliff of a geological fault around its far shore. Directly to the east rose the lofty summit of Mauna Loa, achieving over thirteen thousand feet of elevation above the sea. To the south the gentle slope of the volcano's immense flank disappeared below the ocean far in the distance.

As a boy, I had wished that I could run away to the South Seas like Robert Louis Stevenson or Marlon Brando. My fantasy was to live the good life in a tropical paradise with an exotic-looking girl and have lots of children. Here I was now, an adult in the northern corner of Polynesia, with Jill, whose Eurasian features and long black hair made her look very much like a local. We spent our mornings at one of the beaches swimming and playing with Erica, who was now almost three years old. Our work on the house and the land occupied the afternoons, and in the soft tropical evenings, I worked on a series of paintings of Hawaiian temple sites. Fortunately we had a good rapport with our generous Hawaiian neighbors, whose children appeared frequently at our door with breadfruit or fish. Life was very fine.

Jill became pregnant with our second child in March 1986, just before the rainy season started. By that time, I had pretty much cleared the property and had seventy coffee trees in the carport ready to be planted. Many mature trees were already established, including seven Hayden mangos, four varieties of avocado, three types of banana, a Surinam cherry, a strawberry guava, a lychee tree, and a *wi*-apple, all of which I had fertilized just as the rains began to fall.

It was on a night in March that the "dream" began.

It was the dark of the moon, and the night was very still. Something awakened me just before dawn. I lay quietly beside my sleeping wife, listening. Except for the occasional whine of tires on the highway up the drive, I heard nothing out of the ordinary. I got up and looked out through

the window above the bed but saw nothing unusual. The tropical stars blazed like tiny distant windows through the massive black silhouette of the banyan tree beside the house. Nothing was stirring. . . .

I waited for long moments, then eased down into bed again and turned slowly to embrace Jill. I let my breathing follow hers and was just slipping into a dream when something alerted me once again. I lay quietly in the darkness, waiting, and suddenly I felt the sensations. They felt almost as if they were outside of me, just at the edge of awareness. More than two years had elapsed since that third altered-state experience, and I grew excited as the familiar feelings seemed to come inside and expand within me. I gently disengaged from Jill and managed to turn onto my back, glancing quickly at the alarm clock's luminescent dial, just before my entire body became rigid. As before, my discomfort from the paralysis was more than compensated for by the feelings, which were marvelous, simply marvelous.

I gasped, fighting to breathe, trying to retain some control over my body, as the pressure seized me in its invisible fist. My conscious mind, now fully awake, registered curious designs, spots and lines of light that again flickered in the darkness against my closed eyelids. The rushing, buzzing noise filled my ears again. As I fought for control, I remembered the doorway, the *nierika.* With that thought I suddenly felt myself expanding and moving outward. The lines of light shimmered, becoming more like strange serpentine, spaghettilike patterns. Then these too changed, becoming more angular and chevronlike as a strange arc appeared. A curious rectangular grid coalesced around and through the arc, flickered briefly, stretching into an unimaginable, seemingly infinite distance, and then was gone. The buzzing in my ears abruptly ceased. A brief period of total, absolute silence followed. The pressure that had enfolded me lessened abruptly, at which I felt slightly disappointed.

I heard a sound, a strange click, and then another. Startled, I opened my eyes—and discovered that I was there.

24

2
First Journey
Nainoa's Walk

A YOUNG MAN WAS STANDING AND GAZING OUT OF a cottage window at his world. The dark wall of a distant forest encircled terraced fields beyond his settlement. The colors of the dry season prevailed—large swatches of yellow, orange, and brown stood out from the otherwise omnipresent green. The towering trunks of immense trees at the forest's edge stood mutely before the darkness, which was broken here and there by shafts of sunlight among great buttressing roots. The forest was unusually silent, as if the trees were withdrawing into themselves in preparation for long, dry months of profound meditation. Noting that some of the arboreal giants were shedding their leaves, the man looked up at the single cotton tree in the center of the courtyard outside his cottage. In the breathless hush of early afternoon, he could hear the isolated leathery click of falling leaves.

Another year had finished its cycle, and the nights were growing colder. The natural seasons progressed, but this year the settlement's cycles were decidedly different. Gone was the comfort and security of the harvest time, with the storehouses bulging with surpluses and the smokehouses hung with meats. Instead of the customary feasting and celebration, an atmosphere of fear, uncertainty, and doubt prevailed among the people. Rumors of raiders always surfaced at harvest time, but this year something entirely new had occurred. The man felt a hollow space, a sense of urgency from within him, and he gazed out at the distant profile of the southern horizon, where smoke darkened the sky. His sense of urgency increased.

His cottage was tucked into a level place below an elevated platform dominated by the imposing residence and administrative buildings of the director and landlord of the settlement. The platform was a natural hill, whose summit had been flattened and whose edges had been squared and walled with stone. Buildings that housed the director's extended family and staff radiated outward, merging with the settlement below. The platform stood squarely in the center of the sprawling community. Beyond, the cleared fields extended out like the spokes of a wheel. In the distance, in all directions, lay the great forest.

Today, for the first time in its hundred-year history, the settlement was empty, and the great houses on the long platform were vacant. The director and landlord, High Chief John Hulikanaka Kaneohe, and his family and staff had all departed, as had virtually everyone else. The chief was a tall, big man of the ruling class who held the power within the chain of settlements along the western edge of the inland sea. Like the other directors, he was responsible for the land, for its productivity and care. The same responsibility extended to those who lived on the land and farmed it, including the various artisans, merchants, hunters, servants, and others who lived within the settlements.

Each land division along the inland sea was composed of two halves, a settlement on the water's edge whose inhabitants exploited the rich marine environment, and another community inland devoted to agriculture and livestock. High Chief Kaneohe directed the inland half of this settlement, and his elder brother, the high chief of the entire land division, was in

charge of the coastal half. Each agricultural community extended inland a distance of one day's journey from its sister community on the coast.

Trade within and between the two communities distributed a variety of products. But more important, each of the land divisions could be completely self-sufficient, even in times of famine. This was the ancient pattern that the voyagers had brought from their island homeland. This was the strategy that had ensured their continued survival throughout their long and often turbulent history.

As the man, whose name was Nainoa, listened to the silence, childhood memories raced through his mind. Nothing was the same. All had changed. Dead for ten years now, his adoptive father Kiwini had been a senior clerk with a considerable reputation as a scholar and historian. From him Nainoa had learned reading and writing. Through study he had developed self-discipline and an excellent memory, which was important because most records of the settlements were memorized by the clerks, to be recalled and repeated as circumstance demanded. Although the chief owned some ancient and fragile books, bark-cloth paper for record keeping was nonexistent.

Nainoa's biological ancestry was unclear. Because famine had been a frequent visitor in the earlier days of the settlements, extra children had been passed on to families who could feed them. Many grew to adulthood without knowing their natural parents, especially those from commoners. Such had been his own case, although he had been most fortunate in being adopted into the family of one of the chief's senior administrators and so had grown up being trained to serve in that capacity himself. He was a clerk—in charge of record keeping and inventory of agricultural products —and functioned as personal secretary to the chief. He was well suited to this work.

As Nainoa listened to the silence, a feeling of loneliness swept through him. To ease it, he thought of his relationship to his chief.

Nainoa's training had begun in childhood at the hands of his adoptive father. As he grew older and word of his progress had spread, his abilities

had brought him into close relationship with Chief Kaneohe and his family and, through them, with many of the other ruling families along the western edge of the inland sea. By the time he was grown, the ruler's power had elevated him above the rest of the servants among whom he had been raised. That seemed to have little meaning now.

Just this morning he had stood before the chief, who had sat behind the broad table from which he conducted the affairs of the settlement. The dark, polished surface was bare of the various objects that usually stood there. Many of these were made of metal—a brass elephant green with age, several small horses in various poses, a statue of a woman holding a child. Others were made of glass, ceramic, or wood. When still a boy, Nainoa had often allowed his eyes to wander among these objects. His favorites had included an ancient, painted ceramic cup and a large bowl of koa wood that contained many smaller metal objects. There had also been a wondrous glass fish and a metal tiger frozen in the moment of springing. The chief had noticed his youthful interest and told him stories about them—tales recorded in the minds of clerks and directors who had preceded them. Most of the objects had been in the chief's family since before the Huaka'i, the long voyage that had brought their ancestors from their island homeland to the western shores of America 130 years before. Most were artifacts of the Great Age, a period of history now nearly five thousand years in the past.

Today, however, there had been no stories. The chief had appeared tired and anxious, his unsettled gaze revealing an unsettled heart. Nainoa had waited for the chief to speak, observing the ancient, ivory emblem of royalty that hung about his neck from cords braided from the hair of his ancestors. Even with the ivory hook, the chief's personal power was not then in evidence, for his customary inner harmony was disrupted by the uprooting of the community. For many days the sounds of the people preparing to leave had clamored from the courtyard. Now silence heralded the chief's own imminent departure for the capital.

Resolve finally formed in the chief's face as he turned to the young man before him. The affection he felt for his clerk flared briefly, but his words

were abrupt and to the point. They were alone, and Chief Kaneohe spoke informally.

"Nainoa, as you know, civil war has broken out among our volatile southern neighbors. They have always had trouble governing themselves, and now they have attacked their more peaceful neighbors, our friends in the land division on our southern borders."

The chief considered the bitterness in his words, then continued. "They have always been extremists. Among them, a fanatic, supported by a fanatic following, has now assumed the directorship. We have received reports almost daily from exhausted runners—reports of murder, fratricide, and militaristic displays of power. The usurper and his warrior elite will likely move against us next. They have always considered the warrior's way of greatest importance. Now they are on the move, and there seems to be little chance of stopping them."

The chief and his clerk observed each other across the broad table. The elaborate systems of trade and economic exchange that had held the settlements in balance for so long had finally and completely failed.

"It is very serious," the chief continued. "I do not know what will become of any of us. The world as we know it has changed, and not for the better."

He turned to stare grimly southward through the window of his office toward the horizon. "We have always been involved in food production on this estate," he said. "This periodic resurgence of warrior elite societies is a real problem. Military extremism has no respect for life. It breaks the balance necessary for the survival of us all. It is caused by a failure of leadership at the highest level."

Both men gazed out the window across the miles of empty harvested fields. The last of the livestock had been driven up the north road by its commoner-caretakers, toward safety in the next neighboring land division. The crop surpluses had been moved days before in wagons drawn by oxen. The invaders would find little to eat here on their arrival. The strong political bonds of marriage between the ruling families of the two estates would unite them against their common southern enemy.

The chief turned to his clerk. "It seems that we are at a new threshold, whether or not we are ready to cross it. We will appeal to the governor, and our community will live under her protection for the time being. She is related to me through my mother's lineage. We will be safe there, at least for a time."

Chief Kaneohe's affection and warmth for Nainoa emerged once more. "As a keeper of records, you have contributed greatly, both to my household and to the overall well-being of the estate. As you have matured, your skills of memory and analysis have revealed your superior mind. You possess qualities and potential that clearly distinguish you from the more ordinary people."

The chief paused, and Nainoa knew that he was thinking about his adoption and unknown parentage. For more than a thousand generations, the ruling class had bred for physical size, strength, and intelligence, and the chiefs were, on the average, at least a foot taller than those who served them. Nainoa's own height was close to seven feet, and he had often wondered whether he might be the bastard son of some chief's dalliance with a peasant girl. The chief interrupted his speculations.

"I have come to value your abilities and your integrity, as well as the friendship that has grown between us."

The older man paused once more, and Nainoa knew that Chief Kaneohe did not want to embarrass him with praise. To take on praise, to reflect overly on one's accomplishments, led to selfish thoughts and selfish acts, which led to the loss of internal harmony and inner balance. The chief glanced south through the window again. The smoke above the distant horizon had just appeared.

Abruptly the chief stood and moved around the table, beckoning Nainoa to accompany him into the courtyard. Behind them several servants appeared to carry the table and chair out to a waiting wagon. The chief looked up at the tall cotton tree, then focused his full attention on the younger man.

"Nainoa, I have a proposal for you to consider. On the one hand, you are of great value to me as a clerk, but there are many clerks in my household, and there is something that you might do which could be of even greater value." The chief paused. "I would like you to consider going on a long walk."

The formality and respect with which the chief made this request was a great honor to the younger man. Normally, only a party led by royalty and accompanied by a large number of servants would undertake a journey of formal exploration, which was what the chief meant by a "walk." It would mean a rise in personal power and status for Nainoa.

The Hawaiians had always been a maritime people. Clearing the forest on the American coast had been arduous, and few within the settlements had been inclined to penetrate farther inland. The immense trees were daunting, and travel through much of the forest was largely impossible except during the relatively short dry season. So the interior of the American continent, especially that region beyond the inland sea to the east, was largely unknown except to the hunters and the woodcutters who forayed into it in search of meat, hides, feathers, timber, and medicinal plants. Yet even these hardy adventurers rarely ventured farther than a few days' journey from the coast.

"The purpose of your journey will be to increase our people's knowledge of the interior. In your youth, I know, your relationship with the hunter Nagai took you into the forest often, so you possess the knowledge and the skills necessary for the success of such a walk. You also have the makings of a historian."

Nainoa flushed involuntarily at this praise. Historians were highly regarded, and the implications of the chief's statement were many. The chief continued:

"Because of your abilities, you will remember all that you encounter, the innumerable small details that will enable you to retrace your path through the labyrinth of the great forest. I know that you will find your way back to us at the end of your journey."

The chief's eyes suddenly sparkled with humor and warmth, and he observed Nainoa closely. "Your name will bring you good luck," he said. "You will find your way, as did your esteemed namesake before you."

The name of Nainoa the Navigator was written in the stars. From this ancestor, the knowledge of transoceanic navigation had been passed down to the people. All the great navigators throughout history had traced back their ancestry, actual or spiritual, through the distant past to this man. Nainoa had always wondered why he had been given this name, but now Chief Kaneohe showed that it had been prophetic, casting a strong positive mantle around him and his journey. Nainoa felt even more new power created within him by the chief's statement. The chief understood and smiled.

"I want you to travel toward the east," he said. "Cross the great forest beyond the inland sea and the high mountains beyond. We have always known of these mountains from the ancient maps that the Americans left on our islands during the Time of Contact, but no one knows what lies beyond them. Our voyaging canoes have explored the inland sea, its river systems, and the myriad islands of the archipelago along the coast far to the north and south. But exploratory expeditions encumbered by royalty and servants have been unable to cross the mountains before the return of the rains.

"With your knowledge and skills, you might be able to do so by traveling light. I want to know what lies beyond the mountains. Do you know why?"

Nainoa had often thought about the interior of the unknown continent. He nodded and said, "You want to find the descendants of the Americans and the edge of the forest." The chief nodded, so Nainoa continued.

"Perhaps the Americans were not forest people," he said. "The country beyond the mountains may be drier and less forested. Perhaps we will find their descendants there. Their population was large; our history records that they lived in settlements of immense size in great houses of metal and stone. Yet when our voyagers made landfall, they found no people, nor any of their settlements. What happened to them remains a mystery, and we have no way of knowing how accurate our own history is. Many thousands of years have passed since the fall of their civilization. Much of what we

suppose to be fact may actually be myth. Yet they were here; we know this because our farmers continually dig up strange artifacts. Overgrown remains of their great roads cross the forest—"

At this point, Nainoa perceived that Chief Kaneohe was restless, and he stopped.

Time was short. The chief resumed his instructions: "There is something else about which I am curious. The great voyaging canoes that brought our ancestors here were designed to carry people and the provisions they needed for their survival, both during the trip and after making landfall. No one knew how great the distance was because none of the many previous expeditions to America had ever returned to Hawai'i or sent back a canoe. They simply disappeared, and it was assumed that these earlier voyagers had perished.

"Nevertheless, our ancestors decided to make the attempt. They were fortunate enough to survive, but it was very close. Like their forebears they brought along their crop plants and their domestic animals—all except one. They had to choose between bringing cattle and bringing horses, and because cattle, pigs, and goats provide us with so much, they decided to bring calves, piglets, and kids.

"It was, of course, the correct decision. They hoped to find horses here upon their arrival. It was known that horses had originally been brought to Hawai'i by the Americans. But at landfall the voyagers found no Americans and no horses.

"Horses are not forest animals but are found in open country, in grass lands where they can run. None of us here around the inland sea has ever seen open country grasslands, yet they must exist somewhere. None of us has ever seen horses either, although if open country exists beyond the mountains, it is likely that you will find horses there. The rediscovery of horses would be a truly great accomplishment, one of considerable merit. I want you to bring them back if you can. I want to breed them as my ancestors did."

The chief stopped speaking and smiled at his clerk. Nothing more

needed to be said. To Nainoa's great surprise, Chief Kaneohe then stepped forward and embraced him. Then he raised both hands and blessed him in Old Hawaiian:

> *"E' ho'omaikai keia huaka'i,*
> *E' ho'omaikai keia kane,*
> *Lele walea akua la,*
> *Amama, ua noa."*

> Blessings on this journey,
> Blessings on this man,
> Go easily with spiritual assistance,
> Let it be so.

Nainoa was confused by the chief's unexpected display of affection. His own lowly social status did not merit such honor. Chief Kaneohe turned and crossed the courtyard, motioning to Nainoa to follow him. Passing behind his family residence, they ascended the steps of his personal *heiau*, the place of power where prayer and offerings were made to the spirits.

Stopping short of the *hale mana*, the chief bowed and uttered a short prayer, requesting permission to enter the house of power. Then, undoing the gate, he stepped up onto the raised stone platform and entered through the low door. Days before, the sacred relics, including the bones of his ancestors, had been removed and transported to a new place of safekeeping, accompanied by the *kahu*, the caretaker priest responsible for the *heiau*, its rituals, and its contents.

After a few moments Chief Kaneohe reemerged clutching a large, bulky object wrapped in black bark-cloth. With this bundle he descended the stairs and crossed the courtyard to where his four-wheeled royal wagon awaited him. Obviously, the package would be traveling in his personal care. The older man glanced around to ascertain that they were alone. Only the wagon's six white oxen were in attendance, so he beckoned to Nainoa and unwrapped the cloth.

Within was the famous *pohaku kupua,* the spirit stone of which Chief Kaneohe was the *kahu,* the honored caretaker. Nainoa had never seen it before, and he was greatly honored now in being granted the privilege. The stone was a lava boulder that resembled an angular face and head. It had been minimally carved to accentuate its natural features. The natural layering of the stone suggested a strange down-turned mouth. Instead of eyes a diagonal asymmetric groove crossed its flat face, and it seemed not to have a nose. Its overall appearance conveyed great strength and power.

The chief regarded the grim visage of the stone with a reverent affection. "This *pohaku* has been with my lineage for many thousands of years. I am its current favorite," he told Nainoa, glancing at him to see the effect of his words. "It is difficult to explain. An *akua,* a spirit, resides in this stone. It is a form of awareness that is profoundly different from ours, yet—" The chief broke off, searching for the right words. "I have a relationship with this awareness. Often it comes to me in dreams, but I can also make contact with it when I am awake. The way I do this is through intention combined with sustained concentration. I did not choose to become its *kahu.* The *akua* in this stone chose me. I am showing it to you at its request. I do not know why it has asked this. It has its own motivation. The stone is an object of great power for those who know how to use it.

"This *pohaku* came from Hawai'i on the canoe of my esteemed forebear. On the eve of his departure from the islands, the *akua* within the stone came to him in a dream and informed him that he had its permission to move it, to take it away from the great volcano of its birth and bring it to the shores of America. The stone also told him that it had made this journey before in the company of a former *kahu,* and that it would help him find his way.

"My ancestor told the priests and chiefs of this dream, and everyone was amazed. It was naturally regarded as a very favorable omen for all the voyagers. No one knew of the stone's former journey, but it was clear

that the stone wished to go voyaging again. This was in keeping with its name as passed down from antiquity, Kapohaku'ki'ihele—the stone that travels."

The chief paused again for a long moment, as if listening to something in the far distance. "Perhaps it senses the voyager in you. I do not know. As I said, it has its own motivations and intentions. It came to me in my dreaming. It wanted to meet you." He smiled. "You may place your hands on it and ask for its blessing."

Nainoa was again struck by the honor being accorded him, even though he wasn't sure he believed in spirit stones. Only the chief was permitted to touch this stone. Many questions formed in Nainoa's mind, but there was no time to ask them. He hesitated, then placed both hands on the stone's rough surface. He cleared his mind of thoughts and waited, feeling emptiness form within. Then, with respect, he formally asked the spirit stone to bless him and his journey.

Was that warmth flowing into his arms? He could not be certain. He waited but felt nothing more. He stepped back, and Chief Kaneohe rewrapped the stone in its cloak of black *kapa* and placed it carefully in the wagon. Then he turned to the young man.

"I have instructed the kitchen staff to provision you. Go now, and select from your belongings those things that you will take with you. The servants will load the rest of your things in the wagons. They will be stored in safety until your return. I have had several things that you will find useful placed in your quarters.

"I have also arranged with my brother for a small sailing canoe to be left for you in the secluded cove to the north, where we caught the *hahalua*, the great horned ray. This place is rumored to be the abode of spirits, and if the invaders know about it, they will avoid it. It is still early in the dry season. You may be lucky and catch what remains of the west wind to carry you across the inland sea. Keep an eye out for the *ihuloameniho*, the long-noses with teeth. I look forward to your return."

The chief then turned away and, within a very short period of time, departed with his retainers, leaving Nainoa alone.

.   .   .

Nainoa terminated his reverie and left for the kitchens to gather his provisions. He had decided to remain for this one final night. Tomorrow he would be the last to leave.

In the extensive open-air enclosures that surrounded the earthen ovens of the chief's kitchens, he found traveling fare laid out for him—dried fish, beans, corn, groundnuts, and fruit. There were also several bundles of *poi-ulu,* pounded breadfruit mixed with coconut cream, sliced and sun-dried and wrapped in *ti* leaves for travel. A handsome wooden food bowl filled with *taro-poi* and a small woven sack of salt were included. He would have liked to have some dried pork as well, but he had no wish to tempt fate—it was bad luck to carry pork from one place to another after dark.

After he had consumed these provisions, Nainoa would have to provide for himself from the forest. A small metal cooking pot, a long calabash water bottle with woven carrying straps, two wooden fire plows, and several woven net bags to carry it all completed his supplies.

Suddenly something alerted him. Turning, he caught a flicker of movement in the shadows. He remained motionless, watching carefully, but nothing and no one appeared in the fading light. He was alone.

He remembered an old woman who had befriended him as a child. She had been long gone for many years, yet he felt her presence strongly now. She had a sharp, intense gaze, and her voice was a dry whisper, which now rustled like lizards in the leaves of his mind. She had described the land east of the inland sea as a vast unexplored region of high forest inhabited by the spirits of the vanished Americans who had once lived here. They were not happy spirits, she had told him. Nainoa's people were very superstitious, yet he himself was not inclined to believe in supernatural ideas.

Nonetheless, Nainoa looked around the kitchen and suddenly felt uneasy. In the silence and emptiness unseen things were stirring, perhaps warning him. He decided to leave the settlement right away. He arranged his provisions within the woven string bags and returned to his cottage.

Chief Kaneohe had provided him with two wondrous gifts. The first was

an iron knife in a wooden sheath. Its heavy blade was straight and sharp, as long as his forearm, and it was fitted into a handle fashioned from a whale's tooth. It was a thing of beauty, and he knew it was one of the chief's personal possessions. The second was a spear with a leaf-shaped iron point mounted on a stout hardwood shaft, bound with leather straps and copper nails. It was an arm's length longer than he was tall and was designed for hunting the large forest pigs. It had a short metal crossbar fitted around the shaft behind the blade to stop the beast when it impaled itself with its charge. This spear might provide him with his only defense, should he be unfortunate enough to encounter a tiger, Nainoa reflected uneasily.

Of the metals that remained from the great days of the past, iron was both the hardest and the rarest, because of its tendency to rust. The soft metals, the various alloys of copper, aluminum, silver, and gold, were more commonly found, and the metalworkers of the artisan class made them into tools, wagon fittings, household objects, cooking pots, and personal ornaments. It was recorded that metals had originally come from the earth, but no one had ever discovered from where they had been obtained or how. All the metals that the people possessed were derived from the artifacts of the Great Age, and virtually all were soft. Only members of the chiefly class possessed objects made of iron, and these were primarily weapons, some of which had been treasured within chiefly lineages for thousands of years.

As Nainoa prepared for his departure, he considered the social implications of Chief Kaneohe's gifts and wondered again about his own ancestry. These were not the sort of gifts a chief would usually give to a mere servant. He added to his provisions several pairs of sandals, his woven hammock, a long cloak for cold nights, a coil of woven rope, a tool kit including an awl, a sharpening stone, an antler punch, and a core of glassy stone for making arrow points, a ball of strong cord, several bowstrings, and a good-size nodule of tree resin, to be softened with heat for use as glue. He also had some cosmetic items and a small sack containing various dried herbs and medicines for fevers and wounds. Finally, he had two nine-foot lengths of woven cotton-strip cloth to be utilized as a *malo*, the loincloth worn by all men most of the time.

He stowed these things in the string bags for carrying and slung them around his shoulders, adjusting them for comfort and balance. Around his waist he wound the coil of rope. Around his neck he slung a rain-cape fashioned from a piece of netting, over which *ti* leaves soaked in coconut oil had been tied. He arranged it so that it hung down over his left shoulder. Last, he hung his quiver of arrows across his back on one side and thrust his old digging stick and the new knife through his rope belt on the other.

He picked up the spear, his long bow, and his throwing stick, and hung his water bottle under his arm. He was ready to depart. The urgency of the time was upon him, and glancing around his empty room one last time, he turned and crossed the threshold.

Nainoa strode across the courtyard to descend the stone stairway that connected the administrative center with the rest of the settlement below. As he passed, from habit he checked the storehouses for which he was responsible on their low, elevated stone foundations. All were empty, their floors of fitted planks gleaming as if newly polished. All should have been full at this time, but even the usually omnipresent bundles of thatch for roofing had been taken. Chief Kaneohe had instructed the people to leave nothing for the invaders. Anxiously he quickened his pace.

As he passed the crossed poles capped with balls of white bark-cloth that had been placed before the ascent to the chief's compound, he paused. The cluster of buildings above was dominated by the high roof of the men's house. The women's house was only slightly smaller, and the chief's personal residence was only slightly smaller again. These principal buildings were wooden-framed structures with internal skeletons of hewn beams or bamboo. The dozen or so others, all of thatch, included the storehouses, the residences of Chief Kaneohe's wives and children, the kitchens, and those occupied by the immediate staff. He saw the roof of his own house among them and wondered, with a brief surge of bitterness, when and if he would see it again. He had lived all of his life here. It was his place.

The crossed poles were symbols from antiquity that warned all unauthorized people to keep out. Nainoa observed the smoke above the southern horizon and doubted that those so-called warriors would respect the *kapu* sticks.

Nainoa walked quickly through the settlement toward the north road. As he passed through the district where the weavers had worked and lived, he found a length of strong cord hanging from a post before the house of a friend. Holding it, he felt a sense of contact with the maker and quickly fashioned a carrying sling for his spear, then walked on.

The silence was unsettling, and impulsively he took a short detour by the house of another friend, a woman with whom he had sometimes visited. There, where he had spent many pleasant hours, he found another object inadvertently left behind: On a shelf above her raised sleeping platform was a cup fashioned from a cleaned and polished coconut shell. His gear was now complete.

The warmth he had felt at finding a familiar comfort suddenly evaporated. Without warning the hollow place within him filled suddenly and intensely with grief. Great wrenching sobs constricted his chest. Dropping his bags, he knelt in the dust and wept, releasing the tension and conflict of the last few weeks in a burst of feeling, mourning his people's losses and his own. He grieved—and then after a time he picked up his belongings and moved on. Something inside him had settled, accepting his situation.

Nainoa left the settlement and strode along the north road. Its surface had been scarred by the passage of the population and their livestock as they evacuated the community. He passed the vacant fields, avoiding the ruts and piles of dung, watching for any signs of humans or animals. He observed the distant edges of the forest carefully, watching for evidence of the warriors from the south who might already be concealed there. If they were, they were already aware of him. Nothing moved among the fields, however, and the forest beyond was still unusually silent, as though every living thing had been swallowed up into the earth. Had it been like this when the Hawaiian voyagers arrived, expecting to find the Americans living in their vast settlements? He considered how it must have been for the Hawaiians, weakened by thirst and starvation, to make landfall after the arduous ocean journey of forty days—to arrive and find no one, no people at all, only the huge dark forest that seemed to go on forever.

The north road followed the rolling contours of the terraced farmlands. As he walked, he thought about the legendary Americans and their civilization. There was no consensus among the historians about the duration of the Time of Contact during which the Americans had come to Hawai'i, although most felt it had lasted about two hundred years. The Hawaiians' sense of themselves as a distinct cultural group extended back beyond this time, but none of the great chiefly genealogies could be traced beyond the Time of Contact.

The Americans had first appeared during the reign of a chief called Kalaniopu'u. They had arrived in two sailing canoes of immense size and strange design, under the leadership of a great navigator named Cook. Some historical accounts recorded that Cook and his men had not come from America at all but from another place called Britain. All agreed, however, that shortly thereafter, a great chief named Kamehameha had become governor, and that during his reign the Americans had established themselves in Hawai'i, bringing many different people from elsewhere in the world.

The Time of Contact became known in retrospect as the Great Age because of the amazing things these foreigners had introduced. Their enormous flying canoes could travel at great heights and at great speeds by a kind of power that came from metal objects called machines. There had been big machines and small machines with many different functions. Some machines, called *enjins,* had been used to empower wagons, so that they could move without oxen to pull them. Huge roads had been constructed for the passage of these wagons. Isolated remnants of several such roads had been discovered in the forest around the settlements, completely overgrown and buried by earth to a considerable depth.

Before the Americans' coming, there had been no metal in the islands, no horses, no cattle, no sheep or goats, no glass or ceramic objects, no paper or books, no cotton. But at the end of the Great Age, the Americans had disappeared overnight. The metal machines they left behind had ceased to function and were quickly made into other useful things.

Many people from America, and from other legendary places like Iapana, Ainapake, Ainapilipino, and Okekulelia,* were believed to have been living in Hawai'i when the Fall, the end of the Great Age, occurred. Historical accounts of this time described extensive social strife and political upheaval. Most of the people in the islands died from starvation because the population was too great. A Great Flood, accompanied by a disease, subsequently killed off many of the survivors of the famine.

Nainoa considered the flood theory briefly. It was recorded that the ocean had risen dramatically and that much of Hawai'i had disappeared beneath the waters. Nainoa had read the accounts of this period in Chief Kaneohe's library. In books of finely crafted bark-cloth paper were maps that had been copied and recopied by hand by scholars down through the millennia. Many were replicas of originals left in Hawai'i by the Americans. Of particular interest were the maps of the western coast of America, although these bore little or no resemblance to the coast as it existed now. In the old maps this region was a solid, unbroken coast with a large river system flowing westward from the mountains, forming a large bay at its meeting with the ocean. The last hundred years of extensive exploration, however, had revealed the coast to be a scattered archipelago of mountainous islands, running roughly north-south in long, linear rows. Nor did the ancient maps depict anything resembling the vast inland sea to the east.

Nainoa thought about the voyagers as he wended his way along the road. They had arrived in a fleet of 108 great double-hulled canoes, each holding a hundred people, their crop plants, and their animals. They had settled on the shores and islands along the western edge of the inland sea because the soils and drainage patterns of the land there were better for agriculture, while still providing easy and protected access to the rich inland sea. From their arrival the Hawaiians had given high priority to childbearing, and the population had grown rapidly.

. . .

* Japan, China, the Philippines, and Australia.

Nainoa's thoughts were broken by the roar of a red monkey from the forest, a formidable sound out of all proportion to the size of the animal that made it. It never failed to impress him. He was glad to hear another creature. Aside from the monkey and a long-tailed red and blue parrot flying high above the cleared expanse, he was the only thing moving in the empty landscape.

The road came to an end, but he forged on across the last of the fields, whose cotton had not yet been harvested. He stepped carefully, watching for the snakes commonly found at the edges of settlements. As he approached the forest, Nainoa looked for the rocky ridge that shouldered above the surrounding tree canopy. From this vantage point he would be able to see back down the valley to the settlement.

A rocky stream bed formed a natural boundary between the terraced fields and the forest, and he dropped lightly down onto the water-polished boulders that the dry season had revealed. He crossed easily, passing under a towering cotton tree. Far above, its branches bore green pods that would mature and open, releasing handfuls of cotton fluff in which the tree's small dark seeds would be dispersed on the wind. Typically the massive trunks of these trees rose from an immense base of planklike buttress roots, to soar high into the air above the canopy of the forest before throwing out their own crown of branches. The summit of this one was so laden with orchids and ferns that it resembled an enormous arboreal garden.

The Hawaiians were very superstitious about these *pulupulu* trees. They believed that Makua'uwila, the lightning man, descended to earth from the upper world through the cotton tree, so people were very reluctant to cut them down. Since these trees achieved such a great height, they were sometimes struck by lightning, and Nainoa supposed that this was the source of the belief.

Approaching the base of the giant tree, he admired the impressive thorns that adorned its massive gray trunk. Between two of its flared buttress roots, someone had left an offering, a small leaf-wrapped bundle with a dog's skull on top. He recalled how Nagai the hunter had enlisted aid from the spiritual dimensions through the making of offerings.

When Nainoa was still a boy, a farmer had asked Nagai to help him deal with a resistant illness that had not responded to the medicines of the *kahuna lapa'au*, the herbalists. After asking many questions, Nagai had determined that the sickness was caused by an ancestral spirit in the farmer's lineage . . . a spirit displeased with the man for his failure to make regular offerings to his ancestors.

"For such an illness, one cannot simply wrap an egg in a leaf and be done with it," Nagai had said. "The resistance of the sickness is a clear indicator of its source in the realm of the spirits, and for this reason, the offerings must be great. If we are to succeed, the sacrifice must be lavish."

Nagai had known that the man was well-off, that he could afford to make the offerings, and so a special altar had been made, fires prepared, and the sacrifices had gone on for several days. Many pigs and goats had been slaughtered, cooked, wrapped, and offered, after which an *awa* plant was presented at the ritual's end. It was a scene Nainoa witnessed many times as Nagai's unofficial assistant. In this way, he had learned the importance of making offerings to the spirits . . . and in the right way.

And now, standing in the great tree's shadow, he felt an inner shift in response to these memories and rapped on one of its roots to get its attention. He offered a short prayer to the tree's spirit, requesting its blessing and assistance on the journey ahead. He listened to the silence as if expecting a response and was rewarded by the plop of a guava into a pool among the rocks.

Satisfied, he gathered some of the guavas from their bushy tree nearby and prepared to go. Then, recalling the way in which Chief Kaneohe had approached his family shrine, Nainoa paused. He cleared his mind of thoughts, and with respect he formally asked the great tree for its permission to enter the forest. He waited, but this time nothing in particular occurred, so he turned and walked into the shadows and left humankind behind.

The sun was setting as Nainoa scaled the ridge and arrived at the crest, out of breath and sweating heavily. He unburdened himself of his belongings.

Many years had passed since his last trek into the forest with old Nagai. Because of his recent sedentary life as a clerk, he would have sore muscles tomorrow.

From the ridge Nainoa had a clear view of the settlement across the fields, and he could even distinguish the individual buildings of Chief Kaneohe's compound under the tall cotton tree. From here he could watch and not be seen, so he settled down to wait, unsure of what it was that he was waiting for. To the south, the smoke from the burning buildings of the neighboring settlement was clearly visible, but the wind was from the northeast, so he could not smell it. When darkness fell, the southern sky continued to glow.

In the evenings, Nainoa would ordinarily have been seated around the raised edge of the main room in the men's house, a low fire in the room's center, eating with his associates while they recounted the day's events. Tonight he could have no fire to comfort him. He ate a cold supper of dried fish, *taro-poi*, and guavas, washed down with water from his bottle-gourd. He thought about his friend Nagai, who had taught him about the forest.

Nagai had been a commoner who spent most of his time in the forest, a man who exuded a sense of independence, of freedom and a friendly disregard for most social convention, quite different from Nainoa's formal life in Chief Kaneohe's household. Nagai had been his mentor and had given the young boy permission to develop his own sense of personal freedom, especially in his thinking. Nagai had revealed to him the importance of intention, and that intention is the first step to bringing into being that which exists only in one's thoughts. Nainoa remembered their first meeting. . . .

As a boy, he had been fascinated by that part of the open-air market where the hunters sold and bartered their harvest from the forest. Under long rows of thatched roof, each hunter had a stall where he displayed his goods. There Nainoa had wandered daily, feasting his eyes on exotic things until his chores took him away. Some sections of the market were devoted entirely to herbs and medicinal plants, while others sold meat, game, and produce. Still another area offered feathers, animal skins, and objects made from them—bags, clothing, containers, talismans, and other things concerned with magic. There he had first encountered Nagai the hunter.

Nainoa had come upon a group of men bargaining over a spotted tiger skin that had been tanned and softened and glowed in the sunlight. An older, gray-haired hunter with a full white beard sat immobile behind the yellow and black pelt rolled out on a low table, while two lesser chiefs' sons attempted to bring down the price by stressing this fault or that. The hunter was clearly bored with their line of argument. Looking up, the old man had spotted the young boy watching, whereupon he had said to him, "You look like a good judge of quality. How much do you feel this magnificent tiger skin is worth?"

The young chiefs had fallen silent when they saw he was a boy—and a servant at that. Their manner and posture showed their disrespect. Unfazed, Nainoa had studied the skin with care and then turned to the men. "I do not know how much it is worth now," he had said, "but I suspect it was worth considerably more to its original owner."

The old hunter had roared with laughter, clearly delighted with his response. The two chieflets had looked embarrassed and departed without a word, casting dark looks at the old man and the boy. Nagai had rolled up the tiger skin and asked Nainoa if he had ever been into the great forest. They went together on a walk that was the beginning of their friendship and the first of many trips over the years. From Nagai, Nainoa had learned how to survive in that sometimes hostile and sometimes benevolent wilderness.

Now Nainoa sat in the gathering darkness and realized that he had not thought of Nagai for some time. The hunter had passed away eight years before. Nainoa would have greatly enjoyed the old hunter's company and expertise on this walk.

The night air was warm, and the rocks of the ridge crest radiated heat stored from the sun through the early part of the evening. Nainoa rested in comfort, dozing in short cycles, keeping watch in the dim light cast by the

waxing moon. Eventually the day's tension exacted its toll, and he slept deeply in the middle of the night.

The air turned colder before the dawn, and something suddenly alerted him. He scrutinized the valley below in the starlight, wondering at the cause. He could make out the dark mass of the settlement in the midst of the fields and the road he had traveled. Nothing appeared amiss.

Abruptly monkeys howled from the forest to the south. Nainoa sat bolt upright and focused his attention on that area but again saw nothing. He was on the point of relaxing into another short nap, when a light appeared briefly near Chief Kaneohe's personal residence, then abruptly disappeared. Once again he saw it, and once again it vanished. He watched the platform's dark mass with great concentration but did not see the light again. Had it been a signal? If so, to whom? None of the commoners or nobles of the settlement would dare approach the chief's residence for any reason at this time. The penalty would be severe, and retribution swift.

Weighing the various possibilities, he thought it likely that the uninvited guests from the south had arrived. He considered himself fortunate indeed not to have remained for one last night.

And so in that darkest hour before the dawn, Nainoa sat quietly on the ridge thinking, watching, and waiting for first light of the coming day. When it appeared, he rearranged his gear and slipped into the shadows, heading north toward the canoe waiting for him in the cove on the coast.

As he walked, he heard roosters crowing in the distance.

3
Shamans and Speculations

MY "DREAM" ENDED AT DAWN, WHEN THE CROW-
ing of my neighbors' roosters shifted my
awareness. The transition was abrupt, much
like changing channels on a television. My eyes blinked
rapidly as the rush of sensation faded in slowly diminishing surges. The exquisite paralysis retreated from my body
and finally disappeared. I could close my hands once
again.

It was not surprising that the roosters' shrill crowing
had disrupted my altered state, but I was struck that
Nainoa had heard them too.

I lay still for some time, reviewing the imagery, impressions, and feelings of the dream. I ran through it quickly,
in segments. Unlike my ordinary dreams I could recall it
all and in great detail. It was as though I had been there,
and I mean *really there.* As I realized this, I began to panic
—and my mental constructs about the nature of reality
began to disintegrate.

Struggling to control my emotions, my scientific curiosity came to my rescue and helped me regain a calm perspective on what I had experienced. More than two years had elapsed since my three previous experiences in Berkeley. In the interim I had managed to create neat little mental parentheses around them. I sensed this experience was not going to be as easy to set aside. Although the altered state had come over me spontaneously once again, this time I had found myself intimately knowing a man who would live thousands of years in the future. I wondered if I would ever see anything in quite the same way again.

When I finally got out of bed, I walked out onto our wide lanai and looked down, across the island's green flank, to Kealakekua Bay. It was still quite early, but I could clearly see the white obelisk of Captain Cook's monument on its far shore. The ocean was calm, its dark surface inscribed by wide lines delineating the interface of winds and currents. I had observed this view every day for almost a year, but this morning everything about it struck me as different. The sun had not yet cleared the volcano's rim to the east, and the landscape looked flat, almost two-dimensional, perhaps because there were no shadows.

I did manage to go on with my life much as before, spending mornings at the beach and afternoons working on the house and land. In the evenings, however, I wrote down everything I could recall about the dream.

At first I wondered if it had perhaps been a lucid dream—that dramatic state in which the dreamer knows that he or she is dreaming and can act in and direct the dream. I reconsidered the experience over and over during the weeks that followed, and in spite of my scientific training and nature, I came to believe that it had not been a dream at all.

I had really felt as though I were inside Nainoa's body, seeing through his eyes, hearing what he was hearing. I had listened to his thoughts and felt his feelings. I had even probed his memories—and they were not my memories. I had learned a lot about him and his world through his memories. I had seen his world visually through his eyes and cognitively through his perceptions, judgments, interpretations, and opinions. His thoughts and feelings had an alien quality, a foreignness, that was very

distracting at first, but this was due to the profoundly different cognitive "shape" of his mind, which had been determined largely by his experiences since birth in his own slice of reality, within his own culture. I became aware by degrees that I was eavesdropping on his mind—a mind quite different from my own. At the same time, however, I felt an odd sense of familiarity, as though I knew him very well. Always the professional anthropologist, I had also observed many concrete details of the community, the architecture of the buildings, and the design of Nainoa's clothing and possessions.

I had perceived all this as vividly real, as if I had been fully awake, fully aware, and fully operational in my own everyday, ordinary world. Yet during the time I was in the altered state, my physical body had lain safely in bed, seemingly asleep beside Jill, and I had maintained a dim awareness of it throughout my time with Nainoa.

While I was merged with this man, it was as though I *were* him, and yet my personality had not dissolved, nor had his. The two of us existed simultaneously within one physical body. His personality remained distinctly separate from mine, and he had seemed completely unaware of my presence within him while I was "there."

When I had first opened my eyes in Nainoa's body, however, I tried to control his movements. His body responded with confusion to two separate sets of commands. Somehow, despite my own confusion and excitement, I managed to figure out that the solution was to be completely passive. I merely "sat within" and observed. My limited experience with meditation certainly proved invaluable here, as I was able to discipline myself to become completely still yet fully watchful. Thereafter if I wished to look at something, Nainoa would very shortly walk over and look at it. If I wanted to know something, it would obligingly appear in my mind— and in his.

Had I projected an aspect of myself into my dreaming to create Nainoa? If so, I had certainly created a magnificent ideal. Nainoa was in the prime of his life, in his late twenties perhaps. He was close to seven feet tall and built like a professional athlete. He must have weighed at least 275 pounds and was physically very fit. His skin was dark, a rich burnt sienna, and he wore his black hair long, gathered into a single thick braid that extended down his back. His face was framed by a short beard. His features were strong, with high cheekbones, a broad nose with a high bridge, and a full wide mouth. When he looked into the stream, I had seen his reflection. Oddly, his expressive, almond-shaped eyes were blue.

So were Chief Kaneohe's, I recalled. The chief vaguely resembled a dark-skinned version of the late British actor Jack Hawkins, yet he was huge, his height emphasized even more by his hairstyle. The sides of his head had been shaved or plucked, leaving a Mohawk crest of graying hair that terminated in a short braid in the back. Whereas Nainoa wore a classic Hawaiian breechcloth or *malo*, the chief wore a longish pair of wide woven cotton shorts dyed with a dark red pattern. His carved whale-tooth pendant was not unlike the classic *lei niho palaoa*, that ancient symbol of Hawaiian chiefly status shaped like a projecting hook or tongue. A dyed cotton cloak around his shoulders had hung almost to his bare feet. He had been shirtless, revealing linear rows of tattoos on the right side of his body.

The language that Nainoa and the chief spoke did not resemble either English or Hawaiian, although some words seemed derived from each. Just how had I understood what they were saying? Their speech had seemed to be some kind of "pidgin" or *patois*, but it was very different from any I had heard in the Caribbean, West Africa, or present-day Hawai'i. While I was merged with Nainoa, I had had no idea what most of the spoken words meant, but Nainoa had, and because of this, in some incomprehensible way I had too. As I "listened in" on his recollections, which included conversations with other people, I understood through his understanding.

I am not a linguist, nor am I particularly interested in linguistics, but I wrote down some of the words that I was able to recall phonetically. The word for *machine*, for example, was *mokini* or *mukini*. The term *cotton tree* is my own translation from the words Nainoa used in his thoughts, *la'au'* (or *lao*) *pulupulu*. I have not encountered this name in contemporary Hawai'i, but the tree he was seeing was a kapok (*Ceiba pentendra*), a pantropical species from Africa, Asia, and Central and South America that grows at several localities on the "big island." The term for the chief's personal temple site, *heiau*, was essentially the same as that used in the islands today. So was the word for stone, *pohaku*, although the phoneme *p* sounded closer to a *b*, and the *k* sounded more like a *g*, producing a word resembling *bohagu*. Since the word *pohaku* is still currently in use in Hawai'i, I write it that way here. Similarly, the word *kahuna* was perceived as *kahoon* or *gahoon*, but because this word is well-known, I have chosen to write it as *kahuna* in the account that follows.

I had been "there" for at least sixteen to eighteen hours of his time, yet by the dream's end, less than five minutes had elapsed in my time. I knew this because I had finally remembered to glance at the clock when I felt the sensations coming on. My inner scientist was at a loss to explain this discrepancy.

Nainoa had been alone when I first "arrived," involved in preparations for his walk. In fact, he was alone for the entirety of the "visit," so most of what I learned about him, his world, and his recent history arrived in my mind as disjointed blocks of—to me—completely new information. I absorbed these blocks as if I were transferring information from one floppy disk to another. The information appeared in the form of impressions, feelings, thoughts, opinions, ideas, and memories and would suddenly materialize as a series of vignettes in my awareness. Each would "shade off" gradually into the surrounding ground of my own thought-feeling before the next formed. These scenes came rapidly, in sequence, so that I had little time to consider or think about what I was seeing before the next series began. So I tried to absorb them while I was merged with Nainoa, with the intention of recalling them afterward. It was a little like watching television, but the "show" included far more than just visuals and sound.

So how does one present information of this sort without sounding like a candidate for certification in a mental institution? I offer it as I perceived it. My creative imagination is undoubtedly involved to some extent in this reconstruction because I have had to compose a framework in which to express these extraordinary experiences, yet I did not make up this trip out

of whole cloth. As I write, I often consider whether my imagination has filled in details, expanding the account, but I know when my creative side is engaged and when it is not. I had clearly perceived a world that is quite separate from my own and from my self. I have chosen to write Nainoa's life like an adventure story because that is very much how I experienced it. In this story another man's life and my own form a double helix, a twisted ladder whose edges consist of two lifelines, Nainoa's and mine, with rungs of connection between them at various intervals along the continuum.

The translation of this episode onto paper has been a strange and difficult task. My first attempts were hesitant, the results discordant, as I searched for a way to convey the initially ineffable quality of my merging with Nainoa. Because I had received large chunks of information all at once from Nainoa's memories, and because I did not remember them in chronological order, it took me weeks to "excavate" them from my own recall. I had to work hard to recapture and arrange them in an accessible narrative. Many times, I thought I'd finished rendering the episode, whereupon I would suddenly remember something else, some detail on which I had not focused when the dream was actually happening. It seemed as if my memory had absorbed far more information than I had been aware of at the time. It was all there, buried within me, but also still outside of me, separate and apart from me.

Nainoa's world was so real that if I had not had some prior knowledge of tribal shamans and their curious practices, I would have seriously considered that I was going mad. As it was, I sensed that I had journeyed like a shaman in an altered state of consciousness, but my destination was not the spirit world. I had journeyed across space and time to merge with the consciousness of another person, one who lives right here on the earth, in ordinary reality, but in a slice of the future that is profoundly different from the reality that exists today.

Time passed, and my days in Kona became weeks. My dreaming became normal again, although I spent many waking hours going over the dream, trying to figure out where I had been, if indeed I had traveled to the future.

Nainoa's community was located somewhere on the western coast of North America. To the west lay the Pacific, and to the east an inland sea, beyond which there was a mountain range. The place could have been somewhere in northern California. The inland sea could be the central valley filled with water, and the mountains could be the Sierra Nevada beyond. But the environment had not looked at all like the California coast I knew so well. Where were the chaparral-covered hills, the redwoods, pines, and oak-studded grasslands?

I had looked for familiar landmarks, but the dark wall of the tropical forest beyond the fields had obscured my view of the distance, and the sky had been very hazy. The soft cast to the light suggested that the season was late fall, yet the temperature and overall feel of the air resembled Hawai'i's and was clearly tropical and wet.

The buttress-rooted cotton tree that Nainoa had greeted upon entering the woods was easily the largest I had ever seen—its immense trunk soared to considerably more than two hundred feet, before its massive crown extended for another fifty or seventy-five. This rainforest giant suggested that Nainoa's world was actually in southern Mexico or someplace farther south. The bird that had flown over the field was a red and blue macaw, and no one who has heard a red howler monkey's roar ever forgets it.

I wondered if the inland sea could be the Gulf of Lower California that separates Baja from the mainland of Mexico. A fleeting image from Nainoa's thoughts had revealed it to be encircled by mountains around its southern end, strongly suggesting that it was not the Sea of Cortés. I knew that the southern part of California's San Joaquin Valley was encircled by mountains. If Nainoa's settlement were located on its western side, the inland sea could be an intrusion of the sea within the great valley. I thought of Nainoa's flood theory and wondered how much the sea level would have had to rise to fill it.

Perhaps the sea level had risen because of global climatic warming. As in all arenas of science, no consensus of opinion exists among the experts on the so-called "greenhouse" theory, and the ongoing controversy reflects uncertainty among the various scientific specialists. It is now undeniable, however, that the levels of carbon dioxide, methane, nitrous oxide, and the chlorofluorocarbons are increasing within the earth's atmosphere as a result of industrial activities. The ultimate effects of these increases are unknown, but many scientists predict an increase in the world's temperatures of at least five degrees or more if the levels of "greenhouse gases" continue to rise. Five of the hottest years on record occurred during the 1980s, causing the world's glaciers to retreat and pieces of ice the size of Rhode Island to break off from the vast ice shelves attached to Antarctica.

At the time of my dream, it was the spring of 1986, and these alarming signs had not moved American politicians to try to prevent concentrations of industrial pollutants from increasing in the air. President Reagan and the Congress had been dragging their feet on environmental concerns, saying that the evidence for greenhouse warming was inconclusive and warning that governmental policymakers were being induced to take unwise action on the basis of uncertain scientific evidence. The scientists on the other side of the issue were predicting global catastrophe due to overpopulation, environmental degradation, climatic warming, and rising sea levels.

From Nainoa I had learned that a sudden rise in sea level was connected to the collapse of Western civilization. Scientists have discovered that a worldwide temperature increase of at least nine degrees centigrade accompanied the end of the last ice age, around ten thousand years ago when the melting of the continental ice sheets caused the sea level to rise about three hundred feet. Had Nainoa's culture retained the memory of another inundation much like the biblical account of the great flood that Noah and his family had survived? I determined to find out how great a rise in temperature would be required to melt the contemporary ice caps and snow cover in the polar regions.

Late one evening about six weeks after the dream, the heavy, sweet scent of night-blooming jasmine flowed into my house, where I was working on a painting. It was close to midnight, and Jill and Erica were asleep. My attention was divided, and I was having trouble concentrating on the canvas. My scientific nature is interested in solving problems, and

I kept wondering just *why* this strange experience had happened to me: *How* had the time shift happened, and *why* had it happened now, here in Kona?

I paused in my work to stare at the image emerging on the wet surface of the stretched canvas. I put my brush into a jar of thinner and looked around the room, which was both studio and study. On all the walls were newly executed oil paintings, all focused on the same subject: Hawaiian *heiaus*, pre-Christian sites of traditional religious activity. When I began the series, I had felt compelled by these sites; they had exerted a magnetic draw, and I had allowed myself to be drawn by their power. Around the paintings on the floor were rough-cut pieces of lumber on which stood a group of lava stone sculptures in various stages of execution.

During the past year my family and I had been in the habit of driving down the mountain to the village of Napo'opo'o virtually every day in order to swim in the warm waters of Kealakekua Bay. The village's crescent of sandy beach is surrounded by a Hawaiian archaeological site dominated by a large stone platform called Hikiau Heiau. A bronze plaque, affixed to a pillar before the massive temple, informs tourists that in the late 1770s Captain James Cook read the first Christian service in the Hawaiian Islands at this *heiau*, a funeral for an unfortunate British seaman killed over a difference of opinion with the locals.

All that remains of these *heiaus* today are their dark stone platforms, many of which have been reduced to piles of rubble by earthquakes and tidal waves. Some have been restored, using early travelers' sketches as guidelines, and some include carved images of the old *akuas* and full-scale replicas of the *hale mana*, the house of power, in which the sacred relics of chiefly lineages once resided.

I looked at my paintings. The broad linear planes of color were abstractions of these places of power where the human and the natural came together. The black platform surmounted by the *hale mana* appeared in each. I remembered Chief Kaneohe's *heiau*—was there a connection between these paintings and the dream?

Impulsively I looked up the meanings of the syllables of the word *heiau*.

Hei means "net" or "snare" or "to ensnare or catch in a net." *Au* has several meanings, among which are "period of time," "age," "era," or "the passing of time." *Heiau*—a place of power where one could capture time. I began to reconsider the idea of supernatural power from an anthropological perspective.

In the late 1800s an English scholar named Edward B. Tylor asserted that the foundation of all religion was in the concept of the soul, perceived almost universally as a spiritual essence that differs from the physical body. The idea of a soul, Tylor speculated, must have developed among traditional tribal people as a result of their curiosity and concern with the difference between living and dying, between waking and dreaming. Tylor called this belief in a personal, supernatural essence animism, and he argued that tribal people believed a soul to exist not only in humans but in animals, plants, and inanimate objects like stones, ponds, and clouds.

Then in the early 1900s one of Tylor's contemporaries named R. R. Marett counterargued that the concept of a soul was too sophisticated to have supplied the beginnings of religion. Marett speculated that animism must have been preceded by another concept he called animatism, a belief in an impersonal, supernatural force or power.

A good example of animatism is to be found among the traditional cultures of Polynesia and Melanesia, among whose peoples good luck and misfortune, as well as extraordinary abilities or events, are attributed to *mana*, the invisible supernatural power dispersed throughout the universe, which can be highly concentrated both within inanimate objects or places and within living things. It was traditionally believed that human beings could also be repositories for high concentrations of *mana*. Such persons were said to be able willfully to increase their personal supply. *Mana* could be transferred from one person to another, from a person to an object, or even from an object to a person. *Mana* was—and still is—believed to be transmitted through touch or simply through proximity. *Heiaus* were built above high concentrations of *mana*.

I stared at my paintings and wondered if my daily nearness to the huge

temple platform at the bay was somehow affecting me. My scientific worldview shifted uneasily, profoundly distrustful of this line of thought.

My attention turned again to the rough sculptures I had fashioned from black lava boulders found along the coast. Virtually all Hawaiian beaches were littered with them, and many were already partially shaped from being tumbled about by the waves. I sat back and considered the ritual I always performed when searching for stones.

On arriving at a beach, I always asked permission from the "spirits of the place" to find and take stones—a decidedly animist procedure. Although my scientific side found this amusing and smiled at the whole idea of this ceremony, I always did it. Afterward, I would walk the beach, randomly casting my eyes among the stones until one distinguished itself from the others. Usually an inner form was already partially exposed, and I saw the possibilities of how to use it in an artistic piece. I would continue my search until I found a stone with an irresistible form. Most were too heavy to move, so they remained. But some I could lift.

As a result of my study of Zen Buddhism, I consider stones to be sitting in their own form of meditation—an eccentricity perhaps, but a satisfying one. Accordingly, I always ask their individual permission before moving them. I usually invite the selected stone to accompany me back to my studio, where I promise to modify it only minimally in order to bring out its inner form. Almost always the stones agree. Sometimes I have wondered whether I really select the stones. Occasionally the draw is so strong that the stones seem really to be selecting me.

Usually I let the stones sit around for a while. During this time, my incipient ideas of how to develop them become defined. In sculpting them, I follow a meditative exercise. I unfocus my mind and move slowly into their stillness. Then, after a time, I begin.

It was well after midnight when I began contemplating the *pohakus* in my studio and their possible role in my journey. Each stone possessed its own "power" from the place and the process of its origin. Each had acquired "power" from my mind and muscles as well, from the artist who had

brought out their "essence" animatistically. As objects of contemplation, they would acquire even more "power" through their contact with other people. I wondered if they would give "power" in return to those who made contact. As both an artist and anthropologist, I found this idea very appealing.

It was after two when I finally pulled myself away from the stones and *heiaus* and left the studio. Jill was reading in bed. She was approaching the last trimester of her second pregnancy and looked wonderful. Ordinarily long and lean, she had transformed into a wondrous composite of organic forms.

I went through my rituals of showering, shaving, and toothbrushing and slipped into bed. Jill kissed me warmly, then turned onto her side and drifted off to sleep. I turned out the light and lay down, fitting my body to hers and wrapping her in an embrace. Holding her, feeling her breathing, I fell asleep.

At four in the morning, I awoke. The light was on, and Jill was reading again, unable to sleep. I worked on her back, trying to help her relax. The magic that touch creates progressed into lovemaking, and in its aftermath, we held each other closely and prepared to sleep once again.

I felt myself slipping down, down—and was almost asleep, when I felt the sensations there, just at the edge of my awareness. I lay in the darkness waiting, smelling the pungent night-blooming jasmine floating on the night air. Suddenly the feelings surged with a roaring rush of power, filling my ears with a buzzing hiss. My intellect snapped on, fully awake, fully aware. Any residual dreaminess vanished. I had been waiting for this.

My body became rigid with the creeping paralysis, and I had great difficulty breathing. My hands felt like balloons—I could not close them. Then I could not move my body at all. My eyes were tightly closed.

In the darkness I saw again the curious lines of light interspersed with linear rows of dots. The lines shifted to become zigzags, then straightened out again into the serpentine patterns that extended into the unimaginable distance of the grid. The curious, shimmering arc of light appeared, and I

wondered if I would again "visit" with Nainoa. With this thought I had a sense of movement that immediately merged with a new surge in the sensations. I felt myself being pushed out . . . expanding . . . expanding outward.

The sensations continued to intensify. They were exquisite, simply exquisite. The rushing sound abruptly ceased, and once again complete silence descended. The sensations began to lessen.

Startled and somewhat disappointed, I opened my eyes, and my heart skipped a beat—the bedroom was gone. Huge shapes loomed over me in the mist. A fat water drop landed on the back of my arm—a very muscular arm that was decidedly brown. I was standing in the forest.

4
Second Journey
The City in the Forest

NAINOA WAS STANDING AT A FORK IN THE GAME trail that he had been following toward the northeast. It was early morning, and the forest was filled with mist. The strange sweet scent of some blooming plant floated in the humid air and then passed on. His eyes scanned the wet greenery for the flowers but did not find them.

The constant dripping of water from the leaves high above rattled off his rain-cape, which covered him from his shoulders to his hips and protected his sling bags of provisions. The undergrowth sparkled with moisture, assuring that he was wet from the hips down. It was warm in the forest, and sweat beaded his brow under a makeshift broadleaf hat. Being wet was not his preferred state.

Eleven days had passed since he had left the settlement. He was now farther inland than any of his people had been before. He had entered unknown territory.

From early morning until late afternoon, he would travel, hunting and foraging along the way. Monkeys, lizards, birds, snakes, and large rodents fell to his arrows. From the myriad watercourses that crossed his route, he got fish and turtle eggs, a dry-season delicacy buried along the exposed sandbars. Toward nightfall, he always listened for the distinctive calls of the *moa la'au*, the large jungle "chickens" that often roosted on low branches for the night. It was easy to mark their cries, find them after dark, and simply dispatch them with a stick.

As he studied the game trail through the wet, lush greenery that surrounded him, he thought back to the beginning of his walk.

He had made his way cautiously toward the coast on that first day, pausing often in the forest to listen and watch for warriors from the south. He saw no one and arrived at the cove toward dusk. The canoe that Chief Kaneohe had promised was there—a small sailing outrigger that he could manage alone.

He camped well off the ground that night, sleeping in his string hammock in a tree, out of fear of the omnipresent crocodiles. He woke before dawn and waited for first light before dragging the canoe to the water and loading it with his gear. The forest was cloaked in dense fog, but fortunately he knew the coastline of numberless coves and lagoons well. He paddled out into the mist, steering by memory for open water.

That first morning on the water was eerie, the sky and the sea indistinguishable from each other in the fog, with only the touch of his paddle to the water's surface to keep him oriented as to which way was up and which was down. He paddled quietly, watching for well-known landmarks until the fog dissolved with the arrival of the first breeze.

The wind came from the north, and he unfurled the craft's scooplike sail to cruise southeast through the many islands and waterways he had explored in his youth. He sailed on throughout the day and camped that night on an island he knew. The next morning, with the wind once again in his favor, he opened the sail and set off across the vast expanse of the inland sea.

The eastern shore was invisible in the haze of fine dust that always accompanied the dry season. He sat quietly, steering with his broad-bladed

paddle, watching the western shore recede. He saw no evidence of pursuers or anyone else. The sea was empty, and he felt his solitude with a bittersweet intensity that filled him with melancholy. The wind picked up, carrying him southeast at a good clip. He arrived in the early evening on the swampy eastern shore where he camped on a low-lying island surrounded by mangroves.

The wind had carried him farther south than he would have wished, and so he paddled north the next day, in the company of some dolphins, looking for a river he had explored with Nagai many years before. He saw many crocodiles, but all submerged themselves at his approach. Even on this side of the sea, they were wary of humans because they were hunted for their meat and hides.

He camped that night on another island after feasting on a large fish he had speared in the shallows among the mangroves. The warm water seethed with large shrimp, and he regretted not having a casting net. Continuing north the next day, he had finally found the silty, treelined watercourses of the river's marshy delta in the early afternoon. He turned and paddled up its main channel, noting that the water level was low in the advancing dry season. Large crocodiles and turtles basked on the many exposed bars.

The river had changed to an amazing extent. Its bed had shifted and an entirely new passage had been cut. He stayed in the main channel, using a long pole instead of the paddle when the water became shallow. Waterfowl were abundant, and he shot a brace of ducks for his evening meal, using arrows with pronged points designed for that purpose. He camped that evening on an island where he had stopped years before with Nagai.

At dawn the next morning, he killed a small deer, cut the meat in strips, and dried it on racks built over a fire. He continued upstream in the afternoon, and late in the day, as he approached higher ground, he surprised a herd of elephants drinking at another place where he and Nagai had camped. The great beasts stared at him and abruptly vacated the newly exposed sand bar with loud trumpetings, withdrawing into the high forest beyond.

He disembarked on the bar, studying the sand for other animal signs, especially those of large carnivores. The towering wall of the forest beyond looked dark and forbidding in the fading light. A red monkey roared at him as he pulled the canoe to higher ground, made camp, and slept safely in his hammock in a large tree.

The following day, he laboriously hauled his canoe above the highest watermark to a place of concealment. He cut poles and lashed them to trees to construct a rack to support the craft well off the ground, and he erected a rough shelter to conceal and protect it from sun and rain. The canoe would be there for him on his return, safe from termites and the unseasonal floods that often swept down out of the mountains to the east.

The next morning, he checked his canoe, then began his walk in earnest. Accustomed to walking on the even surfaces in the settlements, he now seemed always to be looking up when he should have been looking down. He tripped, stubbed his toes, slipped and fell, and frequently entangled his sling bags in branches and shrubs. As he had expected, his muscles became sore from the unaccustomed exercise.

Nainoa smiled at these recollections as he considered the fork in the trail before him. His body was becoming accustomed to its new regimen of constant, arduous trekking. He took the more well-trodden route, marking the direction with a knife-cut on a tree, where he would see it on his return.

The mist burned off as the morning advanced, and he stepped with relative ease between the great tree trunks, whose crowns glowed in the sunlight far overhead. Bird calls filtered down in the dim light, taking on a bell-like resonance in the vast hall of the forest. His eyes swept the game trail methodically as he walked, watching for the formidable and virtually invisible serpents that lay in wait in the leaf-litter for the large forest rodents to pass. Many trees were leafless in the advancing dry season, and more light penetrated to the floor, making it difficult to distinguish snakes in the dappled mosaic of light and shadow.

At midmorning he almost blundered into a herd of wild forest pigs. These strange animals looked like a mixture of pig and elephant with short prehensile noses. The adults were large and dark gray; the piglets brown,

with lighter spots and stripes. Until the Hawaiian voyagers had arrived on the coast, they had never seen pigs like these before.

The Hawaiians' records in Chief Kaneohe's library had revealed that their ancestors in Hawai'i had thought many of the American forest animals were mythological creatures until they made landfall on the American coast and found serpents, tigers, crocodiles, monkeys, and elephants. Although copies of the very earliest historical accounts brought from the islands revealed that the Americans had kept many of these creatures on display in cages in their settlements, presumably for prestige and as symbols of their power over nature, no one had believed them.

The histories also recorded the voyagers' surprise at discovering this great forest, whose trees exceeded in height and mass any seen in Hawai'i. The archipelagolike nature of the coast and the discovery of the inland sea had created confusion as well, casting doubt on the navigators' claim that they had made landfall on that part of the American mainland known as California, because nothing seemed as it did on the ancient maps. All the navigators had been in consensus, insisting that they had landed near a large bay on the maps, much altered by the Great Flood.

Great respect and awe were accorded the navigators in his culture. While each of the long double-hulled canoes had its own *haku*, or captain in charge of the overall functioning and well-being of the craft, everyone, even the high chief, looked to the navigators for guidance and wisdom.

He thought about his life as a servant as he walked. Very rarely a servant, through exceptional achievement, would be elevated to chiefly rank, usually resulting in marriage into a high-ranking family. Upward mobility was possible but difficult. Such an honor might be accorded him if he survived his journey and returned with his navigational knowledge of the American interior. Nainoa let the negative thought go and considered the hierarchy of his society. The exercise assuaged his loneliness.

Various levels of rank existed within the chiefly class, determined largely by kinship. The directors were the highest-ranking chiefs within their land divisions and were part of a governing council called the board. This was a name from antiquity, and no one was certain exactly what the word signified. The term was derived from Old English, the ancestral language of the Americans.

The board was directly responsible to the governor, the *ali'i nui*, who was the highest-ranking of all the chiefs and held the ceremonial title of *ali'i ho'omalu'bordi*, the chairman of the board. The present governor was High Chiefess Ruth Kahalopuna, whose family was descended from an old royal lineage of Hawai'i. A gifted ruler with exceptional abilities in both politics and administration, she was also blessed with an exceptional staff derived largely, but not exclusively, from members of her own extended family.

Her prime minister, High Chief Shimoda, advised her in the conducting of the affairs of the entire chain of settlements along the inland sea. His ceremonial title was *ali'i gala'aina*, which implied that he presided over the entirety of all the land divisions. He was responsible for the collection of taxes, the redistribution of surpluses, land rights, fishing rights, and so forth. It would be up to Chief Shimoda to deal with the current crisis within the settlements. Nainoa wondered what he would decree. Warfare was probable. Chief Shimoda was the commander of the governor's soldiers, the *ami*, and he would very likely send them against the usurper to the south.

A cloud of large blue butterflies rose in a shaft of light. They had been drinking from a muddy stream bank before Nainoa's passage had disturbed them. He drew his long knife and severed a thick vine. Fresh water gushed from its cut surface, and he drank deeply and gratefully, then refilled his water bottle. Old Nagai had taught him which vines held water and which were poisonous. He sent the hunter's spirit a fond greeting before continuing his speculations.

The directors were guided to varying degrees by a council of priests collectively known as *kahunas*, who were of chiefly rank themselves. The priests were a mixed lot. Most of them were *kahuna pule*, masters of ritual and prayer, ceremonialists who were in charge of the *heiaus*. These priests were politically powerful and worked closely with the chiefs. They would vote for war.

There were also the *kahuna lapa'au*, the healers, among whom were the mystics. Called *kahuna kupua*, the masters of spirits, the mystics served as intermediaries between the people and the supernatural realm and were accorded great respect for their unique abilities. The mystics were not full-time religious specialists, as were the priests—in fact, they had little to do with organized religion. Their power and knowledge were said to be acquired directly from the spirits, the *akuas*, and from their *aumakuas*, their personal-ancestral, spiritual level of self. Unlike the priests, the mystics were found in all levels of society, and many of them had great power. Old Nagai had been such a *kahuna*, Nainoa had later realized, although he had never called himself one.

It was from Nagai that he had learned the world was made up of things seen and things hidden, presented together as different aspects of one common reality. For the old hunter, the spirits were everywhere, in everything, and he had honored and acknowledged them from moment to moment as he passed through his daily life. This had had a strong effect on Nainoa as a boy. His interest in the *kahuna* mystics had begun then.

The irregular brown shape of a termite nest appeared in Nainoa's path, constructed around the slender trunk of a dead sapling. He approached it, alarming a large group of tiny bizarre-looking monkeys. There appeared to be two different kinds of monkeys within the group. Suddenly, in the space of a heartbeat, a hawk swept through the clearing in a blur of motion and flew upward into the green gloom with one of the diminutive beasts clutched in its talons. The survivors retreated through the foliage, giving their alarm calls.

Nainoa thought again about the warriors to the south. There was a quality to them that was not unlike the hawk. He remembered Chief Kaneohe's comment: The failure of these warrior-focused people lay at the level of leadership. They needed a strong director who could control them, a director with a highly developed sense of ethics.

Nagai had shown him that termite larvae were tasty and nutritious. He broke open the termite nest, gathered the larvae, and ate. Then he walked on, thinking fondly of his old friend and missing him intensely.

In the late afternoon Nainoa's surroundings suddenly changed, and he stopped walking. An emotional charge rose within him. The forest was unusually silent, yet there was no sign of human or animal, no footprints or spoor, no broken branches or bent foliage, no serpents coiled in the shadows, no tiger crouched and ready. As his emotional charge began to dissipate, he saw what had stopped him.

Off to his left the predominantly flat ground gave way to a series of mounds covered by the omnipresent trees. Among them stood a number of vegetation-covered "uprights" that could have passed for tree trunks, were it not for the regularity of their placement.

Nainoa had once explored a similar area with Nagai. The forested mounds had been arranged in a regular gridlike pattern, and they had found some artifacts among the roots of a fallen tree—glass shards, broken ceramic fragments, and lengths of rope made from copper. Judging from this evidence, the mounds were the ruins of an ancient American settlement.

Nagai had said that his fellow hunters knew of other such places, but they avoided them, claiming that they were haunted by hungry ghosts. There were many tales of men who had camped among these strange mounds and had never been seen again or had gone insane and never recovered. Nainoa had no idea how true these stories were, but his excitement rose as he looked more closely at his discovery. He had always intended to return to the ruined settlement to explore it, but in the midst of his busy life in Chief Kaneohe's household, he had never had the opportunity.

Suddenly Nainoa felt diminished, and a sense of melancholy invaded him. Was this abrupt mood shift due to his being near this place? Perhaps unhappy spirits really did reside here. His mind unexpectedly produced a word in Old English—*siti.* It was a term that referred to American settlements.

The game trail continued along the edge of the ruined *siti*. He walked slowly, looking, observing. Here and there, more vegetation-covered mono-liths protruded from the ground in regular rows. He examined one, clearing off part of its surface with his digging stick. It was the remains of a chimney, fashioned of curious brown ceramic blocks held together with mortar.

Nainoa saw a large tree leaning against several of its neighbors and climbed to the level of the canopy to get a better look. More tree-covered mounds interspersed with fern-covered chimneys stretched away into the dry season's dusty haze. In the distance he saw a hill with an immense banyan tree growing out of its summit. He decided the tree would be a suitable place to spend the night, so he took his bearings and descended once again to the forest floor.

He thought briefly of the hunters' stories, then dismissed them and walked into the abandoned *siti*. Perhaps he would find evidence of the Americans that would reveal something about their civilization's demise.

His progress was slow as he made his way through areas thickly over-grown with vegetation. He looked at the trees carefully, searching for domestics—for bananas, papayas, avocados, mangos, breadfruit, mac nuts, guavas, or *wi*-apples—but saw none. This place had been abandoned for a long time. Not far from the banyan tree he blundered into an animal trail that crossed his path. It ran straight as a stick for as far as he could see. He followed it and very shortly came to a place where a large tree had fallen. The trunk had decayed into a long fern-and-fungus-covered ridge lying between two of the mounds. A broad circular hollow in the earth where the tree had uprooted now contained a shallow pool of water. Out of curiosity he approached the pool, startling some frogs that plopped into the water, shattering the silence.

He peered into the pool but saw no fish, not even small ones. The dark, leaf-obscured bottom swarmed with the larvae of many different kinds of insects and frogs. Young trees and shrubs grew around the pool, and several large tree frogs blended into the overhanging branches. A flicker of movement revealed a big-billed toucan observing him speculatively from a liana high above. Some of the large tailless monkeys* called in the distance.

As Nainoa looked slowly around, he suddenly spotted a serpent that was coiled motionless between the roots of a tree, several paces to his left. It was a poisonous species mightily feared by the hunters, who called it *kahaku la'au*, the master of the forest. As thick as his arm and perhaps twice as long as he was tall, the snake was pale, creamy brown with several rows of black scales running along the ridge of its back. Irregular white spots and dark indistinct V's pointed down its sides, rendering it virtually invisible in the pile of leaves. Its head was as big as his hand, and long black stripes trailed back from its shiny, jet-black eyes that watched him impassively as its dark red tongue flicked the air for his scent.

Nainoa regarded the snake uneasily as he moved slowly backward. He was fortunate not to have stepped on it. He slowly strung his bow and notched an arrow—the snake would mean a lot of meat for him and would take little effort to kill. He was on the point of letting fly when a strange thought stopped him. This place had an unnatural feeling to it. The animals and plants here might be unnatural too. To kill anything here might incur very bad luck indeed, something he could definitely do without. Perhaps the serpent was the guardian of the *siti*. At this thought all intention of killing the reptile dissipated. Instead, he sat down slowly and watched the forest master with interest.

The snake remained immobile except for its tongue, which continued to flick in his direction with hypnotic regularity. Nagai had told him that forest masters did not move around much, preferring to remain in one place and wait for their prey to come to them. This one was most likely doing just that, watching for large rodents that came in the dark to drink.

"And what will you offer me for sparing your life?" he said to the serpent. His own voice sounded strange, since he had heard no human speech since leaving the settlement. The snake did not move, nor did any answer form in Nainoa's mind. He continued to watch until the light faded. Then he eased himself up and moved around the pool in the

* Chimpanzees.

opposite direction, watching for more snakes. He was on the point of departing when something in the pool caught his eye.

Looking down into the darkness of the water, he saw a tiny human hand.

A surge of emotion rolled through him. He glanced uneasily across the pool at the snake, then cut a slender wand from a shrub and carefully fished out a tiny ceramic human arm as long as his finger. He studied it carefully and washed the mud out of its hollow interior. One of the fingers was broken off.

Using the stick again, he carefully turned over leaves and bark fragments in the bottom of the pool and was rewarded with another arm, both legs, and a small hollow head on a short neck. The ceramic objects were deeply stained, and he guessed they had been buried in the earth for a long time. After he cleaned them, he saw that they had once been white in color. There were remnants of pigment in the eyes and hair. The eyes had been blue, like his own.

Nainoa turned the objects over and over in his hands. They were artifacts from the past, perhaps ritual objects, charms used by women who wished to have a child. Perhaps they were parts of a toy used by children. Perhaps its blue eyes meant it had belonged to an American chief in the dim past. Some American objects had survived the millennia in chiefly collections. The making of ceramics and glass was a lost art. The materials from which they were made had not been found in the islands; nor had their source been discovered here on the American mainland.

Continuing to search the pool, Nainoa found no more artifacts, so he slipped the objects into a pouch and secured it in one of his net bags. He bade a respectful farewell to the serpent and made his way to the mound. A walk around the hill's base revealed its sides to be irregular, steep, and thickly overgrown. The summit was covered by the banyan tree, whose roots wove in and out of the mound, covering its surface with woody tentacles. In the hollows small trees were struggling to survive. Lizards foraged in the leaf-litter, making rustling sounds. The great tree's limbs had sent down aerial roots, which in time had become subsidiary trunks, so

that the mound appeared to be covered by a grove rather than one giant tree.

As he stared up at it, another strange thought appeared in his mind. From old Nagai he had learned that everything in nature, both living and nonliving, possessed its own unique form of awareness. Nainoa wondered if the huge banyan tree above was aware of his presence. Unlike many of the other trees that had dropped their leaves for the sleep of the dry season, this one retained great green clouds of foliage and seemed very much awake.

Nainoa composed his mind, quieting his thoughts. Then, formally, he asked the tree's spirit for its permission to ascend the mound. He waited but discerned nothing out of the ordinary. He climbed the hill, using the convoluted roots as a ladder, keeping a wary eye out for scorpions and centipedes. On one side of the mound, a small tree had fallen; its roots had pulled away the surface and exposed the interior, revealing large chunks of broken masonry and shards of glass.

Excited, Nainoa speculated that he was standing on the collapsed ruin of an immense building. The sun was about to set, however, and further investigation would have to wait until morning. A colony of ants crossing the mound meant he would have to sleep in the tree, as he had been doing almost every night anyway. His woven hammock adapted itself well to this arrangement, and he felt safe from the big nocturnal predators.

Slowly he climbed up into the tree between the two main trunks until he came to a spot narrow enough for his hammock. With his rope he hung the hammock between two large branches and slung his net bags and weapons within reach. He had grown used to lying suspended out over empty space, safe from predators and away from most of the mosquitoes.

As if to confirm this thought, he heard the distant roar of a tiger in the direction from which he had come. Had it picked up his scent and was now following him? Nainoa stared down at the mound eighty feet below him. Could the tiger climb up after him? As he rearranged his gear, he thought about the several kinds of big cats and their different levels of threat. The most feared were the largest orange-and-black striped ones. The hunters

said they typically avoided humans, but every so often, one would eat a commoner working out near the forest edge. A large party of hunters and royalty would then have to hunt it down or trap it—a risky business in which the tiger sometimes killed more people.

A smaller species of tiger was almost as feared. It had a yellow coat with black spots arranged in circular clusters. Unlike the larger tigers, which were primarily terrestrial, this spotted tiger was quite at home in trees, where it often caught sleeping monkeys and birds. Like their larger cousins, they tended to avoid humans, preferring to hunt and kill forest pigs and deer. Nagai had believed that there were at least two different kinds of spotted tigers, a robust and powerful species, and a more gracile variety with longer legs. Other hunters had not been able to confirm this, as the big cats were solitary and reclusive and rarely seen near the settlements.

Black tigers also lived in the forest. The Hawaiians claimed that these big cats were really evil sorcerers who had taken animal form to track down and kill their victims. Nagai had told him that this was nonsense, that they were simply a black variety of the spotted tiger. Nagai had once seen a black tiger attack, kill, and eat a crocodile—a testament to their considerable strength and power.

Still another kind of tiger lacked both stripes and spots on its torso. It was brown and had black stripes along its white muzzle, white belly fur, and a long tail. These cats were more common and had a distinctive scream, which was often heard around the settlements at night. As Nainoa heard the tiger's roar again, he eased himself into his hammock. He doubted that the Americans had kept tigers in cages or trained them to do their bidding, despite what history recorded.

He rechecked his gear, then looked down and out from his camp. The view was beautiful. In the advancing twilight the forest canopy below stretched away to the horizon in all directions. Here and there cotton trees towered over their smaller neighbors. He could see the forest master's pool quite clearly through the gap that the fallen tree had opened. To the west the sun was setting redly into the haze.

To the east appeared the crooked blue line of the mountains, before

which the land rose in low hills. Nainoa ate sparingly from his supplies as he studied the view. The mountains ran north-south in a long, unbroken wall for as far as he could see.

In the tree above several green tree iguanas were among the branches. Nagai had once brought down the long-tailed, spike-backed lizards with arrows, but his own efforts on that occasion had been less than successful, and he had endured the hunter's quiet mirth. Thereafter Nainoa had practiced until he too could shoot straight up with accuracy. The large green lizards were now observing him with blank stares, their legs and long striped tails hanging down below the branches. They had aligned their bodies so as to take in the last of the sun's heat before the cool night air made them torpid and inactive.

Looking down, Nainoa had an excellent view of the ruined *siti.* The mounds seemed to be laid out in a gridlike pattern: long, straight, parallel "valleys" crisscrossed the area at right angles to each other. Here and there more moss and fern-covered chimneys protruded from the leaves on the forest floor.

A flock of green parrots plummeted by, circled, and settled in the tree above, arguing garrulously. Large fruit bats appeared in the sky. As the light faded, the first, hesitant calls of frogs and insects broke the silence of the forest. The dark blue sky revealed the first stars, and with their appearance Nainoa felt better.

Remembering Nagai's ongoing relationship with the spirit world, he heard his old friend's voice reminding him, "So you want to see the spirits, huh? Well, you'll have to wait until the spirits feel you are ready to see them. Sometimes it is possible to catch a glimpse of them out of the corner of your eye, and then when you look directly at them . . . *poof!* . . . they disappear."

Nainoa was wakeful during the first part of the night as the dry-season moon appeared in the sky. The insects and frogs maintained a din of almost deafening proportions. The fruit bats flew across the moon in an endless stream, heading toward some distant tree that only they knew about.

Once again the tiger roared, and the forest momentarily quieted. As if in response, a red monkey howled its deep grating call. In the silence another tiger roared far away to the north, almost beyond the limits of hearing. In the moonlight Nainoa could see the pool where he had found the ceramic artifacts: When the frog chorus there momentarily stopped, he wondered if the guardian had obtained its meal.

After a while, as the moon shone into his face through gaps in the foliage, Nainoa slept, but fitfully—for a light wind from the east caused the great tree to sway. He awakened around midnight from an anxious dream and lay sweating in his hammock as moonlight coming through the moving branches flashed onto his closed eyelids.

Sleep became elusive, so he opened his eyes. It still came as a jolt to be suspended so far above the forest floor. All the way to the mountains, the landscape was illuminated by monochromatic moonlight. Nowhere could he see the light of a fire of other human beings. The forest was quieter now —the insects and frogs seemed to have exhausted their energy. He felt his solitude with a sad intensity and emptiness and for the rest of the night dozed and awakened in starts.

Just before dawn he finally managed to relax and was slipping down toward sleep when he felt a sudden tingling of the spine and a strange, heightened surge of feeling. As he lay quietly in wonder, the feeling abruptly intensified. His awareness turned toward it, and a strong rush of sensation swept into him, engulfing his entire body in an instant.

His frame became paralyzed, and his arms and legs straightened and stiffened, straining against the confines of the hammock. His hands felt huge, and he discovered that he could not close them. His alarm was offset almost immediately by an exhilaration verging on joy that swept through him. He had never before experienced whatever was happening to him now. He struggled with his body, trying to regain control. Strange flashes of light made designs in the darkness. Then he opened his eyes. . . .

His momentary disorientation was replaced by shock as he found himself standing on the mound eighty feet below. His thinking mind was fully awake now, fully aware. The feelings of pressure, of paralysis, surged

through and around him. With great effort, he forced himself to look upward into the tree, where his hammock was still wrapped around a human form. The surge of amazement increased as he realized that he could still feel the hammock around his body. His mind reeled. The shape slung high in the tree must be his. But how was this possible?

The blood hissed in his ears as he turned to look around. The trunks of the huge banyan rose around him in the moonlight as columns of light and shadow interfaced with patterns of graded darkness. The black and white landscape seemed to express a peculiar flatness. Amazed, his mind was observing, analyzing, reasoning, and accepting that he was both in his hammock and on the mound below. As he wrestled with the force that held him immobile, he knew he was wide awake and that this was not a dream.

He crossed the mound between the banyan's trunks. He was not sure how—his intention seemed to be enough to take him here or there. He felt no fear, but rather a strength and confidence that coursed through his body and out his fingertips. He could close both his hands now.

Suddenly he became aware of a presence.

He stopped and slowly looked to his left, down the slope of the mound, and out into the forest. Whatever it was he had felt, it was not there. The mounds marched away into the distance, reflecting a curious brightness, a subtle movement, a slight transparency, perhaps, that they lacked in daylight. The trees had it too—a flickering urgency.

The feelings of pressure abruptly increased, squeezing him, almost cutting off his breath. He became rigid as a stick of wood. His penis was erect. He considered that he might be dying and felt a slight amusement at the thought of dying while sexually aroused. A rushing sound roared in his ears. With enormous effort he prevailed against the force that seemed to flow within and around him and managed to turn toward his right.

There, in the shafts of moonlight and darkness among the great tree's trunks and roots, stood a tall, dark, featureless form. It was vaguely human in shape, and as Nainoa stared at it, he wondered if it was indeed there or was just some pattern within the darkness that his mind had arranged into a man-shape. Its body was linear and tall, and the head seemed small. It had no arms, legs, or feet. From the old myths his mind suddenly produced a name—*ke'aka*, the shadow.

Shock rolled through him. In the old stories a spirit being, an *akua*, would sometimes appear to humans as a tall black shadow, but he had always considered such tales to be merely fiction. He looked down at the ground to renew his hold on what was real, but he was suddenly terribly unsure of what was real. He looked back toward the shadowy figure. It was still there. As his gaze moved slowly up its form, it seemed to stretch, to grow larger until it was towering over him at more than twice his height. Its outlines seemed to flicker, vibrating with the same pulsing rhythm that surged within him. The blackness of it was as dark as the void of the night sky, but without stars.

It had to be an *akua*—he was actually in the presence of an *akua*!

Nainoa felt the roiling of sensations in his body. Could this *akua* be the source of them? As if to say yes, the sensations pulsed more powerfully. He gasped in ecstasy. The force of the *akua* was holding him immobile, yet it did not feel hostile. He tried to raise his arms and gave a mighty heave, his heart pounding with the effort, but the force was absolute. He could not move. Then he tried to merge with the power coursing through him in order to move his arms—and succeeded. He raised his arms—an inch at a time.

A hint of amusement seemed to emanate from the dark being, where-upon Nainoa's arms were once again secured in a viselike grip—which continued to raise them, lifting them high over his head in a slow, almost languid stretch, until his whole body was dangling in the air with his toes just barely touching the ground. Then the force turned him slowly in a circle, dragging his feet helplessly in the dust. Since it seemed absurd to fight against this immense strength, Nainoa opened himself to it, inviting it to show him what it was.

The response was immediate. A tremendous flow of power far beyond anything he had yet experienced surged through him, and the inside of his head seemed to fill with light. It shone out of his eyes, rays penetrating far into the night sky. Streams of lightning radiated from his scalp, fingertips, and shoulders, crackling and hissing in the darkness. The sensations increased beyond his ability to contain them, and he shrieked with ecstasy—with joy—again, and again, and again. His spirit was soaring, he was flying. He embraced the power, merged with it, taking it all into himself, welcoming its return as if it were something he dimly remembered.

Suddenly it began to withdraw. The awesome pressure enfolding him eased, and the shadow set him gently back on his feet. He found himself standing once again under the tree in the dark, staring at the shadow as the ecstatic sensations ebbed.

Above and to one side of the shadow's geometric shape hovered a small, blindingly bright, almost crystalline round object. Its surface was multifaceted, with all the colors of the rainbow expressed in its myriad tiny faces. The force withdrew from his body completely as the shadow shifted to become an ordinary complex of light and darkness under the tree. As the tree trunks seemed to flicker and dissolve, he looked up at the orb. He had a brief sense of ascending, whereupon he found himself once again lying in his hammock, staring into the face of the moon setting in the west. The first light of dawn was illuminating the sky over the eastern mountains.

Nainoa tossed his head back and forth wildly to see if the *akua* was still close by. His mind was reeling. Tears streamed down his cheeks, and his muscles trembled from having wrestled with the awesome force. He directed his mind to calm itself and his body to relax. He slowed and steadied his breathing and heart. He could still feel the small residual pulses of power, each becoming weaker than the last. As he formed the image of the shadow in his mind, he felt a last faint surge, and then the presence was gone.

The first bird-call floated through the forest. Nainoa stared into the light of the brightening sky to the east and thought he heard the sound of roosters crowing in the distance. He was wide awake.

5
Rock Art

TOO EMERGED FROM THE VISIONARY STATE AT DAWN
accompanied by my neighbor's roosters. I was thun-
derstruck to have found myself again within Nainoa,
this time during an encounter with the shadow.

In the days that followed I could sense my entire view
of reality was changing, accompanied by a strange shell
shock, or more accurately culture shock. I seemed to be
sleepwalking through much of my daily routine, staring at
ordinary things that I had formerly taken for granted,
seeing and thinking about them in an entirely new way, all
the while struggling with an inner turmoil and preoccupied by another reality profoundly different from the one
around me.

As I tried to sort out this new dream, I figured out that
between the two episodes, only a few days had elapsed in
Nainoa's time, yet six weeks had passed in mine. I had no
idea what this time equation meant or even if it was
significant, but once again I had been in a state of expanded awareness in which I had access to all levels of my

own experience and Nainoa's. As before, I had had to become absolutely still in order to observe, inquire, and receive impressions through Nainoa's sensory systems and mind.

I wanted to know what had happened to him after he left his settlement, and this wish had elicited a detailed stream of memories from him. But even as my mind filled with questions, I still had no idea what controlled or initiated the experiences. Both of the episodes had occurred just before dawn, and the more recent one, like those in Berkeley, had followed love-making. Aside from these two commonalities, the altered-state experiences seemed to be completely spontaneous.

Shortly after this second encounter, my family and I returned to the San Francisco Bay Area for a few months, during which time our second daughter, Anna, was born in December 1986. In the midst of everything that a new baby brings into a household, I was wrestling with the conflict between my scientific skepticism and my intuitive feelings about the dream.

During this California sojourn I had no further altered-state experiences, but I repeatedly went over in my mind Nainoa's encounter with the dark being. The towering, humanoid form that I had seen had had a semirectangular body, whereas Nainoa's shadow had an elongated, inverted triangular shape, its "point" down. I chose to interpret this as evidence that Nainoa and I were separate individuals and that he was not simply a product of my imagination, dreams, and projections.

In those last moments before I lost contact with him, Nainoa's mind had disgorged another bit of information about his own people's mythology. Associated with the name *ke'aka* was the clear impression that the dark form represented some sort of guardian—a threshold guardian. What was a threshold guardian? I felt quite certain that I had never read or heard this term before.

I decided to do some research in mythology. Years before, I had heard the esteemed mythologist, Joseph Campbell, speak at the Museum of Modern Art in San Francisco, so I decided to begin with him. I acquired a recent edition of his book *The Hero with a Thousand Faces,* which examines core concepts and recurrent imagery in world mythology, and settled down to read. Within the first hundred pages was an examination of a major element in the classic mythological hero's journey, the encounter with the guardian of the threshold. Two passages particularly struck me:

> With the personifications of his destiny to guide and aid him, the hero goes forward in his adventure until he comes to the "threshold guardian" at the entrance to the zone of magnified power. Such custodians bound the world in the four directions—also up and down—standing for the limits of the hero's present sphere, or life horizon. Beyond them is darkness, the unknown, and danger. . . .
>
> The usual person is more than content, he is even proud, to remain within the indicated bounds, and popular belief gives him every reason to fear so much as the first step into the unexplored.[1]
>
> The adventure is always and everywhere a passage beyond the veil of the known into the unknown; the powers that watch at the boundary are dangerous; to deal with them is risky; yet for anyone with competence and courage, the danger fades.[2]

While the chapter gave numerous examples of the guardian from the myths of many cultures, I did not find anything that quite matched my own experience with the shadow.

One day shortly after reading this, I was browsing through an old issue of *National Geographic* and got a real jolt. An article on rock art included photographs of tall, geometric humanoid forms painted on canyon walls in the American Southwest by Amerindian ancestors, hundreds, perhaps thousands of years ago, and there it was—the same dark shadow-form I had seen in my altered states.[3]

The best-known examples of this ancient art are those of the prehistoric European hunter-gatherer populations of 35,000 to 10,000 years ago. Modern *Homo sapiens* like ourselves, they produced the "High Art of Ice Age Europe," remains of which are preserved in many deep caves, such as Lascaux in France and Altamira in Spain. Prehistoric rock art is found all

over the world, and there is a formidable literature on this enigmatic subject, most of which contains descriptions, interpretations, and reproductions of painted pictographs and engraved petroglyphs—including tall, elongated, dark humanoid forms.

This cave art with its recognizable images of animals and humans also often includes abstract designs that have always puzzled prehistorians. Rows of lines, groups of dots, strange zigzags and grids, spirals and squares, rectangles and curves are inscribed or painted onto the rock walls and ceilings of shelters and caves everywhere. These cryptic symbols also appear on the surfaces of many of the well-known "goddess" sculptures associated with the earlier Upper Paleolithic peoples and the later Mesolithic and Neolithic agriculturalists.

The abstract geometric symbols also resembled the strange lines and dots of light that I had seen against the darkened field of my closed eyes during the initial stages of my altered states. The zigzags and chevrons described by some authorities as a symbolic "language" associated with hypothetical "goddess images"[4] were identical to the snakelike meanders that coalesced into the grid moments before my transition into Nainoa's world through the "zone of silence."

I decided to turn to an authority on shamanism who might know something about altered states and might have an expanded perspective beyond that of the various experts and amateurs who were creating and propounding their own mythology of "goddess" worship. About a year before, when I had returned to Berkeley to give a paper at a conference held in honor of the esteemed professor of African prehistory, J. Desmond Clark, I had heard a presentation about shamanism and rock art by a professor of archaeology named David Lewis-Williams from the University of the Witwatersrand in Johannesburg, South Africa. Professor Clark graciously loaned me several reprints of Lewis-Williams's papers,[5] as well as a book called *The Imprint of Man: The Rock Art of Southern Africa*. The reproductions of the rock paintings contained the same lines, zigzags, spots, and grids that I had seen for myself.

Most of the world's prehistoric rock art sites are not connected with any

FIGURE 1.
Pictographs from Horseshoe Canyon, Utah.

FIGURE 2.
Pictographs from Horseshoe Canyon, Utah, a group known as
"the Holy Ghost and his family."

contemporary artistic tradition or cultural group; nor have they been for hundreds or thousands of years. The sites found in much of southern Africa, however, are clearly and directly connected with the ancestors of the San Bushmen who live today in the Kalahari Desert. This direct cultural connection is vitally important. Unlike most authorities who have attempted to interpret the meaning of prehistoric art, Professor Lewis-Williams has been able to work with the field notes made by ethnographers who visited the San in the nineteenth and early twentieth centuries while they were still making rock art—records that have allowed him to unravel the meanings of the complex metaphors within San art from their point of view, rather than from our Western notions of what their art was all about.

Lewis-Williams's research shows that much San rock art is associated with visionary imagery perceived by shamans in various stages of trance. Like shamans in other traditional societies, San shamans achieved expanded states of awareness, in which they were able to cure the sick, control the movements of game animals, and make rain. San shamans surviving in the Kalahari still perform these functions today.[6]

In order to achieve an altered state, the San traditionally held a medicine dance, at which the women sat in a close circle around a fire, singing and clapping the rhythm of medicine songs believed to contain a supernatural potency called *num*. This potency, analogous to what the Polynesians call *mana*, was activated by the singing and dancing, and when it finally "boiled" or "exploded" in the shamans' heads, they entered the trance state in which they perceived the spirit world directly. Most Western cognitive investigators term such visual phenomena "hallucinations."

Psychological studies of trance states[7] have revealed that as people progress more deeply into trance, they typically pass through three distinct stages in which they perceive different sorts of visual phenomena. The early stages of hallucinations typically include the visual perception of luminous geometric forms known as "phosphenes," usually lines, spots of light, zigzags, grids, and vortexes. These phosphenes are believed to be produced by the stimulation of the nervous system and can be seen with the eyes open or closed. Shamans in the Amazon Basin who imbibe the powerful

EUROPE	SOUTH AFRICA
PHOSPHENIC FORMS	PHOSPHENIC FORMS
TRANSITIONAL FORMS	TRANSITIONAL FORMS
THERIANTHROPES AND SPIRIT FORMS	THERIANTHROPES AND SPIRIT FORMS

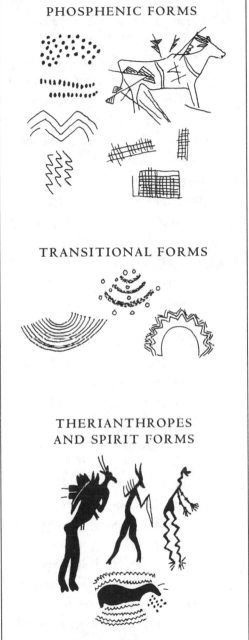

FIGURE 3.

The stages of trance experience suggested in imagery commonly found
in rock art from Europe and South Africa

hallucinogen *ayahuasca* paint very similar designs on their houses and ritual objects, and they identify them as shapes they see during the visionary trance through which they pass on their way to the "other world."[8]

In the rock art of the San, phosphenic forms are not always associated with figures but often appear by themselves. Earlier anthropologists mistakenly identified them as corrals, hunting traps, or huts. Sometimes phosphenic lines superimposed upon human forms have been described as body paint—mistakenly, I believe. That these lines are just as often inscribed upon animals has been largely ignored because, as Lewis-Williams has pointed out, most Westerners simply have no frame of reference for understanding what they might mean.

As shamans enter deeper stages of trance, they typically see "hallucinations" of animals, people, and monsters—and what Lewis-Williams calls "therianthropes," combinations of animal and human forms. The human bodies with animal heads in Lewis-Williams's papers reminded me of the wonderful fantasy world I had as a child, a world peopled by imaginary friends, most of whom were animals and animal-people. During one of the drumming sessions in Michael Harner's workshop back in Berkeley, a young woman named Sandra Ingerman[9] had journeyed into nonordinary reality on my behalf to find a helping spirit for me. Much to my amazement, when she came out of trance, she described encountering one of my old imaginary friends, the one I called the "leopard man." This strange creature had joined me one day at New York's Central Park Zoo when I was about six years old, and it had been my "companion" for several years. Sandy's discovery of this same entity had given another jolt to my scientific worldview, and at the same time I felt that old familiar presence reemerge into my life once again—my secret pal.

Many of the half-animal, half-humans in one of Lewis-Williams's papers seemed to be associated with strange boat-shaped, "moon-shaped," or rainbow-shaped crescents on which phosphenes were often inscribed. Sometimes the U-shapes were like nested sets of curves with superimposed clouds of dots. Single arches often transected the "beast-men," so that the therianthropes seemed to be emerging from them or to be transformed as

FIGURE 4.

The arc may be the *nierika*, an area of invisibility, a place of transformation of human beings into animals. Perhaps the kneeling figure at left is a shaman in an altered state who is conjuring up the vision.
(Redrawn from H. Pager, *Ndedema.* Ackademische Druckund Verlagsanstalt, Graz. 1971.)

they passed through them, their human feet on one side, their animal heads on the other. Sometimes the crescent was rendered to produce a zone of invisibility, into which the therianthropes "disappeared."

On one rock painting a series of antelope legs protruded from the edge of a circular mass over which clouds of dots were inscribed, as though the legs' owners were within the area. Several animal bodies were also depicted as actually emerging or disappearing into the curve, from which a long, red line extended outward. Along this line walked three curious humanoid figures, one of which was clearly a therianthrope.[10]

I wondered, heretically, if these so-called hallucinations were really produced by the human mind, as the psychological sciences professed, or whether they might be autonomous phenomena that existed separate from the self and could be perceived only in expanded levels of awareness.

On the one hand, the fact that therianthropes and phosphenes are found in rock art worldwide suggested that the human mind may exhibit a sort of "psychic unity," as some anthropologists and sociologists have proclaimed. On the other, maybe it was possible that humans everywhere have the ability to achieve what Harner calls the shamanic state of consciousness, tapping into similar places in nonordinary reality in which they experience and perceive similar things.

Another intriguing thought generated by Lewis-Williams's research concerned the U-shaped curves from which entities seemed to emerge and into which they seemed to disappear. Could these forms be the San way of depicting the *nierika*, the doorway within our minds, the interface between ordinary and nonordinary reality? I thought about my own visionary experiences and realized with some amusement that I could use the services of a good shaman.

My family and I returned to Kona with newborn Anna early in 1987, and my next visionary experience occurred shortly after our arrival.

The day began with an early-morning drive to the beach at Napo'opo'o for a swim with three-year-old Erica in tow. Jill was at home with the baby. The road followed the rim of the huge fault-block above Kealakekua Bay, enabling a magnificent view of the Honaunau valley to the south. The cloud that frequently overhangs the valley was already beginning to build on the mountainside, promising rain in the afternoon. The coast stretched south to where the immense shoulder of Mauna Loa disappeared below the ocean. I was impressed, as always, by the monumental mass of the active volcano upon which I was living.

I wondered if the mountain, being "alive," as Nainoa would believe, had its own geologic form of awareness. If so, was it aware of the life-forms on its surface? The Hawaiians have a strong sense of this awareness and have given it a name, Pele. They have a respectful if somewhat uneasy relationship with this volcano spirit, sometimes envisioning it as a beautiful young woman, sometimes as a vengeful crone.

As the road descended toward the ocean, I saw the white pillar of the Captain Cook monument across the cobalt expanse of Kealakekua Bay. On arriving at Napo'opo'o, I turned north, negotiating the one-lane road, and parked under a spreading monkey-pod tree next to the *heiau*. Erica hopped down from the car carrying her swimming ring, and I slung my beach bag filled with towels and snacks over my shoulder. The two of us walked hand in hand past the *lei* stands below the temple site, where I exchanged greetings and news with a Hawaiian woman who sells her hand-printed *pa'us* to the tourists on weekends. During the week, she was employed as a bailiff at the jail in Honolulu, and as I chatted with her, I could feel her considerable presence and sensed the strong calming influence she must have on those with whom she works.

It was the dry season in Kona, and the vegetation above the huge cliff that encircles Kealakekua Bay to the north was a soft yellow ocher. The ocean was calm. As we stepped down from the seawall onto the gray sand, Erica pointed with excitement at the black crabs scuttling among the rocks. It was still early, yet a few friends had already arrived—mostly mothers with children. Most of the beach was covered by sea-worn, black lava boulders deposited there by storms and tidal waves. In the old days, all it would have taken was a word from the ruling chief, and the commoners would have cleared the beach of rocks.

Erica's little friends joined her, and I spent a delightful morning digging holes, building towers, chatting up the mothers, and swimming in the warm, crystal-clear water in the center of a playgroup in which I functioned as the "beach-daddy." As the sun turned hotter, I led my group of small children on a nature walk back through the trees to visit the pond behind the beach. Old maps dating to Captain Cook's visit reveal that this pond was called Wailokoali'i and that it was once considerably larger. Local story relates that it was partially filled in by tidal waves and that the tractor hired to excavate it kept getting stuck. And so it remains, shallow, brackish and wild, with trees, birds, and grasses for companions—and children.

Behind the pond and back in the trees are the ruins of the rock walls and house platforms of the original Hawaiian village. The overgrown site is dominated now by coconut palms, *keawe* and *opiuma* trees, and tall "elephant" grasses. I thought of Nainoa and the leopard man, then looked around half-expecting to see one or both of them.

The children threw pieces of bread to the guppies that someone had introduced into the pond, and I wondered if there was a *mo'o* living in it, a water spirit that disliked tractors. The calls of doves beckoned from the forest, so I walked back around the pond through a stand of *kou* trees that were dropping their beautiful orange flowers onto the surface of the water. I hesitated, then remembered and asked permission. I felt nothing in response, so I stepped into the cool shadows of the now-forested village. It was very quiet among the rows of stone walls, and as I listened to the silence, my eyes automatically scanned the ground looking for artifacts— my old field training kicking in.

I sat on a stone and leaned back against the trunk of a large tamarind tree, watching the children feed the fish, listening to the birds. I looked past the pond, across an open grassy area to the red-leafed *kamani* trees behind the beach, then on to the blue horizon of the ocean. I felt the peace of the place slip into me and considered "being without thinking," the state for which those who practice Zen Buddhism strive. I looked around and wondered if perhaps the effort might better be called "ism." I was surrounded by the masters of ism—rocks, trees, grasses, water—all beings without thinking. Although humans strive for ism without ever being able to achieve it fully, I cleared my mind of thoughts in order to emulate the rocks, trying to be without thinking.

After several minutes a buzzing sound invaded the silence, disrupting my meditation. Was there a hive of bees in the tree's branches? A breeze induced an interplay of light and shadow through its emerald leaves. The greens and yellows seemed unusually intense. The buzzing sound abruptly increased—and then without warning the sensation surged into me. I gasped for breath as my body stiffened. I saw the greens of the trees shatter into shards of glassy light, coalescing into the now-familiar phosphenes. A shimmering, somewhat curved line of brilliance appeared, and I felt a sense of expansion. As the familiar paralysis progressed, I shut my eyes, but the phosphenes remained, moving around me in streaks.

Abruptly the buzzing ceased, and after a long moment of complete and utter silence, I opened my eyes. With a momentary pulse of astonishment, I realized that the shift had occurred.

6
Third Journey
The Spirit Helper

I T WAS NEAR MIDDAY, and Nainoa was crossing a large, open marsh that was now dry and sparsely covered with sedges and grasses. A few strides before him was a small, islandlike rise covered by a stand of trees. Near the edge of the trees, a large, grayish-brown dog sat in the shade. It could have passed for a rock or shadow. As soon as Nainoa noticed it, he stopped walking and eased the spear off his shoulder.

The dog seemed relaxed and watched Nainoa intently. It appeared to be alone. Nainoa looked into the dog's amber eyes, then casually moved his gaze aside. The dog didn't move, so he glanced at it again. The dog looked away as their eyes met, a courteous gesture.

Six days had passed since Nainoa had left the ruined *siti* in the forest. He had seen no evidence of people and wondered if the dog came from a nearby village or temporary camp. He saw no sign of humans at all—no cut trees, no smoke in the distance, no tracks in the dry mud. Nainoa studied the ground and saw lots of animal signs

—the tracks of deer, pigs, birds, and forest rodents. Nearby were the dark, shiny, conelike droppings of a wild turkey. The dog had chosen a good spot to hunt. He met its eyes again, and both looked away.

Nainoa eased into the shade at the edge of the trees and slowly sat down to consider his next move. The dog looked lean, but its condition was good. The fact that it had not run away was curious. Was it descended from one of those hybrid crosses that resulted when wild dogs interbred with their domesticated relatives in the settlements? What was it doing way out here? How wild was it? What good or bad contact with humans had it experienced? What humans?

As the dog and man sat and observed each other, Nainoa thought over his progress of the past several days.

He had reached the foothills shortly after leaving the ruined *siti.* There the well-used game trail had divided, one branch leading south, the other north. The reason became clear when he climbed a tree to scan the terrain.

To the east, a huge cliff ran north and south between the foothills and the high mountains beyond, an unbroken wall many hundreds of feet high. He studied its stark exposure carefully. No ravines or valleys breached the cliff face. It looked as if a vast section of the earth had been heaved upward by some unimaginable force from below. He decided arbitrarily to take the left fork and traveled north for several days, watching for a way up the cliff, but the barrier remained unbroken.

The previous night, while camped within bowshot of a stream bed that the dry season had reduced to a series of shallow pools, he had been awakened by the sound of water being poured into a large, deep storage container. In the dim light, he saw a herd of elephants drinking from the pools. They sucked water up into their long noses, placed them in their mouths, and released the water into their stomachs. Nainoa remained motionless in his hammock and counted twenty in the group, including five babies.

Remembering the chief's brass elephant, he wondered if the chief would

consider domesticating elephants if he could not find horses. Travel through the forest riding atop such a huge animal would be infinitely easier than walking. Nainoa wondered how he and the people could tame them.

In the morning Nainoa had discovered a well-used trail paralleling a substantial stream that led directly east toward the barrier. It was precisely what he had been searching for. He marked a tree with a knife cut and followed the trail up a narrow valley between two forested hills to a steep incline that ran straight across the valley. He walked along its length until he found a large patch of vegetation that had been torn away, revealing stonework marked with the brown stains of iron that had rusted out long ago. It was man-made. With growing excitement, he realized he was looking at a huge wall. Did the forest conceal another *siti* nearby?

Marveling at the size of the wall, Nainoa climbed a steep trail up the hillside to the north and found himself staring down at it as it stretched right across the valley. Beyond it lay the marsh, but there was no evidence of another *siti*. Perhaps there would be some mounds toward the east. He had decided to cross the marsh to find out.

He sat now and considered these things as he watched the dog. Easing one of his woven bags around to extract a chunk of dried fish, he slowly whittled off chips with his knife and slid them into his mouth, letting his saliva moisten them until they could be chewed. A soft breath of air carried the smell of the fish to the dog. It drooled. Nainoa decided to try and befriend the dog.

Sliding more chips into his cheek, he rearranged his gear, rose to his feet, and backed slowly out onto the marsh once again. He spat a moist piece of fish onto the ground, then turned and walked away. After a short distance, he stopped, urinated on a clump of sedge, then spat out another chip and continued walking. He glanced back after a short distance and saw the dog smelling the first chip. The animal had longer legs than he had imagined and looked decidedly wild. It ate the chip, approached the sedge, and after a lengthy investigation urinated on the same place, leaving its own scent marker. It was a male. It took the second piece of fish and followed. Nainoa spat out another chip. Perhaps he would have companionship on his walk after all.

Nainoa circled the rise, then proceeded east across the marsh, heading for the formidable cliff. Through the haze he now saw the shadow of a possible ravine against its face. The dog followed at a respectful distance. At the forest's edge, he walked along the thick, overgrown transition, making for where the stream entered the marsh. No mounds were in evidence.

Upon entering the shade, Nainoa surprised a small pack of large tailless rodents.* As they dashed into the water to escape, he managed to string his bow and kill one with an arrow. He made an early camp below a large tree, found deadwood, dressed out the meat, cut it in thin strips, and cooked it.

The afternoon passed languidly as he slowly roasted and dried the meat. The dog remained outside the invisible circle it maintained around Nainoa and watched him. Toward evening he took the viscera, skin, and bones out onto the marsh and left them for the dog, which accepted the offering, carrying the remains off into the trees to its own place of safety. Then it returned in the dark and resumed watching him, the firelight reflecting off its eyes. Caution prevailed—Nainoa hauled his remaining supply of meat aloft with him as he slung his hammock in the tree.

He woke with the first bird call. He had been dreaming of the settlement and of Chief Kaneohe's compound, seeing strange images of the place he knew so well. The shadowy shapes of wild dogs had been running through the streets, flitting just beyond the limits of his vision, just beyond the edge of what was known.

Emerging slowly from sleep, he looked down and was startled to see that the dog had been joined by another dog during the night. The two of them were now licking each other with obvious affection. The newcomer appeared to be a female and was longer in the leg and muzzle than the male,

* Capybaras.

with longer, shaggier fur. Both were larger than the wild dogs around the settlement.

As he climbed down with his gear and the remains of the evening's meal, the dogs stopped their play and watched him alertly. The female had gray eyes. They did not run away, so he tossed them small chunks of meat while he ate. They gulped them down, and when he broke camp, they followed.

A trail beside the stream led directly east toward the barrier, and by midmorning, he had arrived at its base. He stared upward at the stark, sheer rock face of veined stone that soared above him into the sky. Steep slopes of loose rubble concealed the base of the cliff on which small trees and vines struggled to find a foothold. High above, a flock of small, crescent-shaped birds knifed through the air around an overhang that protected their mud nests. Higher still, a flowering shrub created a red smudge under another overhang, whose walls were covered with dark lichens and mosses. And far, far above, the fringe of trees at the cliff's edge was backlit by the sun, creating a thin line of light against the hazy blue of the sky.

Nainoa tried to see how he could climb that awesome rock face and conceded that it was probably impossible. Yet before him lay a dark, steep-walled canyon from which the stream emerged. Choked with trees, its mouth thickly overgrown with clumps of bamboo, it appeared to cut eastward into the heart of the plateau. Nainoa hesitated to enter it since it was the sort of place where a large carnivore might lurk. The image of *ke'aka* flickered briefly in his mind. Something was in there—he could feel it. Yet in all probability, this was the route to what lay above and beyond.

His canine companions trotted past him in the trees. As he watched them, he remembered a folktale from his childhood about a boy who had found his courage by facing a wolf in the forest. At the canyon's mouth the dogs stopped and looked back at him, then turned and dropped down onto the water-smooth boulders of the stream bed and disappeared. Resolve formed within him, and putting aside his unease, he followed.

He squeezed through the bamboo at the ravine's entrance, watching for snakes. His net bags caught on branches, and he had to free them carefully to avoid tearing them. He glanced down to see the dogs observing him from where the rocky stream bed had diverged from the ravine. He realized with chagrin that they were showing him a route that he had missed.

Nainoa jumped down onto a large slab of smooth rock and began to move upstream with more ease. It was very still, and the air felt humid and oppressive. The canyon bottom was narrow, a long stone's throw across, and its walls rose abruptly on both sides. The water was low, but he could see the height at which it scoured the walls during the rains from the broken branches of trees, revealing that this was a dry-season route only. He fervently hoped that a chance storm would not fill the canyon with water while he was still in it.

Nainoa followed the river bed as it rose. Many of the stones were eroded into beautiful shapes, and he frequently found himself clambering up water-smooth boulders of immense size. Tree ferns and bamboo rose high overhead in layers, and the light was greenish and dim. Aside from the subdued rush and gurgle of water as it dropped from higher pools to lower ones, the air was silent in the midday heat. From somewhere upstream came the rattling call of a fisher bird. He passed a small brown water snake coiled on a stone at the edge of a pool. Several green parrots hurtled by and disappeared. He looked around carefully. The place had an air of enchantment about it.

Being enclosed so deeply within the earth was a new experience, and Nainoa frequently looked upward to the rim of the canyon and the blue sky. In the early afternoon a small herd of pigs rushed past him downstream. He wondered again what lay in wait upstream. Nainoa proceeded with caution, pausing often to observe his surroundings.

Late in the afternoon, the floor of the canyon widened, and he came upon a long pool that was shallow at one end. He studied it carefully as he approached. Along one side was a narrow beach whose sand revealed the prints of many animals, including the broad pugmarks of a tiger, several days old. Large fish hovered in the shallows.

Using his unstrung bow, Nainoa chased one fish down and impaled it, then tossed it up on the sand, where it flopped its life away. Seeing the dogs watching him, he ran down another for them. The afternoon sun shone onto the beach between the cliff walls. It was a beautiful spot, and he scooped out a small earth oven, lined it with dry river stones, and made a large fire in it. He washed the long strip of woven cotton that he had been wearing and spread it out on the hot sand to dry in the sun. Then he bathed in the pool, watching orange dragonflies and reveling in the cool water as he waited for the fire to burn down. His earlier uneasiness began to dissipate in response to the natural beauty of the place, and when the fire was reduced to coals, he wrapped his fish in wet leaves and baked it in the ashes among the hot stones. When the fish was done, he ate heartily, feeding some to the dogs, who devoured it eagerly. As he watched them eat, he wondered if they were there to guide him up the canyon.

Monkeys called in alarm from upstream. Looking up quickly, Nainoa saw an eagle patrolling the treetops along the sloping canyon walls. As the bird dropped down for a closer look at him, a dozen iguanas leaped from their arboreal perches into the deeper end of the pool with loud splashes.

His uneasiness returned as the light faded, and shortly thereafter he found a big multitrunked tree, growing from a fan of loose rubble on the hillside above the canyon floor, in which he could spend the night. As he climbed into the tree, Nainoa thought he felt a presence, and his thoughts turned again to large predators. There was definitely a peculiar tension about this place. He established camp well above the ground.

Darkness fell swiftly in the canyon, and the frogs and insects shouted out lustily for mates. Nainoa looked up at the long strip of blue sky enclosed by the darkening rock walls and relaxed into sleep, thinking again about his former life in the settlement. Longing and loneliness pervaded his last thoughts. He thought briefly of the dogs, and then he slept.

Sometime during the night, something awakened him. Nainoa lay in his hammock alert and waiting. He looked down from his perch but could see nothing in the complete darkness. Far above, the late moon touched only the upper part of the canyon wall, beyond which a swath of starry sky appeared.

Recalling the tiger's prints and the presence he had felt earlier, Nainoa uneasily put out his hand to confirm the presence of his spear, whose nail-

and leather-studded shaft reassured him. Hearing nothing that would have awakened him, Nainoa made a conscious effort to relax, slowly stretching and extending his arms and legs against the confines of the woven hammock. The tension in his body let go, and he prepared to slip down into sleep once more—when he felt a pulse of the same sensations that had preceded his encounter with the shadow in the *siti*. As if they had been waiting for him to recognize them, the sensations within him increased rapidly, and he came fully awake. At that moment, he heard an odd sound.

Tok!

It was a soft, hollow percussive noise, as if a wooden bell or drum had been lightly struck. The sensations continued to grow within him, and he felt his body stiffening, becoming paralyzed. He fought it briefly, but soon found himself gripped once again by the incredible, ecstatic pressure. Hearing a rushing sound, he wondered if the night wind was blowing through the trees on the canyon walls far above.

Strange flickering lights began to dance around him in the night. He watched them as the roaring in his ears grew louder by the moment. Now it sounded like swiftly flowing water. Had an unseasonal rain in the highlands upstream produced a flash flood within the canyon? He shut his eyes tightly and tried to struggle with the force that held him, tried to will it away—when inexplicably the noise ceased. The night became absolutely silent once again, and the feelings of force lessened somewhat. Startled, he opened his eyes.

The canyon floor was filled with the soft golden light of very early morning. There was just enough mist to hold and reflect the sun's radiance, creating a vibrant, luminous intensity. Yet something was different about the landscape. The trees along the canyon walls seemed too regular, too straight, too geometric. He felt different, too, infused with confidence and physical strength. Perhaps it was due to his long walk—he observed with satisfaction that he was in better shape than he had been for years. He must have fallen back asleep and reawakened shortly after the dawn.

But then he felt another surge of those same odd sensations and decided to gather his gear and descend to the canyon floor. With that intention he abruptly found himself at the base of the tree. The ground seemed oddly springy . . .

Tok!

Once again, the hollow, wooden sound echoed through the canyon. He glanced in the direction from which it had come and caught movement off to his left. He thought uneasily of the tiger prints but saw only the trees and rocky hillsides. Looking up, he saw his hammock and his form clearly outlined. Once again he realized he was safe, his spear within reach, the web of the hammock around his body . . . he was safe . . . he was safe. . . .

He looked again at the trees. Some of their leaves seemed a vibrant blue color, while others had an orange tint to them. He had never seen foliage like this before. Perhaps it was an effect of the golden light reflected in the moisture-laden air. There were no shadows.

Tok!

The sound summoned him. Who or what was calling him? He listened intently to the silence as he peered around, his visual perception expanding into all directions at once. He decided to move upstream, into the trees along the canyon wall to his left, and started walking through the golden morning light—or was it afternoon? His awareness shifted, and he was sure it was dawn, a wonderful dawn filled with promise and adventure. The sensations of power in his body grew with the thought.

Tok!

Something was definitely moving through the trees off to his left. Nainoa watched it out of the corner of his eye without looking directly at it, and this time it did not disappear. It was large and as tall as he was, and it was following his progression, keeping in step, flowing gracefully through the trees. It stopped when he stopped. It walked when he walked.

Tok!

He looked away from the movement out into the forest where the light was now shafting down from some unimaginable height. The power pulsed in his body, and the buzzing sound had resumed in his head. As he walked, stepping over fallen trees, brushing by feathery ferns, the tall presence

continued to accompany him off to his left. Luminous mushrooms glowed in the dark places. He wondered what to do. . . .

Tok!

A few strides ahead lay a clearing, perhaps created by a fallen tree. He stepped into it and stopped. Somehow he knew that this circle of golden light was the place where he was supposed to be. The presence was still to his left at the edge of the trees. Nainoa waited. It did not move, so he turned slowly and looked directly at it.

Tok!

He became taut as a bowstring. At the edge of the clearing, half there and half not, stood a strange form. He glanced away, and it disappeared into the broken pattern of light and dark. He quickly looked back again, and there it was. He glanced away, and as before, it seemed to dissolve. Bird calls came from far away. He slowly looked back. It was the tiger.

His mind and body flooded with fear—but it was abruptly replaced by confused relief as he realized that the face into which he was looking was human! And yet, not quite human . . . His perceptions expanded with a jolt.

Standing on two legs like himself, the tall, tawny being was covered with a broken pattern of large spots. Partly concealed by the trees, the lower half of its body appeared somehow separate from the upper half. Its legs and feet were tigerlike, with enormous claws. Its thick tail twitched with nervous feline energy, perhaps as a result of his close observation. One massive forearm rested along the trunk of a tree and terminated in a huge "hand" that was not a hand—at least, not a human hand. Were those short, thick fingers? He was not sure, but they ended in a set of impressive claws that retracted as he looked at them—perhaps a gesture meant to reassure him. Its head and neck appeared slender and gracile compared to its robust, powerful body. The small head bore a face with essentially human features.

It seemed to Nainoa that the essences of tigerness and humanness had been blended somehow into an impossible yet very definite composite whole. He thought, "The tiger man"—and with that concept, the being before him altered slightly in the dappled light and shadow.

It smiled.

It was a human expression, but at the same time not quite human. Yet the smile reinforced Nainoa's growing sense of calm. He tried to speak, to ask questions, but could not. He looked into the tiger man's eyes and abruptly felt another awesome rush of sensation, just as when he had faced the shadow that night in the ruined *siti*. He became rigid, the blood hissing in his ears. He dropped his eyes as he dimly remembered something from long ago, but couldn't quite grasp what it was. . . .

He raised his eyes again to regard the tiger man and felt an odd sense of companionship with it. At that moment the tiger man moved from the cover of the trees and walked up to him. As it drew closer, Nainoa's sensations increased. The beast-man came to within one stride of him and looked directly into his eyes. Nainoa stared into eyes as green as leaves, and other images took the place of the face in front of him.

He saw a pond surrounded by trees, orange flowers floating on its dark surface. Hearing laughter, he looked up and saw a small group of children throwing something into the water. Beyond them were trees with red leaves, and beyond them the vast blue ocean. Invisible boundaries were dissolving. Dark stone walls and ruined house platforms were around him among the trees. What did this mean? Glancing up, he saw an immense cliff above the treetops, but it was unlike that of the canyon that surrounded him. The stone was dark—very dark. . . .

The sensations of power subsided, and the images abruptly evaporated. Deep exhaustion invaded him. His sense of rising was followed by feelings of settling, of descent. He felt the hammock around his body once again. He saw the tiger man's image, this time in his mind.

As he drifted into sleep, he felt, rather than saw, its smile. . . .

7
Napo'opo'o

I EMERGED FROM THE ALTERED STATE ABRUPTLY and sat
bolt upright under the tamarind tree. I quickly looked
around for the children. They were still at the pond,
just where they had been only moments before. I had been
gone for at least thirty-six hours in Nainoa's time, yet
only a minute or two seemed to have passed in mine. The
power within me was decreasing in surges, and my blood
hissed with excitement. At some deep level, I was also
shaken, deeply shaken. . . .

A fragment of Joseph Campbell's quote on the threshold guardian emerged in my mind—"the zone of magnified power." I did indeed appear to be passing through
something like this zone on my way to and from "there,"
but the guardian was no longer in evidence. Could it be
that I had passed some test during that first altered-state
experience back in Berkeley and was now granted access? I
seemed to be making what Michael Harner would call an
extended "middle world" voyage, traveling to another
place in ordinary reality but traversing time to get there.

I stood shakily and rejoined the playgroup by the pond, glancing from time to time into the surrounding trees as if to make sure that I had really returned. The leopard man had appeared to Nainoa, although he was different somehow from my old imaginary friend. As a child I had always perceived this entity as leopardlike, with a leopard's empty rosettes and graceful physique. For Nainoa, he had assumed a different outward form, and yet in an inner sense he was not different at all. The patterning of his spots and his robust figure had been distinctly jaguarlike. Was this what he was really like, or had he simply taken a form that Nainoa would find meaningful? Nainoa's memory lacked the terms *leopard* and *jaguar,* so he had identified him as the tiger man, a close equivalent. I looked over my shoulder into the forested village site and remembered from my childhood adventures that the leopard man always stuck to the bushes if he could.

When I was nine years old, my friends and various grown-ups told me repeatedly that imaginary friends were not real. I remembered railing against their disbelief. Of course they were real! I experienced them as real. The leopard man was not a mental construct or a product of my own creative imagination, I understood, but an independent being with his own personality and his own agenda.

A traditional psychiatrist or psychologist would be inclined to dismiss the leopard man as a mental construct whose ultimate source lay within my imagination. A Jungian or transpersonal psychologist might call him an archetype—one that had arisen in my mind spontaneously from the depths of the collective human unconscious. A traditional shaman, on the other hand, would recognize him as an autonomous spiritual entity that had decided to become my spirit helper.

Ethnographic information on shamans from around the world reveals that spirit helpers tend to take forms meaningful to the human with whom they have a relationship. They are often called power animals because they are commonly perceived as animals or as some combination of animal and human—as beast-men or therianthropes. These spirit helpers reputedly work with and protect the shaman and are the source of great power and knowledge.

Every human culture seems to generate its own folklore about encounters between humans and nonordinary beings like animal spirits, elves, fairies, spirit guides, gods, deities, demons, angels, and spiritual teachers. Perhaps the "extraterrestrials" or "visitors" that some people report seeing in our culture also fall into this category.

As I considered this, my daughter Erica was feeding the fish in the pond. She already had a well-developed inner world, richly peopled by imaginary friends, and she spent long hours by herself talking and interacting with them on our jungly property up the mountain. Her teddy bears and other stuffed animals were simply material symbols of those friends, who were very real for her when she was engaged with them. I wondered when the culture at large would succeed in imposing its consensus over hers and shutting down her other world.

Mythology conveys that dealing with spirits is risky because they can be beneficent or demonic, depending on one's focus and intentions. Joseph Campbell described spirits as "the powers that watch at the threshold to the unknown," on the one hand, and as "the forces of transformation which can enhance growth or inflict disaster," on the other. As teachers and guardians they may bestow power and knowledge, but as demons or threshold guardians part of their job is to turn back questers who are not yet capable of encountering that which lies beyond the doorway. I suddenly remembered something else Joseph Campbell had said years ago in San Francisco:

"Anyone incapable of understanding these spirits as 'gods' tends to perceive them as 'devils.' Those individuals who are 'unready' are unable to traverse the zone of magnified power and enter the nonordinary spiritual realms . . . and for these unworthies, the doorway remains closed."

As I considered this thought, the wind shifted, both literally and metaphorically. Regardless of what the leopard man's ultimate nature might be,

I knew that that strange being was a definitive part of my own experienced reality. And now it was part of Nainoa's as well.

I allowed the children to take the lead on the next stage of their walk and followed behind them, lost in thought. This third episode had occurred in the daytime a full five months after the last one. This time Nainoa had briefly visited with me here and had perceived my world through my own conscious awareness, just as I had made contact with his. Could the process actually work in both directions? Why not? Had the leopard man played the role of facilitator, guide, catalyst—or spirit helper?

We arrived at a place among the boulders above the ocean that the children knew well. I sat down on a large flat rock in the shade of a *kamani* tree while they foraged spontaneously, much as children of hunter-gatherer peoples in remote parts of the world do, using stones to crack open and eat the tree's nuts.

Back on the beach, I saw Jill arrive with baby Anna to take up a spot in the shade near the base of the *heiau*. Erica noticed them too, and the playgroup returned through the trees with me in tow. We all had a swim in the warm, sparkling ocean, during which I recounted to Jill what I had just experienced. She listened soberly, and privately I wondered if she thought I was going crazy. I was acutely aware that I might have thought her crazy if she had recounted such things to me.

Then, I took a step back and wondered if I was in fact going crazy.

Jill could see I was in a terrible state of inner conflict, and when Erica announced that she was ready to return home for lunch, she offered to take the children to give me some time alone. I accepted, and she departed, leaving me in my quandary. I returned to the village and sat on the same stone under the tamarind.

I closed my eyes and tried to open the inner doorway, to reconnect my awareness with Nainoa's. Nothing happened. I looked into the trees and visualized the leopard man in the forest nearby. I invoked his help. The sound of breaking wood interrupted my concentration, but when I scanned the area, I saw nothing out of the ordinary. I was alone. I heard it again and quickly looked around, but again I saw nothing. Perhaps someone beyond the limits of my vision was gathering firewood.

I resumed meditation and tried to induce the altered state. I closed my eyes and practiced one-pointed concentration, clearing my mind of all thoughts and emotions. Then I practiced relaxation to clear my body of tension.

I had achieved only moderate success by the time the mosquitoes came after me, so I abandoned the spot in the forest and returned to the flat rock under the *kamani* tree above the ocean. I lay down on my back on the smooth black stone and looked up into the leaves, watching their rhythmic movement in the light breeze off the water. I listened to the waves breaking.

Perhaps ten minutes passed. I was on the brink of dozing off when the first sensations heralded the shift. Simultaneously I heard the loud sound of wood breaking. I waited, my excitement rising.

The feelings grew stronger. I listened to the waves breaking, and the sensations suddenly rushed up my spine and exploded into my brain. Ecstasy seized me, my body stiffened, my hands inflated. In a moment of vertigo I lifted off—or rather, I fell backward through the stone, through the darkness, as the flashing light-forms appeared and converged into lines that extended into the unimaginable distance. The usual phosphenic shapes appeared, while the sound of the breaking waves receded into total silence. Then I saw only darkness.

The first perceptions were of coldness—my body felt very, very cold. I could close my hands now, and I seemed to be holding something. It felt like wood. I heard a strange bird call. I shivered and opened my eyes. I was there.

8
Fourth Journey
The Serpent of Wisdom

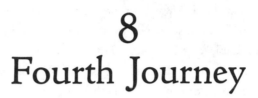

IT WAS AFTER DAWN, AND COLD AIR WAS FLOWING down the canyon from the highlands above. Nainoa shivered in his cloak and rain-cape as he broke another fallen branch and fed the fire in his earth oven beside the long pool. He had never been so cold.

The dogs sat at a respectful distance and accepted the donations of fish that he tossed in their direction. He watched them and wondered again if they had been waiting for him, if they were guides between the forested world below and whatever lay above and beyond the barrier—or if they were themselves spirits. They never came closer than ten paces, and he never attempted to touch them.

On descending from his tree at first light, Nainoa had examined the ground carefully but had found no indication of tracks other than his own and those of the dogs. Part of him was profoundly troubled about the tiger man. Since his encounter with the shadowlike being in the *siti* the week before, he had felt himself being drawn into a relationship with forces that he did not clearly understand.

That he was dealing with spirits was beyond doubt. The dark humanoid form was no ordinary forest creature. It had shown him the existence of power that was extraordinary and terrifying. He wondered if it was the guardian at the doorway into the realm of the spirits. The *ke'aka* seemed to have tested him in some way to see how he would react. The tiger man was as formidable as the shadow but somehow more personable. Could its appearance indicate that he had passed a test and would be allowed to step further into unknown realms? Perhaps the old woman of the village kitchens had been right—perhaps these forested regions were haunted by spirits.

He stood and arranged his gear, feeling strong and well suited to this adventurous way of living. How could his life as a clerk-secretary compare with this? In spite of his worries, he felt wonderful. He drowned the fire, with apologies to its spirit, and set off up the canyon with the dogs.

He traveled up the canyon well into the afternoon, then reached a high rockfall that he scaled with difficulty. Afterward, the canyon widened, and he followed a long level stretch in which the stream deepened into a long dark pool surrounded by trees. Seeing no sign of crocodiles, he was on the point of approaching the pool to run down a fish for dinner when he noted that the dogs had stopped well short of the water and were staring intently up into the trees. Both glanced at him, then pointedly abandoned the stream bed to take a route well away from the water. They scrambled up and over another rockfall close to the wall and disappeared up the canyon.

Bringing the spear down from his back, Nainoa slowly approached the spot where they had stopped and looked up, and still he almost missed it. Just ahead, in a large tree that partially overhung the pool, was an immense serpent.

He drew in his breath with surprise. Unmoving, the great snake seemed a part of the tree. In the dim, sun-dappled interior of the canyon, its dark greenish-brown bulk with large black spots and smaller yellow blotches was almost invisible. Its body was as thick as his own and looked big enough to consume an entire deer or even one of the long-nosed forest pigs—or possibly a man. Since much of the serpent was concealed in the pool, he could not see its length, but he guessed it to be more than fifty feet long. Its head was as long as his forearm and displayed a long, dark diagonal stripe behind the surprisingly small golden eyes. It was longer and thicker than any of the snakes whose skins he had seen in the settlements.

It was probably waiting for its meal to appear at the pool to drink, Nainoa realized, to pass by underneath the tree as he had almost done. He looked around uneasily—were there any more of them? He felt heightened with a curious nervous tension and slowly hunkered down to watch the monumental beast.

This *naheka* was definitely of chiefly rank among snakes. Perhaps it was the king of the serpents himself, or the queen. As the light gleamed off its closely set scales, Nainoa suddenly wondered if it was real. Perhaps it was a supernatural being, the "landlord" of the canyon, a spirit creature out of legend and myth. This place did have an air of unreality about it. Perhaps he had blundered through some door into the mythic lower world of the animal spirits. In the mythology of his people the serpent was the symbol of wisdom. Such a large one had certainly lived a long time and must therefore know a great deal. Nagai had told Nainoa that these huge creatures never stopped growing throughout their long lives.

Nagai had also told him an ancient story about a great serpent who had lived in a cotton tree in a mythic place called Eden. Some scholars held Eden to be in Milu, in the lower world of the animal spirits. Others felt it was up in Lanikeha, in the upper world of the gods, heroes, and spiritual teachers. Some versions of the story found a middle ground, holding that these mythic levels were connected by the tree whose roots were in the lower world and whose crown of branches was in the upper, its trunk passing through various tiers of the dreamworlds in between.

Kahunas believed that everything in the everyday world had an ordinary aspect "here" and a nonordinary aspect in the spirit realms, Nagai had explained. Every night, when a person was asleep, their awareness crossed into this nonordinary level during dreaming. This middle world of dream was also thought to be where a person's spirit passed at the moment of death, residing there for a time in order to adjust to the new state and to accomplish certain things before ascending into the realm where the *aumakua*, the ancestral spirits, resided.

The serpent of wisdom was rumored to travel up and down the great tree between all these levels. Thus it was familiar with all the aspects of reality—higher, middle, and lower, both ordinary and nonordinary. As Nainoa observed the huge snake uneasily, he wondered whether it was on its way up or down the tree. Had it temporarily slipped through some doorway to feed?

In one of the myths the serpent gave the gift of knowledge to Eva, the first woman. She, in turn, gave it to her lover Maui, the first man. In another version, Maui actually stole the knowledge from the serpent through trickery. Maui was always doing outrageous things in the myths and legends and was probably the only person capable of pulling off such a deed. Fortunately, the great serpent was amused by Maui's antics and forgave him, serving for a time as his spiritual teacher. Under the serpent's guidance Maui was finally able to shed his old skin (like the snake) and become fully aware, fully formed, and fully informed as to his own true nature. In this way Maui became a renowned *kahuna* himself in his old age, even though he had been a rascally adventurer for much of his life.

In still other myths the serpent was associated with a great spiritual teacher named Iesu, who was also known as "the white master." Iesu was a woodworker who became a great *kahuna* healer once he had received the serpent's wisdom. In some accounts the serpent took Iesu to the garden in the upper world, where they met with one of the serpent's former students, a great sage named Kotama, who was often known by his honorary title, *Kapukanui*, the great gate or entrance.

Like Maui, Kotama had been a real man once, a prince who had lived thousands of years before in a fabled land beyond the ocean to the west. During his lifetime Kotama had renounced ordinary earthly pleasures to pursue spiritual knowledge and power, which the serpent imparted to him one day while he was seated in meditation under a cotton tree. Kotama then became a great spiritual teacher, and when he died, he took up residence in the garden in the upper world, where he sits eternally in deep meditation.

When Iesu and the serpent arrived in the garden, Kotama greeted the serpent warmly and served as Iesu's teacher, instructing him in the methods of stillness necessary for the achievement of inner awareness and self-knowledge. After many years, Iesu returned to earth to teach mercy and compassion. Iesu's *mana* was so great that he was able to walk on water and could fly through the air like a bird. Iesu could even restore a recently deceased person's soul to their body and bring them back to life, Nagai had said.

In other legends the great serpent acted as a creator being, responsible for bringing forth life itself. As creator, the serpent became the rainbow serpent, Kanaheka'anuenue. Normally invisible, it can only be seen opposite the sun when the sun's energy joins with the water of life as it falls as rain or mist from the upper world. Then the rainbow serpent is seen as it combines light and water into the foundation for all living things. . . .

A short howl brought Nainoa's thoughts back to the present and his shaggy companions. It was the first time he had heard the wild dogs make a sound. The shadows were lengthening with the passing of the day. The serpent before him might indeed be a supernatural being, but he wanted to put real distance between himself and it before nightfall.

Nainoa rose slowly and stretched his legs, then turned right to follow the detour the dogs had taken, well away from the huge snake. He watched it carefully as he passed, but it never moved. When he arrived at the stream bed beyond, he looked back and noticed that it had freshly shed its old skin. He reflected that like the serpent, he too was moving on to the next stage in his existence, beyond his former life of predictability and boredom. Looking at the great snake one last time, he cleared his mind and sent it a respectful farewell. He felt more settled internally after his communion with the serpent, but what their meeting meant remained unknown.

The canyon floor rose abruptly in several giant steps, over which feathery, dry-season waterfalls dripped. Nainoa climbed carefully. The dogs continued to find the easiest passages, and he felt grateful for their company. Almost immediately afterward he came to the canyon's end. The stream bed rose to within a long bowshot of the rim, and he suddenly found himself facing sheer rock walls, up which he saw no apparent route. His disappointment was profound at the thought of retracing his steps and losing four days of travel time. Because of the serpent, he was acutely vulnerable. The box canyon made a perfect trap.

He followed the stream to the base of the rock wall, searching for a trail. Spiky clumps of plants with knifelike leaves grew from cracks. Lizards darted among the fallen rocks at the cliff's base. The stream formed a wide, wet stain, streaming down the rock wall above.

At this point the dogs passed him and disappeared around a corner that he had missed in the flat light under the canyon's shadow. He followed them up the steeply slanted rock face to an irregularity that, had he been alone, he would have overlooked. Copious amounts of dry dung there attested to the regular use of the route by deer and pigs.

Removing his sandals, Nainoa rearranged his gear and carefully climbed onto the narrow ledge, using the full grip of his bare feet. He proceeded cautiously, inching along, leaning into and hugging the smooth rock to keep from slipping. He glanced up and saw the dogs looking down, watching his progress. Crossing the wet spot was treacherous, and he almost fell twice.

Slowly, carefully, he finally reached the top of the rock face and pushed through some thorny shrubs onto a level space. He looked out at a clear view—he had achieved the rim!

Exhilarated, Nainoa dropped his bags, sat down on a stone ledge, and looked around. The ground was rocky, the soil was thin, and the trees were considerably smaller than on the lowlands. There were open, level, grassy areas dotted with rock outcrops and bushes, beyond which the land rose again toward the high mountains. New, undescribed territory lay before him. An unfamiliar bird trilled in the stillness.

Looking back from his perch into the canyon, he saw the dogs far below, moving away from him. As they stopped and looked up, he remembered gratefully that they had been his "guardians of safe passage" past the great snake and the seeming dead end. Perhaps they were returning to their lower world, to await the next traveler. The dogs flowed gracefully down the rocky stream bed and disappeared.

Since the day was fading, Nainoa stood, picked up his things, and made his way cautiously through the bushes and shrubby trees away from the canyon's edge. To his right was a line of palms, revealing the stream's course above the rim. To his left he saw a small hill with a tree growing from its summit. He decided to camp there.

First he wanted to bathe and replenish his water supply. He headed for the palms, amid which the stream had widened into a substantial pool, with a narrow sand bar along one side. He bathed, located a nest of turtle eggs in the sand, and ate a dozen of them raw. Refilling his water container, he took along more of the eggs and headed toward the hill.

Looking west from its summit, he could see across the plateau to the vast darkness of the lowland forest beyond. The haze had cleared somewhat, and in the far distance a sheet of light shone off the inland sea. He could just discern the long ridges between it and the coast. Somewhere among them lay his home. He had covered an impressive distance in the past eighteen days. To the south, the vague outline of a dormant volcano was barely visible. Although he had traveled far north since leaving his canoe, the mountain peaks to the east seemed just as distant as when he had first seen them from the *siti* far below.

Nainoa hung his hammock and possessions in the tree and descended in search of dinner. Within moments he had found a large snake under a decaying tree trunk. He returned to the top of the hillock, made a rock-rimmed pit below his tree, and started a fire. He set water to boil in his cooking pot, then skinned and cleaned the snake, cut it into segments, and added the pieces to the water with a pinch of salt, smiling at the irony of this meal after his encounter with the great serpent in the canyon. He offered a short prayer of thanks to both snakes. The longing thought of breadfruit and *taro* made his stomach sigh with regret. The snake and the turtle eggs would have to suffice.

As Nainoa ate in the gathering dusk, he missed the wild dogs company. The mountains seemed closer and higher in the reflected afterglow of the sunset. Night fell quickly. One moment, he could see clearly in the gathering dusk, the next it was pitch-black. Settled in his hammock for the night, he watched a large herd of deer, a buck with ten does, emerge from cover to head for the thick line of trees that marked the course of the stream. He lay comfortably as a slight breeze moved through the closely packed upper branches of the tree, causing it to sway gently. The wind made an eerie sound.

He thought of the tiger man and his vision of the strange pond in the woods near the ocean. He wondered what it meant, where it was.

Suddenly the powerful visage of Kapohaku'ki'ihele, Chief Kaneohe's stone, appeared in his mind's eye. The word *pohaku* contained roots that could help him understand his experience. *Po* referred to the spiritual dimensions, to the dream worlds of the gods, heroes, spiritual masters, and the animal *akuas*. *Haku* meant lord or master. The term *pohaku* thus implied that stones were in some way the lords of the spirit worlds, the masters of *Po*. Perhaps his "meeting" with Kapohaku'ki'ihele somehow was leading him to his visions. Chief Kaneohe had said that it had sometimes come to him in his dreams. . . .

Nainoa finally fell into a fitful dreaming, in which he was again climbing the canyon and confronting the serpent. He awoke repeatedly, unable to fall deeply asleep. In the darkness sometime before dawn, some clouds appeared from the northwest, and a light unseasonal rain began to fall. He covered himself with his rain-cape, whereupon the rain ceased. As he was dropping off to sleep once more, the rain began again with the lightest of sprinkles, rattling off the oiled *ti* leaves of the rain-cape.

His hunger returned and his stomach growled as he thought of one of his favorite meals, beans cooked with hot peppers, onions, and salt, with sweet fried bananas on top. His stomach's moanings brought him fully awake. To distract himself, he thought once more of the *pohaku* and his vision of the pond, trying to figure out what had been so odd about the children. He invoked the image of the stone in his consciousness, feeling its rough surface between his hands.

Finally, toward dawn, he slept and could smell hot beans cooking—the odors penetrated his dream state strongly. A sound like frying onions, a sizzling or buzzing that he first thought was the light rain making cool points on his face, arms, and legs, turned unexpectedly into the power sensations. Lights flashed in the darkness as the familiar paralysis invaded him. He thought of the tiger man and wondered if he would meet him once again. The sensations reached deeply into him, carrying him . . . carrying him as the lights flashed by. There was an eternal moment of complete and utter silence—and then he heard a human voice.

Someone said something. It was the first human voice he had heard since his departure, besides his own. Startled, he opened his eyes to find himself seated at a finely crafted table. A bowl of steaming black beans sat on the table before him.

Consciously he thought, What an extremely vivid dream! Then, as he looked slowly around, he came fully awake. Sitting at the table with him were a woman and child. He had the sense of another—but another what or whom, he was not sure. The woman was wearing virtually nothing except a wide band of cloth that covered her like a second skin from her chest to her legs. It was brightly colored, with a bold design of green and blue. She was very slender, with small high breasts and long lean arms and legs. She had long black hair, and her hands and fingers were small and well formed. She wore two thin gold rings on the third finger of her left hand.

Her dark eyes glanced at him. They were beautiful and long like the rest of her. Her cheekbones were prominent and wide, giving her face an angular appearance. Then, he realized with shock what was so unique about her: Her skin was very light. He had never before seen anyone with such pale skin.

He glanced at her child. Somehow he knew the girl was hers, but he wasn't sure how. She looked very much like her mother, with the same eyes and pale skin, but her hair was brown. Nainoa looked back at the woman and was startled to feel stirrings of sexual desire toward her.

When she looked up and cocked a long eye at him speculatively, he became aware that he was staring. He dropped his gaze to find a beautifully crafted metal spoon on the table next to the bowl of food. Without thought or intention he took the spoon and began to eat. The beans were spicy and delicious. The spoon appeared to be made of silver.

At this point he noticed his hands, and renewed shock rolled through him. They were very pale, and there were two gold rings on the middle finger of the right one. They were not his hands.

His rising agitation was compounded by the fact that the woman and child were eating with him at the table. Men and women did not eat together in the settlements, except at ritual or ceremonial occasions. Men ate in the men's house, and women and children ate in the women's house.

As Nainoa absorbed his situation, the woman turned to her daughter and said something. He had no idea what she was saying but listened carefully. He picked out a few words and realized she was speaking in Old English, the language in which the early histories were written. He was able to get the gist of what she said, although her pronunciation was exceedingly odd.

The woman rose from the table and walked over to a large, brightly polished metal cabinet. She touched a small projecting object, and blue fire appeared on the cabinet's surface. She placed an odd, long-necked metal pot on the fire. The cabinet must be a machine for cooking.

He looked quickly around the room. Shelves lined the walls with stacks of plates and bowls that appeared to be ceramic, and beautifully formed cups of clear glass, many of which were all the same size and shape. He had never seen such a large collection of artifacts from the Great Age in one place; nor did he know what most of them were, although some of the finely made wooden bowls looked familiar. He reached out and picked one up, feeling the thinness of the wood, marveling at the symmetry of shape. On turning it over, he saw words cut into the center of the underside: "Dan Deluz," under which was inscribed "*Koa* wood." His pulse quickened. This wood came from Hawai'i. Chiefly families treasured the large *koa* bowls that had accompanied their ancestors on the great journey from the islands.

Nainoa replaced the bowl and glanced out the windows through long thin slats of clear glass. Beyond was a mountain slope covered with trees. It seemed to be late afternoon, and low gray clouds that promised rain obscured the mountain's summit. He saw rooftops in the near distance among coconut palms and mangoes and some other trees he did not know.

The view was unfamiliar, and yet it seemed somehow very familiar. He looked again at his hands and arms. Was he dreaming? He ran his hands over his face—where was his beard? There were stories and legends of strange, dreamlike experiences, in which people found themselves within other bodies. He had always assumed them to be symbolic or wishful tales.

With an effort he calmed himself and began to observe, his historian's mind taking in details. The woman and the child abruptly rose and walked into an adjoining room. He stood and followed without making the decision to do so. His body was covered with strange, closely fitting clothing. He seemed to be wearing an upper and a lower garment, both of which were fashioned of finely woven cotton that had been dyed a dark blue. He was amazed to see that the lower garment was a pair of pants. He had never worn pants. Only members of the chiefly class wore pants.

The upper garment had short sleeves and a simple neck, and it appeared to be marked with an image. He studied it and discerned a design that included a palm tree and a circle—the sun, perhaps. There were words as well. They were upside down, and he craned his neck, pulling the garment around until he could read them. Above was written ALOHA THEATER, and below, in smaller letters, he read: KAINALIU HAWAI'I. He felt his mind tipping over. Was it possible?

The woman walked over to a series of shelves on which there was a large box with a gray square on its side. She touched the box, whereupon the gray square filled with light, becoming a vivid blue. An image formed, one that moved and changed. Voices came from the box. His mind reeled in astonishment.

He looked into the blue light and beheld small people. They were talking about something, but he could not understand them because they were speaking so quickly. They were strangely dressed. Before he could study them, the image changed, and he was staring at a brightly painted wagon. It was moving very fast on a wide, black, very smooth road. No oxen were pulling the wagon—it could only be moving with an *enjin*. More machines of different colors appeared in the moving image, and his excitement increased. The woman and child watched the images in silence.

Nainoa tore his eyes away to look around the room. The walls were made of closely fitted planks of wood; the shelves were filled with many, many books. He was stunned at the thought of the knowledge they contained. A large picture on one wall appeared to be of a *heiau*. He glanced out a window at a lush green landscape dominated by more mango trees and coconut palms. Farther away, a large lychee tree stood loaded with dark red clusters of fruit.

He walked over to examine the door. It was made of thin metal strips and finely woven metal netting through which he could see. The design of the latch was most curious. He pushed the door open and walked outside.

To his immediate left stood two machines of the sort that he had just seen moving down the road in the box of light. One was large, one small. He walked slowly around them, studying them, completely wonderstruck. He ran his fingertips across their surfaces. They smelled odd.

The wagons appeared to be made almost entirely of colored metal with windows of clear glass, and each stood on four black wheels made of some hard yet resilient substance. There were seats within. The wagons were on a smooth black road in which small stones were embedded in a matrix. He followed the road with his eyes; it turned uphill and disappeared through a grove of avocados and tree ferns. A large *wi*-apple towered over the wagons from the other side of the road.

He studied his surroundings. The land around the house appeared to be a small farm that was somewhat overgrown. There were several varieties of banana, and coffee trees stood around the other side of the house.

Stepping back, he saw that parts of the roof were covered by thin planks of wood while another section was made of folded sheets of some kind of metal. Never before had he seen so much metal. Near the door was a small rock garden of oddly shaped black stones, among which decorative, flowering plants were growing.

A raised walkway ran down the length of the house, and he proceeded along it past a small banyan tree until he found himself on a wide wooden platform. The wall of this side of the house appeared to be made almost entirely of huge sheets of glass, through which he could see the house's interior. Within was a sleeping room dominated by a large bed on a raised platform of wooden beams. The walls featured more pictures of *heiaus*. A long table contained piles of books.

As he drew back from the glass wall, he suddenly saw his own reflected image—that of a tall, beardless, trim man with very pale skin, short-cropped brown hair, and dark brown eyes. Nainoa's mind raced as he stared into those dark eyes, marveling at the vividness of his dream. But was this a dream? It was entirely too real. But how was this possible? He studied his reflection but could see no expression of the surprise and shock that he was feeling. It was not his face.

He suddenly felt the mesh of the hammock around his body, and part of his mind became aware that he was still safely ensconced in his tree above the barrier. "And who is this?" he thought, surveying the image in the glass. He saw the eyes narrow, and unexpectedly a word formed in his mind, a name perhaps—"Hank . . . or Henk."

"And what am I doing here in his body?" he thought.

His deliberations were interrupted by an odd thundering from above. Looking up, he saw a flying machine appear over the forested ridge just below the clouds. It was white and blue in color and shaped like a bird or a fish. Strange red and green lights appeared and disappeared, and it made a loud, roaring sound, probably from its *enjin*. It moved quickly far above the house, then changed direction and headed west toward the setting sun. It was then that he noticed the ocean for the first time, stretching to the horizon, its surface ablaze with reflected light.

At this moment, a section of the glass wall slid aside, and his daughter came out.

His daughter?

She slipped and fell in the rainwater pooled on the platform. She began to cry, and without thought, he rushed to pick her up and comfort her. She had bitten her lip and was bleeding. He carried her into the house.

As he walked through the house, he felt the floor covering on his feet, a seamless mat of very soft, dense blue wool. As if he had done this many times before, he returned to the kitchen, to a tall white cabinet in the wall, and pulled open the top door. Cold air poured out onto his feet, and his hands extracted a flat blue box that was also extremely cold. It was a gridlike collection of smaller boxes that contained an opaque, cold substance. Without thinking about it, his hands twisted the box, and with a sharp cracking sound, shards of the glassy substance tipped into a finely wrought silver bowl. The child reached into it and popped one of the shards into her mouth. She stopped crying.

Reaching in again, she held a shard up to him. It dripped cold water onto his arm. He took it into his mouth, registering amazement, and gasped. It was very, very cold. Some other part of his mind produced a word—*ice.* Where had the word come from?

At this moment he became aware once again of the sensations of power, increasing perhaps in response to his rising excitement, filling his chest with pressure.

The woman appeared and said something to him as she scooped the child into her arms to comfort her. A thought appeared—these people were Americans. They were Americans! Their pale skin, their curious features, their Old English, their machines—he suddenly knew these people were Americans, living in Hawai'i sometime before the fall of their civilization! He was in someone else's body in the time before the Fall in the ancestral homeland of Hawai'i!

The woman went back into the other room and pushed her fingers against another large box. Almost immediately, tiny lights appeared on its surface, and music filled the air. He had never heard anything like it before. He had no idea what instruments were being used to play it or even where they were. A box that made music. Another machine!

He listened to the music as he walked back outside and looked in wonder at the tropical landscape. "This is Hawai'i," he thought. "This is the homeland of my ancestors."

A light sprinkling of rain fell from the heavy clouds overhead, and as he felt it on his skin, he remembered that he was lying in his hammock in a tree above the barrier. With that thought the sensations of power increased enormously within him, the scene before him dimmed, and he momentarily lost consciousness. Silence descended as the music receded into the distance. The flashing lights reappeared briefly, and then he was suddenly, fully on his hilltop once again, feeling the water drops, hearing them rattle off his rain-cape. The black silhouettes of trees appeared against the first light of the new day.

He was back in his tree, his heart pounding as he stared out at the grassy woodland. A woodpecker darted up and landed on a limb next to him in the fine unseasonal rain. The pungent smell of wet grass pervaded his senses, and as the first rays of sunlight appeared through the mist, a fly landed on the back of his hand.

He observed it carefully, trying to regain a sense of what was real. It was an ordinary fly on a brown hand. It was his hand.

9

Kealakekua Bay

Y OWN CONSCIOUSNESS RETURNED TO MY SUPINE
form on the black slab of lava beside Kealakekua Bay. Raindrops tingled on my bare skin,
and upon opening my eyes, I saw that the sky was dark.
The cloud buildup on Mauna Loa's western flank had
reached the beach, and a light drizzle was falling. As I
pulled my thoughts together, the rain came down in earnest, rattling off the leaves of the trees above me. Unheed-
ing, I sat up on the stone and stared at the ocean.

I remained there in the rain for some time, reviewing
what I had just seen. As usual, my reactions were divided:
My mind was in turmoil, but my emerging mystical nature was thrilled to have had another encounter—one in
which something new had occurred. Whatever the "process" was, it had somehow been reversed, and Nainoa's
mind had briefly traveled across time to visit here within
my body in my world. And this had happened while my
conscious awareness was still merged with his, so that I
had observed him watching my world through my eyes.

And it had happened during the daylight hours of the same day, twice. Both times, Nainoa and I had experienced a crisscross while each of us was in an altered state of consciousness.

Nainoa's "visit" had not occurred in my immediate present, February 1987, but in my past, sometime before Anna was born. Nainoa had noted that the lychee tree on my land was in fruit, so it must have been in May or June 1986—between my first and second contacts with him "there." Had Nainoa's consciousness actually been "here," or had he seen a segment of my life excavated from my memory while I was merged with him "there"?

More questions took shape. Were Nainoa's and my states of mind equivalent to the expanded awareness of traditional shamans? Was this marvel possible only because each of us was a suitable contact for the other? In what ways were we suitable—because of our intentions to know and explore without preconceptions or goals, for the empirical experience? But tribal shamans induce their travels with goals and intentions to help cure the sick or to obtain knowledge and power, not just for the experience. Also, our travels to each other seemed to happen spontaneously and without the other's knowledge. Nainoa had no idea that time travel was even possible, yet he had done it. The same had been true for me, which suggested that intentionality alone was not enough. Was something or someone else involved in enabling the journey? Could the leopard man be the key?

From the flat rock under the *kamani* tree I watched the rain pock the ocean's surface, feeling tormented by my experiences and the unanswerable questions they raised. Then, unpredictably, my spirits lifted. At some level of my being, I no longer cared how or why these things were happening to me. It was enough just to experience them, enough just to know they were possible.

Having relinquished the desire to force an explanation, I got an idea. Nainoa as a historian was preoccupied with the collapse of Western civilization. I as a scientist was deeply concerned with what the immediate future held for human beings, and with the degradation of our environment around the world. Could this be part of the causal connection between us?

Being the father of small children had changed me profoundly. I had been an almost entirely egocentric person, absorbed in my work and other concerns even after Jill entered my life. Now I was a fully involved parent. Being compelled to put my own ego needs aside in favor of someone else's, for twenty-four hours a day, seven days a week, had been quite a change, a considerable stress balanced by considerable joy. The first altered-state experiences had occurred during these shifting priorities, resulting in profound shifts in my awareness and belief systems. Had this time of disruption been used by "the spirits" to shake up my inner world as well?

My children, I was very much aware, were going to grow up in a deteriorating world. Humanity's social, political, economic, religious, and environmental problems, I knew, have at their core a single cause: There are too many human beings on the planet—far too many. The preeminent human problem is that our population is wildly out of control. All the world's other problems stem from this central complex issue.

My background in environmental and evolutionary biology has provided me with a certain perspective. I know with chilling certainty that unless the issue of human overpopulation is addressed and the trend reversed, the ancient planetary system of checks and balances will do it for us. The evidence exists within the fossil record and within the population dynamics of contemporary ecosystems—evidence that is undeniable. Overpopulation results when individuals within a species maximize their reproductive potential. Species that engage in catastrophic overpopulation usually "crash." Extinction is a real possibility. There seems to be no special built-in evolutionary mechanism to prevent individuals from reproducing at peak, so the evolutionary process therefore has no built-in mechanism to guard against extinction.[1]

Sitting in the rain, I brooded on the rapidly approaching fate of humanity. The nature and scope of the problem have been evident for more than twenty years, yet few people wish to hear about it or believe it, let alone act on it. Western civilization, about which Nainoa is so curious, is now being driven by greed and fueled by denial.

It is possible that the planetary rebalancing has already begun. The HIV virus, responsible for AIDS, has already begun to kill off the sexually active sector of the population. At the time of my altered states, the late 1980s, the disease was depopulating large areas of Africa, despite the efforts of health officials to inform the local people about its nature and mode of transmission. At the time of this writing, cases of full-blown AIDS increased by 60 percent in one year, from 2.5 million in 1992 to 4 million in 1993, new cases proliferating at the rate of ten thousand a day. The virus is now firmly rooted in both the homosexual and heterosexual populations on all the continents of the world: In Asia, for example, AIDS cases increased 800 percent in one year, from 30,000 in 1992 to 250,000 in 1993, and in Thailand, 50 percent of the hospital beds are currently occupied by AIDS patients.[2] This fact has formidable implications.

The self-righteous blindness to the issue of overpopulation on the part of many of the world's religious leaders binds their followers' minds in oppressive and archaic dogmas. The continued attacks by religious fundamentalists on birth control, Planned Parenthood centers, and laws designed to protect women and allow the safe termination of unwanted pregnancies reflects our political leaders' inability to take a strong stand on this most important of issues.

"A failure of leadership at the highest level . . ." Chief Kaneohe's phrase echoed in my mind. The ultimate buck would stop with our political and religious leaders in positions of power and authority. For them, it implied a "karmic burden" of immense proportions.

In addition to my concerns about overpopulation, at that time in 1987 there had been much discussion of the "greenhouse" effect. The European nations were accusing the United States of frustrating their efforts to reach an accord on fighting global warming. They proposed radical measures to limit the gas emissions from an overpopulated, industrialized society in order to counter the greenhouse effect, yet President Reagan and his advisers were balking, saying that the measures would require major changes in the American way of life and in the nation's industrial structure. Since the United States is much larger than Japan or any of the European nations and relies more on cars and trucks for transportation than on rail, the U.S. government chose the easier course and followed an ill-informed president in denying the mounting scientific evidence, labeling it inconclusive. Egocentrically and selfishly, the government failed to take the necessary action.

"And that will be that," I thought. "The handwriting is on the wall, and nothing will be done because of a failure of leadership at the highest level. Ultimately, that could bring Western civilization down—that, and our greed."

I sat in the rain and stared moodily at the ocean, trying to visualize a likely global warming scenario. No one knows how high the seas might rise or how fast, but a large percentage of the scientific community believes that it is no longer a question of *if* it will happen but *when* and *how much.*

In the late 1980s the United Nations Environment Program released a study to senior governmental officials from more than one hundred countries who were attending the annual meeting of the Governing Council at the UNEP headquarters in Nairobi. The report concluded that it was already too late to stem the impact of global warming. It recommended that all the world's nations should start preparing for rising sea levels, damage to crops caused by the greenhouse effect, and increasing atmospheric and oceanic temperatures, as a result of the accumulation of industrial emissions and carbon dioxide, which were trapping the sun's heat in the atmosphere. The study estimated that the warming oceans would rise by at least three feet in the next sixty years, flooding coastal lands occupied by more than one billion people.

"And what," I wondered, "if that statistic is a gross underestimation?" Perhaps Nainoa had connected with me because I had been alive when Western civilization fell. I thought about my children and shivered in the warm tropical downpour.

· · ·

The rain let up, and I rose and stretched, shaking myself to release the negative thoughts. The wide terrace of black lava boulders looked different in the flat overcast light, and my eyes automatically looked them over for potential sculptures, although I had examined these stones before and seen nothing new. It was low tide, however, and so I decided to survey the newly exposed stones below the water's edge. I climbed down the ridge of wet boulders and walked into the ankle-deep warm water where it met the sand. Clearing my mind, I asked permission. Almost immediately, my attention was drawn to the left, as if it were being physically pulled in that direction.

I sloshed back toward the cleared area of the beach, scanning the rolled stones lying in the water, half buried in the sand below the tideline. Suddenly, an internal alarm went off, and I stopped walking. I had had similar experiences while surveying for fossils and artifacts out in the eroded sediments of the East African Rift. Something would trigger my attention, and I would stop and scan the ground for the stone that did not belong there or the bone that might or might not be hominid. I did this now, out of habit, letting my eyes glide across the tideline, searching.

I almost missed it . . . and then—there it was.

Something was very familiar about a boulder that was half buried in the sand. For long moments, I just stared at it awash in the waves, savoring the moment of discovery. This was a state beach, and according to the laws of the state, nothing was to be taken from it. But the stone was below the tideline, and if I did not take it, the rising tide would rebury it in the sand or wash it into the deeper waters of the bay.

I decided to follow my ritual—to ask the stone for its permission to move it—and much to my surprise, I felt a strong emotion not unlike affection pulsing from it. The emotion was so intense that it momentarily staggered me.

Recovering, I again asked permission, and again I registered strong agreement. I waited for the last wave to recede and then bent down and grasped its pointed end. Using all my strength, I freed the boulder from the sand's wet grip and turned it over—and felt as if I had been punched in the stomach.

It was a natural block of basaltic lava that had been tumbled by the waves, rubbed against fellow stones, and abraded by water and sand until it vaguely resembled a face—albeit a rather inhuman one. Instead of eyes, a diagonal groove traversed its flat visage, while the mouth was only suggested by a peculiar layering of the stone. There was no doubt—it was the spirit stone of Chief Kaneohe that I had seen in my vision of almost a year before. It was the same yet different, and then I saw why. While most of it was already formed by the natural action of the waves and the sand, the mouth was uncarved.

Again I asked, and again I felt answers form in my mind. It seemed that I would be the sculptor—and that I would be the stone's first *kahu*.

10
Fifth Journey
The Tree of Life

ABOUT THREE WEEKS LATER, I AWAKENED JUST BEFORE dawn and was listening to the rain when the sensations appeared in my body again. As before, they intensified into a constraining pressure, then abruptly and dramatically into a feeling of power. I fought for breath as the ecstatic rush began. Rows of red dots appeared against the dark field of my tightly closed eyes—and then I had a sense of lifting off, of achieving great speed. Phosphenic shapes merged into lines of light that wavered as my eyes looked this way and that. The grid appeared briefly, stretching to the horizon; I passed through the place of silence, and the shift occurred.

I heard the sound of running water and smelled something cooking. I opened my eyes. Nainoa was resting beside a substantial stream, observing a small, brightly colored frog. He was cooking a large fish directly on hot stones in the middle of his small campfire. It seemed to be late afternoon, and the stream was surrounded by steep hillsides choked with vegetation. This forest looked distinctly different from that of the lowlands. The trees were smaller and more closely set in dense stands.

After the initial shock and delight at reconnecting with Nainoa, I projected a desire to recall his recent experiences. A thought-line began to flow, and I "watched," enthralled. . . .

As Nainoa waited for the fish to cook, he remembered setting off toward the mountains the morning after his vision of Hawai'i, sorting his impressions of the extraordinary experience as he walked. Like his encounters with the shadow-being and the tiger man, this one had brought with it a heightened sense of awareness and bodily sensations of power. But unlike the other times, he had had the additional amazement of finding himself within another person's body, seeing with the other's eyes, hearing with his ears, tasting his food with his tongue—in another world and another time.

In the literature and legends of his people there were stories of others who had had such extraordinary adventures—there were precedents! Several legendary heroes had made visionary contact with ancestral spirits who had conveyed lost knowledge to them. He had always assumed these to be myths, but what if they were true? What if it really were possible to make contact with one's ancestors through the dreamworlds? Since the American lived in Hawai'i, he was an ancestor in the general sense of being an honored elder, but could the American actually be one of his own ancestors? Had he somehow managed to make contact with an ancestor of more than five thousand years ago?

He recalled a story about a woman named Kalasera who had lived more than a thousand years before. There had been a crisis in the home islands, and civil war had broken out between two of the most powerful ruling families. Kalasera, a *kahuna*, had strong kinship ties to the family that lost the war, all of whom were executed. Only Kalasera was spared because of her rumored powers, yet she was enslaved along with the others, even though she was the only person of rank among the survivors of her land division.

Years of suffering followed. Many slaves died. One night Kalasera had a vision in which she found herself in the body of another woman who had lived in the past. This woman was Kalasera's ancestor, and from her Kalasera acquired much knowledge of the healing arts. She went on to become a medicine woman well known throughout the islands. At that time, by chance, the governor, High Chiefess Claudia Akahiakuleana, was ill with a wasting disease. Kalasera cured her. Kalasera then successfully petitioned the governor, became high chief of her land division, and released her people from bondage.

Might he be one of these rare voyagers for his people? Nainoa attempted to remember everything that he had seen and heard down to the smallest details, reviewing them until he was satisfied that they were fixed in his mind. Then he checked to see if the fish was ready to eat yet.

During the first few days of his ascent, walking had been easier on the high ground, so he had stuck to the ridges and south-facing slopes, descending to the streams for water and fish only at the end of each day. The tiger man had appeared often in his mind as he trekked, seeming quite manlike at some times and entirely feline at others. Nainoa no longer felt quite so alone at these moments and invited the spirit to accompany him as an imaginal companion, as if he were striding through the forest with a tiger by his side. His skeptical side was amused by these daydreams and wondered if he had been in the forest long enough.

This afternoon, he had looked down from a ridge and discovered an ancient road. The contour of the forest canopy had revealed it. Nainoa saw that it led to the next hill, which was abruptly truncated as the road cut right through it. A great deal of the hill had been removed to accommodate the road's passage, which must have required an immense amount of human labor, he thought in amazement.

He moved quickly downslope to investigate and shortly found himself standing at the edge of an eroded cliff, over which snaked the thick roots of a strangler fig. He used the roots as a ladder and descended carefully.

The remains of the road were less evident when viewed up close on the ground. Unused for millennia, trees grew on its surface. Water coursing down the hillside had cut a gaping crevasse through the terrace, and many feet below the present-day buildup of reddish soil, broken rocks, roots, and other organic debris, he glimpsed the ancient road surface.

Nainoa had dropped into the eroded cut to observe it closely. It resembled the dark, hard surface he had seen next to the house in his vision of Hawai'i. He moved along the crevasse, carefully searching both sides, and found a curious flat object of corroded metal, inset with cloudy yellow glass, like a small flat box that did not open. Nainoa put it in one of his net bags, but as he continued to explore the hole, he found nothing more. He decided to follow the road along the contour of the hill. Perhaps he would find another *siti* site.

He encountered more washouts, all of which he examined for artifacts. He found dense scatters of glass in several of them. He took some thick green fragments to make arrow points with his antler punch. Many of the washouts had undercut the hard road surface and created large caves. As he explored these, he alarmed clouds of bats, which flew into the sky in dark, stormlike funnels. In some undercut places the roadway had collapsed, and jumbled sections of the hard surface were partially exposed through the greenery. Some had traces of yellow pigment. The road had obviously been designed for more than just wagons and livestock. He recalled the machines he had seen in his vision.

He had continued walking east along the road and toward evening had descended to the stream below to bathe and catch a fish. . . . A delicious aroma pulled him from his reverie. The fish was cooked, and he ate it in the company of the small, brilliantly colored frog. Then he washed quickly, refilled his water bottle, and climbed until he was within sight of the road, making camp again in a tree.

He awoke in the darkness sometime later. The scent of some night-blooming plant filled the forest. Nagai might have known what kind of plant it was. In fact, Nagai would certainly have had some insights into his strange visionary experiences.

Nagai had encouraged Nainoa to take an interest in the mystics, although when Nainoa expressed interest in studying with a *kahuna kupua* to acquire their knowledge and extraordinary abilities, Nagai had found this amusing. Any who wished to have the *kahuna* knowledge, he said, would first have to be deemed worthy by the spirits, because the only real teachers of such knowledge were the spirits themselves.

Nainoa heard the hunter's deep, grating voice in his mind as he lay in his hammock in the dark mountain forest. . . .

"You want spiritual knowledge, huh? You cannot get it from reading books or hearing stories of others' experiences, although this can point you in the right direction and help prepare you. Knowing that the spirits exist and wishing to acquire knowledge from them are good ways to begin to become a *kahuna*, but you can only hope that the spirits will notice you, that they will take an interest in you. If they don't, no amount of effort you make will give you firsthand knowledge of them. But if they do decide you are worthy, they will teach you themselves.

"Before the spirits reveal themselves to you and allow you to acquire *mana* and knowledge, they will watch you to see what sort of person you are. They will test you, and the test is always arduous. Life itself, and how you live it, is part of the test. The spirits will review your intentions, because what you attract to yourself and experience depends to a large extent upon your aims and goals. Intentions are very, very important. They will determine what happens.

"When the spirits decide that the time has come to teach you, they will approach you in their own way to see if you are ready. Pay attention to what happens to you. Until then you must wait."

Nagai had told Nainoa a story of a chief named Kaneakama who had lived long ago in Hawai'i. Kaneakama had lived his life in a selfish manner. Established in his habits, he was arrogant and liked to gamble.

"Kaneakama went out one day," Nagai had begun, his eyes alight with enthusiasm, "and he came across a gathering of chiefs at a playing ground on the side of a great mountain called Mauna Loa." Nagai's voice dropped to a conspiratorial whisper as he confided, "The spirits had plans for Kaneakama and decided that the time had come.

"Kaneakama joined the games, determined to acquire great winnings for himself at the expense of his rivals," Nagai continued, with a knowing grin. "The games went on for three days and nights, but in contest after contest Kaneakama was defeated, until he lost everything he owned—his land, his possessions, his livestock. He even lost his wife's possessions and land. The only thing he had left was his body. For the first time in his life, Kaneakama felt fear. He was face-to-face with an enemy. If he bet his body and lost, he would be killed.

"At this point Kaneakama went to drink some water to refresh himself, and because he was exhausted, he fell asleep under a tree. He had a dream in which a spirit came out of the tree and said to him, 'So you have finally been beaten, huh?' Kaneakama agreed, 'Yes, I have.' The spirit then told Kaneakama that the *akuas* had intentions for him and that he was destined for great things among his people. The spirit remonstrated strongly with Kaneakama and told him that he would have to live his life in a different manner from that day forward. The chief, confronted with the flaws in his character, underwent a profound change. The spirit saw this and told Kaneakama that he would win back all his wealth, possessions, and land and that his rival would be defeated.

" 'But I have only my body to bet,' said the unfortunate Kaneakama, 'and if I lose—'

" 'Do not fear,' said the tree spirit. 'Make the bet and see what happens.'

"Kaneakama awoke from his dream and wagered his own life against all that he had lost to his enemy. He won. They played game after game, and in each, Kaneakama defeated his rival," Nagai concluded with delight. "That night, as the victorious chief slept, the tree spirit came to him again and began to instruct him. In time, Kaneakama became a renowned *kahuna* mystic, and he maintained a special relationship with the tree spirits for the rest of his life."

Nainoa smiled and ran his hands over the bark of the tree in which he was camped. He could see nothing in the total blackness, but the pungent perfume that was floating in the darkness grew stronger until it overpowered his senses. Unexpectedly, he felt the sensations of power stir and then surge, filling his body with their rushing, soaring force. The terrible yet wonderful feeling seized him and, as before, slowly squeezed. He gasped, trying to breathe, trying to open his eyes as his body stiffened.

Part of his mind remained detached and charted the power's progress from his feet to his head and back again, as well as the rapid, sweeping waves of sensation and the roaring sound that gradually diminished as time passed. As before, strange lights flashed and danced past him in the dark. Then he had a feeling of falling—of dropping rapidly through the swirling darkness of a vortex. His fall slowed within moments, and he managed to open his eyes. He was back on the forest floor. The familiar golden haze of light that did not create shadows glowed around him. He looked around excitedly, searching for the tiger man among the trees, but the spirit was not there.

A strange sound drifted through the trees to his right—a deep, resonant tone. He had never heard anything like it before, and he turned toward it. He sensed motion around him within the forest, a strange, flickering vibration discernible only with his peripheral vision. Abruptly, he sensed the trees as aware and the forest as a vast composite being with its own consciousness—as an alertness composed of the collective awarenesses of all the living things existing within it.

With this realization came the certainty that at this moment the forest was aware of him.

The deep tone sounded again. It seemed to be two separate inflections, both very low, vibrating against each other. Just ahead, Nainoa saw a grove of huge cotton trees, and again he felt the sound. It seemed to come from the trees.

A strange form appeared on the forest floor before him, a tall vertical shape much like the shadowy *ke'aka,* only green. It seemed to be made of leaves, all of which were trembling slightly, giving the impression of a densely foliated bush considerably taller than himself.

As he drifted closer, the green pillar altered slightly, and a face appeared among the foliage. It was an alien, inhuman face—a green face made entirely of leaves. It observed him with an alert intelligence. Startled,

Nainoa abruptly recalled the stories of Makua'nahele, the forest spirit, who was sometimes seen by the hunters.

As Nainoa stared in wonder at the green face, it altered, as if ruffled by a breeze, into an almost-smile, which made it seem even less human than before. It looked as though it were a part of the forest that had come alive, assuming a vaguely human form to communicate its awareness to him. It flickered and changed shape—at one moment it appeared to be leaves and at the next it appeared more geometric, as if it were made of irregular shards of green glass that allowed the light to shine through it.

Once more the strange tones sounded from the trees, and the green leafy visage smiled again—with more success this time. The spirit gestured upward with an armlike column of leaves that swirled as though blown by the wind.

Following the gesture with his eyes, Nainoa looked upward into the light, and the sensations increased almost beyond his ability to bear them. He felt as if he could fly—and then suddenly, he felt himself lift off the ground. He was flying—he was actually flying!

A deep, wild joy seized him as he floated upward between the great gray columns among shafts of green and golden light, carried on the deep vibrational sound, on the song of the cotton trees. He felt their awareness focused on him as he continued to ascend. Then he was high in the air— high up above the level of the canopy. All around him, the trees' great arms reached upward, dividing into thousands of outstretched fingers, each tipped with hundreds of thousands of leaves.

During Nainoa's first long adventure with Nagai into the forest, the hunter had been giving him a long description of a tree's roots, trunk, branches, and leaves and how they worked. When he finished, Nainoa had asked him, "Where are their eyes?" Old Nagai had laughed long and hard with delight, and then his eyes had narrowed thoughtfully. Someday he would see them, he told the boy.

Now, staring wildly around at the verdant mosaic of leaves that surrounded him, Nainoa saw them as millions of green eyes gazing upward at the sun.

An eagle shrieked, and away in the distance, rising from the canopy, an immense column soared up toward the sky's zenith. Gasping in disbelief, Nainoa realized it was a tree—a tree of gigantic proportions. Great buttress roots joined the stupendous trunk high above the level of the canopy of the forest, and its crown, lost in the sun, was a blinding cloud of brilliance surrounded by flying things.

Tears streamed down Nainoa's face in response to the incredible beauty of what he was seeing. This huge pillar could only be the great tree of life that connected the different levels of reality. The world tree existed. It was real.

A profound yearning pervaded him, and his awareness merged with that of the forest. At a deep level of being, he came to understand many things. The resonant tone that had been carrying him split into fragments, producing a succession of strange sounds and words that whispered and echoed around and within his mind. Was he hearing ancient names? Among them, he made out a Hawaiian name—*Kiliwia*. As the word formed, the vision began to dissolve. He felt himself merging more and more deeply, becoming part of the whole—and that "whole" was green . . . green.

Everything was part of himself, and he himself was part of the all. Feelings of great bliss, green bliss, permeated his being. From somewhere, he heard singing—a mighty chorus of many, many voices, within which could be discerned the deep vibrational song of the trees. But the forest itself was gone, dissolved into the greenness. Colored images of brilliant light and blinding darkness emerged—and always that sound, that deep sylvan murmur, carried him on. He was floating on it, his mind no longer forming questions but merging—merging into it, whatever "it" was.

Suddenly the green light became more sharply defined, then coalesced into linear forms that grew thinner and thinner until a vast field of lines stretched away from him in all directions into the darkness. Each strand was a brilliant fiber in a web of intersecting lines, along which glowed knots of light. His perspective shifted, and the perceived knots became stars—all the stars in the universe connected by strange lines of light.

Nainoa thought-extended himself along one of the fibers toward one of the glowing orbs. Abruptly, he found himself standing in a strange, desolate night landscape. A wide, seemingly infinite plain stretched toward the horizon in all directions. The land's surface appeared to be covered with gray ash or dust. The sky was black and thick with stars. To his left was a roughly circular depression, its contours softened by the dust. In the distance a range of geometric mountains glittered in the starlight.

Nainoa looked up at the stars, his gaze moving from one area of sky to another. He could not recognize a single constellation. All were totally alien. He glanced back at the mountains—the peaks seemed made of metal, polished, reflective.

In the ash at his feet, he saw a large chunk of rough, jagged stone pocked with holes. With enormous effort, he reached down and seized the stone. It felt very, very cold. Slowly he lifted it, as though he and it were under water, and then let it go, watching it fall slowly, disappearing into the dusty substrate, which rippled at the impact. The ripples spread outward in all directions. The ground began to crack open, and the dust all around him poured slowly into some unseen cavern below. He, too, began to slip into the abyss, and he felt panic. There seemed to be nowhere to get a foothold to escape. His only way out was up—and up he went.

As he flew upward, the scene before him dissolved, and he found himself suspended in the void. All was blackness, in every direction, forever. He was nothing, less than a speck of dust, and with this awareness came a terrible feeling of emptiness, of aloneness, and frightening sorrow. Just as his desolation became unbearable, a minute area of dim light appeared in the distance. As he moved toward it, it grew brighter, but remained ever-distant and unreachable. He felt a strong sense of yearning and a nascent joy. His longing created a spark of light within him. . . . The light grew, and as it grew, so did the joy.

Nainoa stared at the distant light in the darkness of the void, building light and joy within himself—for how long, he did not know. Regretfully, he finally felt himself begin to withdraw, and below he saw again the vast net with its wondrous glowing knots streaming away infinitely. Suddenly he experienced himself and his inner light as one of those glowing orbs. Many brilliant fibers stretched away from him into the darkness. He was part of a vast pattern laid out before him. He was intimately interconnected with everything—everywhere—forever.

Joyful at his own being and at the existence of everything, he thought of the forest and of the forest spirit. Once again he heard the deep murmuring song of the trees. Then the net dissolved in a flash of light that momentarily blinded him.

Through the transparent tree trunks that reappeared, he could see into the distance. The trunks slowly solidified as his sight recovered from the blinding light. He felt the hammock around his body again, and he closed his eyes. The surging feeling was diminishing, receding, and when he opened his eyes again, he saw that the golden light was fading . . . fading.

Below him he saw the forest *akua* peering up at him from the forest floor. With great effort, Nainoa raised his hand in greeting and acknowledgment. The green pillar flickered and flowed, raising an "arm" in response. Then whatever had given the leaves their form and life-force vanished, the pillar disintegrated, and only the leaves remained—a whirlwind of green shapes swirling on the warm breeze into the golden light.

Nainoa closed his eyes again, savoring the sensations as they drained out of him—and when he reopened them, it was dark, and the night had resumed its normalcy. His face was wet with tears, his body was shaking with the strain, his mind was numb with amazement.

As the air turned colder before the dawn, Nainoa dried his tears, wrapped himself in his cloak and rain-cape, and drained of emotion, slept.

The mountain forest was filled with mist when Nainoa awoke again, and water dripped steadily from above. He gathered his possessions, unrigged his hammock, and descended to the ground, which betrayed nothing—no disturbed leaves, no footprints aside from his own. He resettled the rain-cape around his shoulders to ward off the drip and stood quietly within the embrace of the tree's buttress roots, thinking.

As happened in the mythic adventures of his people's heroes, his trek through the forest was being punctuated by visionary nighttime experiences. He struggled to compose himself. Was his own mind playing a role in the creation or reception of these visions and their link with the supernatural stories of the past?

In classic Hawaiian the creative function of the mind, the imagination, was *mana'o'ulu'wale.* He broke down the phrase for clues to its inner meaning. *Mana'o* meant "thought" or "idea," but it could also mean "mind" or "meaning." Included within it was the word *mana,* or "supernatural power." *Ulu* implied "growth" or "increase" but also conveyed "inspiration or possession by the spirits." *Wale* had many meanings. It could mean "alone" or "only" in this case.

Thus, the concept of imagination implied "information, thoughts and ideas that had their sole source in the spirit realm." Nainoa stood motionless under the dripping trees and considered his seemingly spontaneous experiences as "thoughts or ideas that originated from the spirits"—as "mindgrowth in response to inspiration by the spirits"—as "inspiration."

He thought of the ruined road in the forest and the fallen civilization of the Americans and their machines. Many stories about these ancients portrayed them as deities with supernormal powers. It was difficult to separate fact from fiction within those stories—and to distinguish what was real from what was imaginary in his own visions.

The early sun broke through the mist, and he stared at his own shadow stretched out on the ground. The shadow was an aspect of himself, considerably longer than he was tall. It was real, and yet it was not. He could not detach it or pick it up. It had no existence apart from himself, and yet there it was.

He was beginning to think about the spirits he was encountering in a way that his fellow historians would consider heretical. What if "the world of the spirits" were actually just another aspect of the real world—a hidden level of reality accessible only through that part of the mind able to perceive "the shadows"? As he stared at the jungle-green world whose grandiose scale dwarfed him, he thought of his encounter with Makua'nahele. What if the spirits were simply unperceived aspects of everyday physical objects and actions? What if they and their world were unseen shadows or reflections of what existed here on the physical plane? His mind trembled at the implications of these nonordinary thoughts.

To the Hawaiians the *akuas* were supernatural beings who existed in the nonordinary realms. They had more *mana*, more power than humans, and thus more control over both the supernatural and the natural worlds. Some humans, however, could tap into the power that these spirits possessed, especially individuals of high ethical stature who lived in harmony with everything and everyone around them. Such persons could acquire *mana* directly from the *akuas* and then use it to help their people. *Mana* was highly concentrated in living things and could be accumulated by those who knew how. The success of all *kahuna* mystics' endeavors depended on the abundance or scarcity of *mana* within them.

Perhaps the "sensations" that gripped him during the visionary experiences had been *mana*. Could it be that he was being empowered—*ho'omana*? Could it be that he was being initiated—*ho'okumu*?

The literature of his people abounded with stories of the mystical covenant between humans and animals. His skin prickled as he remembered an account from the great Huaka'i that had brought the Hawaiians to America.

During the last days of the great journey, the seas had been rough, the weather overcast and stormy, and the voyagers exhausted from bailing and close to starvation. Suddenly a great shark appeared. It swam among the canoes, turning on its side to look at the travelers. At first the people were terrified, assuming it had come to finish them off. Then a *kahuna* mystic who possessed great *mana* named Helena Kuamangu went into trance and talked to the shark. It revealed that it had come at the request of the spirit stone, Kapohaku'ki'ihele, and that it would guide the fleet to land. Although they were famished, the people sacrificed a pig and fed the shark, whereupon it turned, and the canoes followed. At night they lit torches so they could see the shark, and after three days they made it to land.

Was the land itself the source of his visionary experiences? Were the spirits of the land responsible for his contact with the American? The forest spirit had revealed part of the mystery behind the world of everyday reality—the interconnection of all the beings in this world and the interconnection of each world with the others.

The spirit of Nagai had become part of Nainoa in his memories, in his inner eye. Nainoa turned to this inner Nagai now and asked him about the tiger man. As the image of his old friend formed within his mind, he could feel his presence nearby and hear his voice quite clearly. The hunter's answer was completely unexpected. Nagai spoke directly to him in a mixture of old Hawaiian and the *olelo* spoken by the commoners.

"Kanaka'taiga? The tiger man? Ah yes. *Auwe noho'i e!* I know who you mean. So you want to know about him, do you? Well, do you remember the day we first met in the market over a tiger skin? Yes? Well, the spirits are always around, and the spirit of that tiger overheard your comment about his beautiful skin. Your sincerity and sense of integrity impressed him, and he developed a fondness for you.

"Through that tiger's spirit, the *aumakua ka'po'e taiga*, the high spirit of all spotted tigers, has taken an interest in you. It has accepted you into its custody, so to speak. You have acquired a very powerful ally indeed. The tiger spirit has great strength, and its courage, skill, and power are legendary. But here is something interesting. The tiger spirit is mostly *ku*, mostly *unihipili*, mostly bodymind. It longs for more of the *lono*, more of the *uhane*, more of the higher, thinking level of mind. It seeks balance.

"Because of this, the tiger spirit likes to associate with scholars, which is another reason it likes you. Manjusri was one of its famous favorites. He was an aspect, the manifestation of wisdom, of the great spiritual teacher Kotama Kapukanui, the one the tiger spirit refers to as the Buddha."

Nainoa was amazed by this unexpected answer. Nagai's dry chuckle was so real that it startled him. Suddenly, he felt as though something or someone else wanted his attention. He opened his mind to whatever it was. The sunlight shone through the mist. The trees had almost stopped dripping. He waited—and had again a sense of immediate presence. A pulse of excitement ran through him. This was new. Contact was happening in broad daylight.

The image of the tiger man appeared in his mind, with its strange inhuman expression, that almost-smile. But though he felt its benevolence, this contact had a mood of urgency and warning. The tiger man turned dark, almost black. He heard Nagai say, "The tiger brings a unique tension to the forest. It works silently and patiently. You must be like the tiger not only when you hunt but also when you simply are in the deep forest."

A new silence had descended on the forest. Nainoa moved ever so slowly back into deeper cover among the roots of his tree and gradually lowered the spear from his shoulder. In this level of reality tigers were the undisputed top hunters. There was one nearby—he felt it. Long moments passed as he remained motionless, peering through the tangled vines that overgrew the massive tree trunk. Finally, a flicker of movement in his peripheral vision revealed the tiger. It too had been motionless, observing the forest from the ridge of the old road before descending to the stream to drink. It now walked soundlessly through the undergrowth, its spotted body so well camouflaged in the broken pattern of light and shadow that it alternately appeared and disappeared as it flowed down the slope, passing close enough for Nainoa to see its pale green eyes. It was a male, and it walked powerfully and confidently.

The great cat instantly became immobile when it caught his scent. More long moments passed as it slowly surveyed its domain. Nainoa's heart thudded as he waited for the tiger to approach his hiding place. Then a slight breeze sighed through the trees, placing him downwind. The tiger lost his scent and continued past him, stopping occasionally to listen, finally vanishing over the edge of the hillside without detecting him.

Nainoa slowly relaxed and waited until he was sure the tiger was beyond hearing. Then he moved quickly, silently, back up to the road and east into the mountains. The forest came to life again as he walked, and he imagined the tiger man in the trees, moving with him, providing company—and now something more: protection and prescience.

After achieving distance Nainoa stopped, cleared his mind, and formally thanked the *akua* for its assistance. He invited it to accompany him on his journey of investigation through the mountains. As the strange image of the half-human, half-animal formed within his "imagination," he felt the tiger man agree—and noted that the spirit was brightly colored once again.

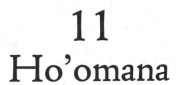

11
Ho'omana

THE POSSIBILITY THAT NAINOA WAS MY DESCENDANT had never occurred to me. I must admit that the idea of having a descendant alive and well millennia in the future was appealing. It made my life an evolutionary success story, suggesting genetic and spiritual immortality. An ancestor-descendant relationship might also explain why the connection between us had occurred in the first place. With this new orientation, my experiences took on another dimension.

Could Nainoa and I both be undergoing some sort of shamanic or spiritual initiation? One that we had to experience jointly? Could mine be occurring through Nainoa —through my own descendant—as a vehicle? Could this be another cause of our connection?

I had once asked Michael Harner, anthropologist to anthropologist, how he perceived the nature of his role as a spiritual teacher in the shamanic tradition. He had replied without hesitation that his job was to facilitate, to assist students in stepping onto their own spiritual path

—to expose them to time-tested methods used by "traditionals" so that each seeker could achieve his or her spiritual initiation through direct experience. That accomplished, the initiates were on their own, and Harner's job as the teacher in ordinary reality was essentially finished. Genuine spiritual knowledge and power could be imparted only by the spirits themselves, as Nagai had revealed to Nainoa.

Interestingly, it doesn't seem to matter whether visionaries are Christian or Islamic, Gnostic or Taoist, Hindu or Buddhist, Jewish or Egyptian, Chinese or African, Amerindian or Hawaiian. Their otherworldly experiences all echo the ancient shamanic way of "journeying" in an altered state of consciousness and perceiving what lies beyond the boundaries of ordinary reality. What they perceive there tends to be shaped by their specific cultural lens and worldview. In other words, we see reality as we are taught to see it by our parents, teachers, and friends. Reality is what we think it is —and how we think and perceive is formed largely by the culture in which we live.

Most mainstream psychologists and other cognitive scientists believe that visions are all "in the mind." They assert that the "other worlds" of visionary experience are cognitive in nature, that they are imaginative projections whose source lies within the mind of the person having the visions. North American Lakota Sioux, for instance, perceive spirits and spirit worlds that conform with their psychosymbolic worldview, as do Siberian Tungus tribespeople, the Yoruba of Nigeria, and others. All visionary worlds of dream, trance, art, ecstasy, and imagination adhere to their own inherent, culturally determined rules and structure and how the individual's consciousness interacts with that culture.[1]

The strange botanical being that I had seen through Nainoa reminded me of the leafy visages of "the green man" that stares from the walls and ceilings of ancient churches all over Europe.[2] Had I projected the nature spirit into Nainoa's vision, or had he appeared under his own initiative? And what about the great tree, which seemed to be the mythical world tree, the classic *axis mundi*, believed to connect the lower, middle, and upper worlds of traditional shamanic cosmology?

I have no problems with the cognitive scientists' rather egocentric (or cognicentric) interpretations of visions, but other questions are important to consider, too, when exploring visionary phenomena. For example, just *where* is the mind? Most mind-body medicine and psychological researchers agree that it does not lie solely within the brain, but that consciousness is also formed by physical communications from the body. What was the source of the imagery and information that had clearly not come out of my own memory banks? A psychologist would say it was produced *by* my creative imagination. A shaman would believe the inner doorway, the portal to other levels of reality, was allowing my visionary experiences to come *through* my mind rather than being created *by* it.

A cognitive investigator would very likely argue that there was a doorway within my mind only if I believed there was. A traditional Huichol shaman might be more inclined to say that the *nierika* was there whether or not I believed in its existence. Before my initial altered-state experiences in California, I had understood nothing of all of this. Although I had taken Harner's workshop, the passage into the nonordinary levels of reality had been presented in our meditations as a mental image of an entrance into the earth that led to a tunnel to the mythic lower world of the animal powers. I had had no tunnel in my later visions. Although my initial encounter with the dark geometric, humanoid form and my subsequent "journeys" to the other worlds were very similar to those of classic shamanic experiences, I had learned of these similarities only *after* already experiencing them. I feel quite certain that I had not absorbed some suggestion that set up this whole affair. I was coming to believe that there is indeed a doorway within the minds of all people, and that a greater spiritual reality may exist apart from our individual beliefs and culture and psyche.

I was coming to believe, with traditional tribal shamans, that the visionary realms and the spirits residing in them are real and have an existence and agenda quite separate from the human being who perceives them. A Jungian or transpersonal psychologist might take a position that the visionary worlds that shamans visit are a kind of dreamworld existing within the unconscious minds of all human beings—within a kind of "collective

unconscious" to which all, theoretically, have access. A cognitive scientist would say that these places were created by the human mind, not discovered by it. For the traditional shaman, however, the spirits and their visionary world are real, not individual inventions. The shaman experiences the nonordinary reality of the altered state as a discrete but hidden universe, peopled by spiritual beings at various levels of development and awareness, from whom one can acquire wisdom, power, and assistance.

Someone asked Michael Harner a question about this at the workshop years ago. The anthropologist's expressive eyes had twinkled as he answered, "I am inclined to believe that there is more to the universe than that which exists within the human mind."

Perhaps Nainoa's and my most recent visionary journeys had given us a firsthand look into the nonordinary world and a direct encounter with what mystics have called "cosmic consciousness."

Six months passed without further contact with Nainoa. During this period, however, I finally carved the stone.

On the day I found the *pohaku* awash in the waves, I had carried it into the old Hawaiian village and placed it under the tamarind tree just beyond the pond. There it remained for several months, visited daily by me and the children on our nature walk while I slowly established a relationship with it. I do not know why I did this. I just did.

One day the time seemed right, and I invoked the stone's spirit in my stone-moving ritual, asking its permission to bring it away from its beach and to my home. Its strong agreement flowed into me in response. I did not wish to be seen taking it from the site, so I arrived at the beach early the next morning before anyone was there and carried the stone to my car. When I got home, I placed it near my front door in the rock garden among the other beach stones. There it sat for a while, untouched. It had made its first voyage, however, from the wild place of its origin into the world of human beings in my Volkswagen van.

The curious bond between us continued to develop. The bond was not

merely my thrill at possessing an object for which I felt attraction. The linkage involved a process between myself and the stone. My first hesitant attempts at dialogue were necessarily experimental, but I had an ongoing, moment-to-moment awareness of presence. In the beginning I simply let my attention rest upon it meditatively while thoughts and feelings related to it moved through my mind. As the thoughts and feelings took on recurrent patterns, my personal awareness of it deepened.

One night the stone came to me in my dreaming, and upon awakening I saw it in my mind's eye in its completed form. I'm not certain whether this form came from my memory of how the stone appeared in Chief Kaneohe's possession or whether it was slightly different. I got up, went out to the stone, and asked its permission to sculpt it. I felt a strong, positive reaction, so that same afternoon, I carried it to the tree stump I used as a base for sculpting. With bush hammers, I did a minimum of reducing of the "chin." A little chisel work brought out the "mouth," and it was done. Most of the stone remained untouched, just as I had found it.

I then replaced the *pohaku* with its attendant sculptures in the rock garden, staring east toward the summit of the volcano of which it was a part. In my thoughts, I addressed it using Chief Kaneohe's name, Kapohaku'ki'ihele—the stone that journeys. And as the stone's first custodian—or *kahu*-elect—I too would have ordinary and nonordinary journeys and discoveries in *everyday* reality.

Soon after I rendered the stone, late in 1987, I attended a conference held at the Keauhou Beach Hotel, on the coast near Kailua-Kona, an insiders' affair put on by Hawaiians to honor the knowledge and achievements of their Polynesian ancestors. As an outsider, I was fortunate to have been invited—it was the efforts of a curator-photographer friend working for the Kona Historical Society Museum that got me an invitation. The conference was well attended by an interesting gathering of people, most of whom were of Polynesian descent.

Professor Rubellite Kawena Johnson of the University of Hawaii spoke about the *heiaus* and about the Hawaiian gods and ceremonies. Hawaiian elders Papa Kala Naliielua and David Mauna Roy spoke about the traditional Hawaiian worldview and the intimate connection between Hawaiian culture and the land. They described the Hawaiians' respect for nature and how the Polynesians had taken care of the land, seeking harmony with it so that it would take care of them. They spoke of the Hawaiian concept of spiritual unity with their *aumakua*, their ancestral spirits, and how life and *mana* came out of everything in nature.

Another session was held by four crew members of the now-famous double-hulled voyaging canoe *Hokule'a*. This sixty-foot re-creation of a traditional Hawaiian transoceanic sailing vessel has completed many round-trips between Hawai'i and Tahiti, as well as a long voyage to New Zealand and back. The *haku* of the canoe, Captain Shorty Bertelmann, was there, as was the watch captain, Tava Taupu. Sam Ka'ai spoke strongly about the place of the sailing canoe in traditional Hawaiian society and revealed that the ancient Order of the Canoe was being re-formed, to "refill the bowl with what had been lost."

I was completely unprepared for what occurred next.

A trim, handsome young man of Hawaiian descent was introduced. His name is Nainoa Thompson, the first Hawaiian in more than six centuries to navigate a great sailing canoe over the vast oceanic expanses of Polynesia without modern-day instruments. The respect and the awe in which this man is held is great. As navigator of the canoe, he is the most important crew member, the one into whose care the success of the voyage and the lives of all the voyagers are entrusted. He is the wayfinder. I had never heard of him before that moment.

Partially trained by a traditional Micronesian navigator named Mau Piailug, Nainoa Thompson rediscovered the ancient Polynesian navigational system that used the stars, moon, clouds, winds, ocean swells, and currents. He re-created the wayfinding method that had brought his ancestors to Hawai'i in several waves of migration, beginning around A.D. 300.

Nainoa Thompson spoke in a soft voice about his voyages and his ancestors and about harmony. He spoke with integrity, with power, and with humility—and he never mentioned himself. He talked about the canoe and the crew, the ocean and the heavens. All of these became one, he said, balanced and unified during the voyages. He suggested that this unity was the goal and the success of the journey—a goal in which each person was as important as everyone else.

The Hawaiians in the audience were misty-eyed with pride for him and, through him, for themselves. The *mana* generated by their collective emotion was palpable in the room.

After his talk I waited for an opportunity to approach him. We shook hands and exchanged pleasantries. I could not possibly have broached the subject of the strange events in which I was involved, but I was profoundly moved by meeting him. I wondered if he was the one who would be remembered and revered through time as Nainoa the Navigator. I wondered what moved through his mind and through his dreaming as he guided the double-hulled canoe across the vast expanses of the watery world. I wondered what it would be like to be out there with him. What would my own dreaming produce under those circumstances? Could the Nainoa of the future somehow be induced to "visit" within me—to visit his namesake—to voyage with the navigator?

The last session at the conference was conducted by a Hawaiian healer, a *kahuna lapa'au* named Morrnah Nalamaku Simeona, who shared her knowledge and skill in *ho'oponopono*, the traditional Hawaiian method of conflict resolution.

She spoke of the unity and balance of life and how everything in life begins with thought and intention. She discussed the three levels of being —the physical, the mental, and the spiritual—as they are conceived within traditional Hawaiian spiritual knowledge. She spoke of how these three aspects are manifested within human beings: the spiritual as the superconscious mind or *aumakua*, the mental as the conscious mind or *uhane*, the physical as a material form, the body, and a nonmaterial form, the subconscious mind or *unihipili*.

These concepts are not unique to Hawaiian culture and are well known to Western psychology, but hearing Morrnah Simeona's talk made me want to know more about Hawaiian shamanism and the body of knowledge called Ho'omana.

After her talk I politely asked her to clarify a point she had made about healing. She gave me a curious look and then reached out, took my hand in both of hers, and closed her eyes. Long moments passed. Then she smiled and looked at me again, her alert gaze boring into mine, and asked me if I knew what *aloha* really meant. "It means 'to be in the presence of the divinity,' " she explained. "*Alo* means 'to be in the presence of' and *ha* is 'the divine breath of life'—*alo-haaa.*" She paused as if to see the effect of her words.

"Problems always begin in the mind, in the mental aspect," she continued. "Physical and psychological problems have their source in negative thought-forms. Illness is an effect of these distorted thoughts. Unfavorable thoughts arise in the conscious mind and are then held in the subconscious, from which they can be transferred into the physical body. Because of this, true healing always has to begin at the spiritual level.

"One must ask the divinity for help. Then the divinity sends down its *ha* through one's *aumakua* level of self. From one's spiritual aspect, it travels into the subconscious level of the physical. This deep level of the mind can then erase the negative thought-forms and emotions it holds, such as anger and fear, replacing them with light. This is how the cause of illness is dealt with and how all true healing is accomplished."

She smiled again and released my hand. Someone else asked her a question, but for long moments her gaze remained locked with mine as she looked into my soul. I do not know what she saw there, but she nodded slightly and beamed warmly at me before turning away.

I remained rooted to the spot while the crowd surged around me like water around a rock. I felt something within my body—something that had flowed from her to me during those brief moments. I recognized it as the sensations of power. I realized that I had received *mana* from her, transmitted through her touch. I felt something deep within me open in response.

The sensations remained there, just below the surface, throughout the rest of the day.

This experience marked the beginning of my investigation into Ho'omana. As a verb, this word's translation is "to place in authority" or "to empower." As a noun, it has come to mean "religion" or "sect." Another term sometimes used is Huna, a word that means "concealed knowledge," "mystery," and the "key to something hidden."

Ho'omana was developed and utilized by the traditional Hawaiian *kahuna* mystics. The word *kahuna* by itself simply means a master of something. A *kahuna kilolani* is a master stargazer; a *kahuna pule*, a master of ceremony, a *kahuna kupua*, a shaman or master of spirits. When the word *kahuna* is broken down into its root meanings, *ka* means "the"; *hu* means "something surging" or "boiling over" or "rising to the surface"; and *na* means "calm," "centered," or "settled." The word *kahuna* thus contains an interesting duality not unlike the old yin-yang symbol of Taoist derivation.

I began my investigation of Hawaiian mysticism with the written works of Max Freedom Long, L. R. McBride, David Kaonohiokala Bray, Martha Beckwith, and Serge Kahili King.[3] I also met several practitioners of Ho'omana, including Lanakila Brandt and Serge King, both of whom offer guided experiential workshops. I attended several of these in the beginning of 1988 and gained a considerably expanded perspective on shamanism.

Some will disagree with my interpretations of how the *kahuna* mystics of Old Hawai'i perceived reality. When two people attempt to interpret any metaphysical idea, each may arrive at a different conclusion. As the venerable Chinese mystic Lao-Tsu observed 2,500 years ago, "Existence is beyond the power of words to define. Terms may be used, but none of them is absolute."[4] Yet allow me to try to define the undefinable.

The Western world is essentially objective in its approach to defining reality. Westerners believe what they can see. Ho'omana understands reality as levels of objective experience on the one hand and as levels of subjective awareness on the other. For the Hawaiian *kahunas,* the physical, objective level of ordinary everyday reality, which science regards as the only "real" reality, is only the first of several possible levels of experience and awareness. At this physical level everything is perceived as separate from everything else. I am "here" writing this book; you are "somewhere else" reading it.

Serge King describes the subjective level of thoughts and emotions as the second level of reality. This is also the level at which psychic phenomena such as telepathy, clairvoyance, and psychokinesis are experienced. Like ordinary physical reality, this too is a level of action, but at the second level, everything is in contact with everything else through threads of an "energetic or etheric substance" called *aka* in the Hawaiian language.

In Ho'omana, everything in the universe is connected to everything else through a vast net or web formed by these *aka* threads at the second level. These connections can be brought into being both by thoughts and intentions—they are "activated" by attention. Sustained concentration, such as that practiced during meditation, theoretically increases the strength or volume of the contact.

Nainoa's vision of an immense grid extending out into space, as well as the more modest grids, zigzags, and lines of the phosphenes I saw at the beginning of my altered states, not to speak of those strange geometric grids and lines on Neolithic pots and figurines and in cave sites and rock shelters might all be visual perceptions of the *aka* field. Perhaps the grid is a psychic map to follow to wherever one wishes to go in the "other levels" of reality.

Nainoa's name for the dark "shadow" figure was *ke'aka*. A Hawaiian dictionary revealed that the word *aka* translates as "image, reflection, or shadow," which corresponded to my own spontaneous naming of it. Perhaps the "spirits," lacking a physical, material body, were formed of *aka* substance and were thus perceivable only in an altered state—or to use Nainoa's expression, "someone able to perceive the shadows."

Another Ho'omana concept illuminated the "expanded time phenomenon" I had experienced during my episodes with Nainoa. At the second level of reality, time is synchronous—that is, everything that ever happened in the past as well as everything that will ever happen in the future could all be going on at once, interconnected through the *aka* field. Because of this, as King has pointed out, there are no beginnings or endings at the second level of reality (or awareness)—only cycles and transitions. Applied to the concept of reincarnation, this perspective suggests that one's past and future lives could theoretically be going on all at once, interconnected through the *aka* field at the second level of reality.

Perhaps the *aka* field could explain how I often knew when the phone was going to ring and who was calling, or how Jill and I so frequently caught ourselves thinking the same thoughts simultaneously. Perhaps we were essentially listening in to each other's second-level mind patterns through the *aka* threads that connected us.

Since time is synchronous at this level of reality, the *aka* connections can extend across time as well as across space. Perhaps this is the path by which certain individuals can remember fragments of their past lives. Perhaps it offered me a way to comprehend my connections with Nainoa.

I still had not absolutely surrendered my speculation that Nainoa was an aspect of myself, a subpersonality whose source lay within my own mind. Yet I also began to consider that Nainoa might actually be one of my reincarnations living a future life five thousand years down the road. Could this be what a true ancestor-descendant relationship represented? Could reincarnation depart from genetic lineages and move randomly between different lines through time? And if I were experiencing an ancestor-descendant relationship, how had the connection been established in the first place? Why had it suddenly been activated when I was forty-four years old? When I talked about these issues with Jill, she observed that the first altered state back in Berkeley had occurred when she was pregnant with our first daughter, and that the series of visitations within Nainoa had not occurred until she was expecting our second. Had it been necessary to reproduce—to create descendants—before connecting with the future world?

I resolved to tap into Nainoa's memory banks to find out his culture's beliefs, if and when the opportunity presented itself.

In Ho'omana, the third level of reality (or awareness) is the "spirit world." Called *Po* in Hawaiian, it is the nonordinary reality to which traditional tribal shamans journey, while in an altered state of consciousness, to meet with spirits. This is the level of mental-astral travel, which King describes as a level at which everything is perceived symbolically. What a *kahuna* shaman calls *ike papakolu*, "third-level awareness," may be what Michael Harner calls "the shamanic state of consciousness" or what Australian Aboriginals call "the dreamtime."

In Hawaiian cultural belief the realm of the spirits is divided into a lower, a middle, and an upper world, very much in the tradition of tribal shamans everywhere. The lower world is called Milu, the realm "under the earth" where the shaman journeys in trance to acquire helping spirits for himself and to meet with power, usually in the symbolic form of animals, plants, objects, or spirits. The middle world is Kahiki, the nonordinary aspect of the physical plane of everyday, ordinary reality. This is the dreamworld—the place we go when we dream, either nightly when asleep or in a structured, goal-oriented sense, as the shaman does when awake. Everything that exists in ordinary reality *here* is felt to have a dreamlike or mirror-image equivalent *there*. It is also thought to be the place where one's spirit finds itself immediately after death, the *bardos* of the Tibetan Buddhists or the *kamaloka* of Christian mystics. The upper world is known as Lanikeha. This is the archetypal level of the gods, goddesses, and mythological heroes and heroines. Here one also encounters the sages, the great spiritual teachers, the ancestral *aumakua* spirits, and the spirit guides.

In Ho'omana thought, there is yet one more level of reality, the fourth level, *ike papakauna.* King describes this as a purely subjective state of mystical awareness of the essential oneness of the universe and of everything in it. It is the holistic-spiritual dimension in which everything is experienced *as* everything else.

King has called this the level of shapeshifting and identification—the level of awareness in which accomplished shamans can make contact and merge with schools of fish in the water or with deer in the mountains in order to bring them to the nets of the fisherpeople or to the hunter's bow

—a decidedly different way of fishing and hunting. This is also the level at which one can make contact with the divine field, that vast emptiness charged with potential that Taoists call the Tao; Buddhists call Buddha Mind; Amerindians call the Great Spirit; the Muslims, Allah; the Christians, God; the Jews, Yahweh; and which others have called cosmic consciousness. At fourth level everything is perceived as part of the one, and the "one" as part of every thing.

It is what the fourteenth-century German mystic Meister Eckhart meant when he said, "The eye with which I perceive God is the same eye with which God perceives me."[5]

Almost six months had passed since my last episode with Nainoa, in spite of my constant intention to renew the contact. Every night I went to sleep wondering if *it* would happen, but it didn't. My intentionality alone did not seem to be enough. Perhaps I didn't have enough power yet or enough control. Perhaps I needed assistance.

In early 1988 I was sitting in my study writing these thoughts. I rose and went outside and walked around the house to where the stone stood in the rock garden. A light wind rattled through the palms overhead as I greeted the stone's powerful visage in my thoughts, in second-level awareness. I remembered Chief Kaneohe's instructions to Nainoa when he met this same stone at the onset of his walk. I looked around carefully. Jill and the children were shopping for the evening meal. I was alone.

I squatted before the stone and placed both hands on it, feeling its rough surface. I remembered the moment of finding it, and I felt my strong connection with the place in nature from which it had come. I closed my eyes and cleared my mind of thoughts, waiting for long moments, but felt nothing unusual. Perhaps the awareness within the stone was waiting for me to do something—but what? I greeted it again, then formed the desire to regain contact with Nainoa. I asked with what I hoped was humility and purpose, and with good intention.

I felt no response, but then, I didn't really know what to expect. Talking with spirits in stones was a new experience, and like Nainoa, I still wasn't all that sure I believed in spirit stones. I stood up and surveyed the *pohaku* for a few moments more, then went inside to start dinner.

Perhaps it was coincidence, but that night in the hour just before dawn, the contact happened once again—and in the usual way.

12
Sixth Journey
Spirit Flight

NAINOA WAS STANDING ON A LONG, HIGH RIDGE of broken rock just below a mountain peak. He was breathing heavily, having just completed his ascent. Around him in every direction, as far as he could see, were the endless mountains. Vultures, hawks, and large black birds soared by on the wind, the light catching their eyes as they spotted him. A chill wind was coming from the northeast. Wrapping himself in his cloak, he sat down to reduce his exposure.

Far below, a deep blue lake sparkled in a steeply walled valley. Its green borders were dotted with game. A stream appeared to exit from its eastern side, suggesting that this was the highest part of the mountains. The watercourse curved around to the north before disappearing into the forest. To the northeast lay another large lake surrounded by high peaks, but he could not discern what lay beyond.

Nainoa had followed the remains of the great road east, expecting to find more *siti* sites along the route, but aside from the surviving sections of the broad roadbed

terrace, all traces of the former inhabitants of this land had been obliterated, covered by the forest and earth. This morning he had looked up at
the extensive outcroppings of naked rock that loomed many thousands of
feet above him and decided to climb to the top of the nearest, to have a
look at the view and gain some idea of what lay ahead. The peaks had soft
grassy shoulders that stretched in long treeless slopes down to the needled
forests below, from which grew trees with rough bark, needlelike leaves, and
curious scaly wooden fruits. As far as he knew, none of the hunters or
explorers from any of the settlements had ever described seeing these trees
before.

It was midmorning when Nainoa had started upward, zigzagging back
and forth across the steepening slope, trying to find the easiest passage
through the trees, trying to catch his breath. He saw many sheep with big
curled horns, and an odd kind of chicken burst into noisy flight from
thickets. By midday, he had reached open grasslands above the treeline. The
view grew more spectacular by the moment. The sun was hot despite the
cold air, and he had to stop often to rest and catch his breath. He longed to
see horses, but only deer were near the trees' edge below, and sheep above.
The animals did not seem to be afraid of him as he passed close to them—
they probably had never seen humans before. The slope grew steeper, and
Nainoa stopped more and more often to regain his breath.

In the valley below a large animal emerged from the trees and crossed the
open grassy borders of the lake to drink. Deer had moved out of its way,
their proximity giving him some idea of the size of the creature. Suddenly,
he realized with some shock that it was a bear. But it was not at all like the
dark forest bears of the lowlands with which he was familiar. This one was
huge, with yellow-brown fur, and he considered himself fortunate indeed
that he had not run into one directly.

The grasses gave way to loose, angular stone shards as the slope became
steeper, and Nainoa seemed to slip backward almost as much as he progressed upward. He counted out ten paces at a time, then he stopped and
breathed deeply, leaning on his spear; then he continued another ten paces,
proceeding carefully up the treacherous slope, searching for small mats of

grass growing out of the stones on which to place his feet. He arrived at last on the windswept ridge and dropped his possessions. Leaning on his spear, he marveled at the sweep of mountainous terrain.

It had taken him nearly a month of hard, steady trekking to get this far. The dry season would last for only three to four months, after which the rains would return, flooding large areas of the lowland forest and making travel through those regions impossible. This meant that he had only about fourteen days to walk before he should begin his return journey. He knew he could find his way back, but once the rains returned . . .

He put the thought from his mind. Three to four days' travel would bring him to the peaks to the east. The edge of the mountains that he had seen on the old maps could be there. He decided to continue his walk at least to that point and stood up to stretch his legs, his muscles jumpy after their forced climb. It was a long walk down to the lake, and the afternoon was waning. Because of the bear in the valley below, he decided to make camp here.

Gathering his belongings, he walked up along the ridge to the peak, a massive outcropping of dark rock that soared above him another several hundred feet or so into the sky. He spied a broad ledge and, on clambering up, discovered a warm, south-facing platform there, out of the wind. An abandoned bird's nest of large branches took up much of the space, and the scattered bones of monkeys, goats, deer, lizards, and rodents provided mute evidence of the former occupant's diet. The nest itself made for an adequate supply of firewood, and Nainoa decided to camp on the ledge for the night.

He took apart and stacked the nest, created a sleeping space, and arranged his camp in well-practiced movements. Then he rested from his arduous climb, as the sun-warmed rock at his back took the chill out of his body. He studied the clouds and watched the landscape change as the afternoon progressed and the sinking sun threw the mountains into shadowed relief. Suddenly the sun's rays reflected off a small, glassy shard half-buried in the soft dusty substrate deposited by the wind nearby. He picked it up, and his pulse quickened once again.

It was an arrow point made of black glass. He rummaged in his net bag and extracted the stone core he had brought from the settlement, comparing it with the point. The raw material was similar, but the point's design was unique. No Hawaiian had made this. It looked as though it could have been made yesterday. A careful search of the wide ledge revealed no more flakes of glass—most likely the point had been here a long, long time. Perhaps some hunter had come up here long ago and loosed an arrow at the birds who had built the nest.

The wind died as the sun went down, and Nainoa made a small fire, ringed with stones. Into his cooking pot he put several skinned and gutted rodents that he had gathered that morning, added some water and salt, and simmered them slowly. They weren't bad; the meat tasted spicy and resinous. Still, he would have given a lot for a breadfruit roasted in the coals.

After eating, he sipped the warm water from the pot and watched the changing light. He fed the fire, wondering if anyone could see the blaze. He stared at *mahina*, the moon, and a fragment of an ancient poem in Old Hawaiian came up in his mind. It contained an archaic expression for "moonlight"—*malamalama o ka mahina.* He considered the word *malamalama.* By itself, it implied "clarity of knowledge," but it also meant "spiritual enlightenment." Perhaps he was on *kealakupua*, the path of the mystic, moving toward enlightenment.

The darkening land below and the brightening universe above intensified the strongly spiritual feeling of this place. It would make a magnificent spot for a *heiau.*

Nainoa began to think about the religious practices of his people. As he reviewed what was known about religious symbology, he thought about the cross that had been brought to Hawai'i by the Americans as part of their strange religion. According to the earliest books they owned, which had been written shortly after the Fall, the Americans had worshiped Io, the vast, impersonal emptiness of the universal void from which everything in existence had come forth. They had considered Io to be a supreme, fatherly creator deity of some sort, and invoked it in a prayer they commonly used that began with the phrase:

Our father who exists in the upper world,
sacred is your symbol . . .

Many Hawaiian scholars had written about this one line and many believed
that "our father" did not represent the void but actually referred to the sun
as a deity, to the source of *mana*, the life-force, which, in combination with
kawai'ola, the water of life, made all life possible. Another theory seemed
more in concert with the *kahuna* mystics' beliefs, central to which was the
understanding that everything in nature existed at three different states of
being—physical, mental, and spiritual—with each level expressing both an
outer and inner aspect. For human beings, for instance, the outer physical
aspect was the *kino*, the material body, and its inner counterpart, the energy
body, the *kino'aka*, a kind of invisible, duplicate body carrying the life-force
that enlivened the individual.

At the mind level of being, the inner mind was strongly integrated with
the physical body at a level of awareness called *unihipili* in classic Hawaiian,
or more commonly the *ku*, or "bodymind." The *ku* experienced the outer
world, stored memories, and was the source of emotions and feelings.
Through the *ku*, one also received information about the nonordinary levels
of reality. It was the level of the mind through which visionary experiences
occurred.

The outer aspect of the mind was focused primarily on the outer world.
This was the mental, intellectual level of the human self and was called
uhane, or more commonly, the *lono*. This aspect of awareness was the
thinker, the analyzer, and the decision maker, receiving information about
the outer and inner worlds through the *ku*. It was *kealaka'i*, the director in
control of a person's actions and behavior, whose decisions are translated
into action by the inner *ku*, which works directly with the physical body.

Nainoa paused in his thought-line. The information was coming up out of
his mind more concisely than ever before. He put more wood on the fire
and looked carefully around. He thought he felt a presence, yet he was
alone. Was it Nagai's spirit, or someone else, or a spirit that lived on this

mountaintop? A stream of ideas, imagery, and memories came up into his consciousness through his *ku*.

The spiritual level of the self was called *kane'wahine* in Old Hawaiian, a term that implied a personal spirit that is both masculine and feminine. The more general term *aumakua* was commonly used to designate this aspect, and each person, each manifested thing in nature, both animate and inanimate, was thought to have one. The *aumakua* of each manifested thing existed in the spirit world, in Ao Aumakua, and unlike the physical and mental aspects of the self, the spiritual aspect did not die.

In mystic thought, living and nonliving beings on the physical plane of existence were the outer aspects of their inner *aumakua*. Each person, each plant or animal or river or stone, originated as a thought-form, whose source was its *aumakua*. Everything in nature was manifested intentionally into the everyday world of physical reality by its *aumakua* in the spirit world. In this way, everything was essentially dreamed into existence by its non-ordinary spiritual aspect.

The mystics also believed that each of the three aspects of the self—body, mind, and spirit—could increase and grow, change and evolve, in response to experiences occurring at each of the levels of being. In this way, each aspect was to some degree responsible for co-creating the others. As a person lived his life on the physical plane, his experiences were projected through his inner *ku* into his *aumakua* level of self. This aspect then increased and changed in response, existing as a kind of repository for that person's life experiences, including those derived not only from the present life but also, to some extent, from past lives as well. As such, one's *aumakua* contained a spiritual memory of all personally accumulated experience and knowledge.

In addition, each person's *aumakua* was connected with every other *aumakua* through a vast interconnecting matrix of power or energy called *koko'aka*. All the personal *aumakuas* of all human beings everywhere thus formed a collective entirety known as *kapoeaumakua*, the human spirit. This great, multifaceted composite being contained the collective knowledge of all humanity. This wisdom was theoretically available to every individual person for the asking. The trick lay in knowing how to make direct contact with one's own *aumakua*, because such information could be accessed and received only through that aspect of the self.

The mystics revealed that contact with one's personal spiritual aspect occurs through the *ku*, and that information from one's *aumakua* usually takes the form of dreams, ideas, impulses, thoughts, and inspirations. The *aumakua* was thus the source of inspiration and intuition. In this way, one's spirit could function from time to time as a personal teacher or guide.

Nainoa felt inspired by this thought, which implied that his own *aumakua* could be involved in his visionary experiences and, perhaps to some degree, in his ordinary ones as well.

He paused again. It definitely felt as if someone were directing his thoughts, gently, as if a voice he couldn't quite discern were speaking with him, within him. Could it be Nagai's spirit, or his own *aumakua*? As he listened closely, the voice became distinct, and he heard it say that time does not exist in the spirit world in the same way that it does on the physical plane, that "there, time is all at once."

Nainoa considered this revelation. It suggested that he could gain access to knowledge from the past or from the future through his *aumakua* in the spirit world. Perhaps his own desire to know about the time before the Fall had helped him travel back to ancient Hawai'i, and his *aumakua* had provided the connection to an American. Nainoa remembered the American invocation in its entirety.

> *Aumakua*, who exists in the upper world,
> sacred is your symbol.
> Let your wisdom and intentions be manifest here on earth,
> as they are there in the spirit world.
> Nourish me each day, and assist me in being compassionate.
> Help me to achieve right conduct, and protect me from evil.

For you are the source of my power and my being
Forever . . .
Amama.

The Americans must have been aware of the three levels of the self. Perhaps they were not invoking a father-sun deity or the universe; perhaps they were attempting to make a connection to their personal, inner, spiritual aspect—their *aumakua.*

He considered the phrase "sacred is your symbol." The inner and outer levels of the mind, the *ku* and the *lono,* were often symbolized as carved *akua* images on the platforms of the *heiaus.* The *aumakua,* however, was most often represented by an upright, uncarved stone or one that had been minimally trimmed to accentuate its vertical appearance. Large public *heiaus* and smaller personal shrines dedicated to the *aumakua* usually displayed a standing monolith that functioned to remind all who saw it of their vital, inner spiritual selves and their connection with the spirits of the ancestors. It helped them shift their awareness to contact their personal ancestral spirit self.

The *aumakua* was also sometimes symbolized by *manu,* the bird that could fly down from the upper world bearing knowledge, thoughts, and messages. Many historians had theorized that the cross could symbolize the bird and thus represent the Americans' concept of their personal *aumakua.*

Many others had pointed out that the cross could also have represented the four directions—the east, north, west, and south—and been both a physical, practical symbol and a powerful spiritual symbol for the harmony created when the spiritual qualities of the four directions are brought into balance. Others had theorized that the cross might be a composite symbol in which the horizontal represented the "middle world" of ordinary earthly reality, and the vertical symbolized the lower world below and the upper world above. The cross could thus be a single image of all three levels of reality.

One could also view the vertical part of the cross as the *aumakua,* the monolith, Nainoa thought, whose base penetrated below the horizontal ground of ordinary reality to the lower world and whose apex projected upward toward the heavens.

Nagai had also described the cross as an abstraction of the great world tree that connects the upper, middle, and lower worlds and is associated with the cross of the white master, Iesu. The spirit of Iesu was said to have traveled up through the world tree to the upper world at his death. However, other *kahunas* thought it far more likely that the cross symbolized Iesu's *aumakua*, his bird-form that he reassumed when his spirit withdrew from his dying physical aspect and flew back to the upper world.

Nainoa liked this idea, too, because it implied that the cross was the actual form in which one's *aumakua* self existed within the spirit world, within Ao Aumakua.

Nainoa's people had many rituals that used symbols to control or manipulate supernatural power or to shift individual awareness from the everyday plane into deeper realms. Many rituals also celebrated events such as the birth of a child, the onset of puberty, a marriage, and a funeral, all presided over and controlled by the priests.

The priests of the *heiaus* followed a fairly rigid ceremonial schedule throughout the year. They staged the rituals according to the phases of the moon and always accompanied them with lengthy prayers, offerings and sacrifices, the retelling of old myths, chanting, drumming, and *hula*—physical activities designed to impress one's *ku*, a necessary ally in the shifting of awareness. These events also brought the community together and helped reinforce group solidarity and disperse negative feelings, such as antagonism between rival households. Finally, the rituals reinforced the political power and higher levels of status enjoyed by the chiefs and priesthood.

There was also a dark side of spiritual practice. Sorcery was considered evil in the settlements, but it still existed. Sometimes a sorcerer would accumulate *mana* and would ritually direct it at others with the intention to do them harm. People who suddenly suffered misfortune were likely to look around for the person who wished them ill. They might then use countermagic of their own or that of a specialist to send the negative thought-forms back to their source.

When Nainoa returned to the settlements, he knew the priests would most likely try to discredit his visionary experiences, since he was not of the priestly class. They were not likely to allow him any spiritual status. They tightly controlled religion in the settlements, and only they could perform the sacred rituals. Only they were officially permitted to act as intermediaries between the community and the supernatural, but the *kahuna* mystics would be interested. The mystics came from all class levels and tended to keep a low profile because of the priests' political opposition.

Nainoa rearranged some of the smaller branches into a long pile on which he placed his hammock. He wrapped himself in his cloak and rain-cape, made himself comfortable, and stared into the fire. He had been holding the stone arrowpoint in his fingers during his deliberations, and he now speculated about its maker. Perhaps he was sitting where that hunter had sat. Perhaps that hunter, too, had been drawn up to this place of power.

Nainoa drifted into sleep and slipped immediately into dream. In his dreaming he climbed the mountain again. As before, he slipped backward on the loose stony shards, and as he started to fall, his muscles jumped, awakening him. Again he drifted off, only to awaken once more as his body tensed. Annoyed, he fed the fire, then willed himself to relax, willed himself to sleep—and very shortly, he did.

The wind picked up during the night, moaning and whispering around the rocky crag. The temperature dropped as the rocks cooled, and toward dawn Nainoa became chilled. He awakened to feed the fire. As he sat and shivered in his cloak and cape, he regretted choosing this exposed place to camp. He studied the heavens and located the water dipper, *na Hiku.* Tracing the path of the dipper's handle, he found *Hokule'a,* the star that was said to pass directly over the ancestral homeland of Hawai'i. Well up in the sky now were the Pleiades, *na Huihui a Makali'i,* the cluster of little eyes whose appearance at sunset had marked the beginning of the harvest. In an old story, the world tree grew upward and passed through the hole bounded by these seven stars. Recalling his vision of the great tree and the strange green man made of leaves, he finally drifted back to sleep, only to be reawakened almost immediately by the shriek of some huge bird. Nainoa stared wildly around him, scared out of his wits, wondering if the owner of the nest had returned to discover that he had burnt much of it. But he saw nothing in the darkness and decided it must have been the wind. He concentrated on relaxing, and just as he was slipping off, it began. . . .

First he felt light, as if he were floating, weightless. The now-familiar feelings of power rushed into him, and his intellect awakened fully, instantly.

He remained motionless, his eyes closed, enjoying the sensations of power, of floating, of hovering above the ledge. He tried to imagine the bird that had made the terrifying shriek, and in his mind's eye appeared a huge *io*, a white hawk with brilliant golden eyes. Its outspread wings and tail seemed very long, and as his *lono* mind observed dispassionately, the bird did indeed resemble a cross.[1]

His eyes flew open, but he saw no bird there, only the stars, myriad dots of light filling the darkened sky. He closed his eyes again, yet the brilliant spots remained—as did the floating feeling. How marvelous it would be to be able to fly like the *io*, he thought—to be able to soar out into the void from this mountaintop.

And with this thought, he did.

Nainoa merged with the rush of feeling, and stretching out his arms and fingers, he lifted effortlessly into the wind. His eyes snapped open, and below him he saw the mountaintop and a ledge on which someone was huddled in sleep. It was his sleeping, dreaming self, he knew—and he was safe.

The power sensations were expanding, filling him with pulses of pleasurable feeling. The rushing of the wind hissed in his ears. Then he suddenly plummeted toward the rocks. His brief alarm became exhilaration, however, as he opened his wings—his wings?!—and veered off, shooting down with amazing speed over the steep slope of broken rock. He banked and ascended, lifting himself up, climbing higher and higher until he was far above his mountain, making great lazy circles on the wind. His spirit was soaring too. Joy filled him near to bursting, and he screamed—and the shrill shriek of the *io* echoed and reechoed from the surrounding peaks.

Far, far below the minute details of the mountain forest were clearly visible: He could see individual flowers among the grasses near the lake; small striped rodents running for cover among the rocks; the spots on the backs of fish in the water. As he looked around, his visual field shifted to encompass the valley and the mountains. Yet on looking down again, he had the same extraordinary perception of detail.

Nainoa sailed out over the mountains, half of him shaking with something close to fear and the other half cresting with happiness and excitement. Again, the hawk's shriek ripped out of the fabric of his being, an offering to the universe, to be repeated again and again—joy—joy—joy. Back on his mountaintop, the small figure was still sleeping wrapped in his cloak on the ledge. The fire had gone out again, Nainoa saw. He looked away toward the dawn, and intention formed within him. He had to see what lay beyond the distant peaks.

Far below the remains of the road were a thin broken line, alternately exposed or covered with trees. There wasn't much of it left. In many places massive landslides obscured it, and at one point it disappeared under the lake. The lake's eastern stream drained down the mountain, creating its own path, discovering the least resistant rock, to form another lake in another valley, and another.

He veered off to the north, toward the huge lake he had seen from his mountaintop. Ringed by high mountains, it sparkled a deep vibrant blue. Even from this height he could see great numbers of fish in the shallows. Among them, extending out from the shore, were long, parallel rows of posts that had been driven deep into the lakebed beneath the surface of the water. They appeared to be the remains of *uapos*—docks. The remains of the road were barely discernible, running along the shore, then rising and cutting east through the mountains. He lifted on the wind then, and as he headed over the last rocky peaks, he gasped aloud.

The eastern flank of the mountains dropped steeply for thousands of feet, forming a vast wall that ran north and south as far as the eye could see. Beyond lay a different world. He had come to the edge of the forest.

Great seas of grass stretched dry and gray to the eastern horizon. As the sun's first rays broke over the edge of the world, the immense expanses turned a beautiful soft yellow ocher, and the hawk shrieked again in response—and again. Smaller mountains appeared east of the great range, some sparsely wooded, many lacking trees entirely. Although grass dominated the land, galleries of trees marked the watercourses like dark snakes crawling across the dry open plains. To the south lay part of another long lake.

His vision magnified the trees, many of which had dropped their foliage for the dry season. Here and there, strange, grotesque trees had greenish, vastly swollen trunks studded with thorns, their stubby leafless limbs loaded with podlike green fruits.

Then he saw the animals. At first, from his great height, he had thought them to be bushes or trees dotting the open spaces. But now he saw that uncountable numbers of animals were everywhere, blackening the open plains. There were herds of wild cattle, and strange sheep with large curved horns. Unusual pigs with long curved tusks and knobs on their long faces moved around deer and other large black goatlike animals with long ridged horns twisted into spirals. And there were elephants, many herds of elephants.

Flying low along the edge of the woodland at the base of a hill, he saw a group of tigers the color of the grass, the male with a great cape of dark fur around his head and shoulders. A memory emerged of Nagai teaching him about the constellation *na Leo*, named after a "mythical" beast, and his mind surged as he realized that lions were real.

He flew up and over a complex of hills, from where he could see light shining off another body of water to the far northeast. Toward the west the mountains formed a dark forested wall that loomed above the dry open country below. On the wooded hillsides, groups of large doglike monkeys, with long muzzles and ruffs of fur around their heads and shoulders, were foraging in low thorny trees, eating small seedpods that looked like peas.[2]

He passed out over the grassland to where more herds of unfamiliar, somewhat deerlike animals grazed. A group of wild dogs approached the herd from the north, and catching their scent, the entire herd broke into a run. Nainoa's heart jumped with elation: These could only be horses! He recalled the metal horses on the chief's desk and the drawings in his library. With awe, he watched their beautiful flowing motion and powerful forms. He had found horses! He followed them as they outran their predators, admiring their power, wondering at their seemingly indomitable strength. After his long and arduous search, it was difficult to leave them.

Finally, still elated, he soared up to an even greater height to cross a range of hills and a broad bowl-shaped valley. It was bordered on the west by the mountain wall and a huge peak, whose eastern side appeared to have fallen away, creating large white scars. A shallow lake in the valley's center was surrounded by open grassland that was covered with animals. Halfway over the lake, something about the landscape caught his eye.

Nainoa circled higher, and when he glanced back toward the lake's treeless eastern side, a jolt of emotion shook him to the core. There, well back from the water, was a village.

A cluster of small dome-shaped structures that seemed to have been made from tree branches stood next to fire-pits ringed with stones. His heart leaped with excitement, then sank as he realized that the dwellings were abandoned.

Where were the people? He soared higher, lifting into the wind with a sense of urgency. He saw into vast distances, searching for other people. He could not see them.

Returning to the site, he saw it was certainly recent because such flimsy structures would not have lasted a year. The wind and the termites would finish them off quickly.

Confusion filled him. Something else was not right. There were no cultivated fields, no terraces, no watercourses for irrigation. What could this mean?

Soaring higher, he saw once again the long mountain-locked lake and, to the southwest, his mountaintop. His urgency was transformed into a sudden yearning, a deeply felt need. He was being drawn back—back. As he flew with great speed, the wind roared through his feathers—then it was rushing through him, as though he had become a hollow tube.

The image of this hollow vessel consumed him, swallowed him, and he plummeted into it, riven by fear. Strange spots and wavy lines of light coalesced into a single brilliant strand that led him onward through this hollow tunnel. His descent slowed, slowed, until suddenly before him appeared his mountaintop and ledge.

Next to his sleeping form, the tiger man was curled up in a feline posture. The *akua* looked up at his approach, and its form shifted and flowed until it appeared more manlike. Nainoa felt himself settling, and abruptly, he was there on the ledge, shaking with the cold and excitement, drawing deep gasping breaths. His body shuddered from the strain of his exertions. One arm was asleep, tingling strongly as it came back to life.

The power withdrew in diminishing pulses. He lay quietly, his teeth chattering in the cold, until it was completely gone. When he glanced toward the tiger man, he saw that only the eyes and spots remained, swirling like pools of water until they too disappeared.

Nainoa stood up, stamped his feet, and hugged himself in the cold. The wind had stopped, and a pink dawn was filling the eastern sky. His mind reeled at the memory of his flight, and he wrapped himself more tightly in his cloak, as if to reassure himself of his own solidity. To return fully to the present, he built a small fire. As he fed it the remaining sticks from the nest, he heated water with some herbs. When it was fragrant, he sipped it, staring at the view. He knew now with certainty where he had to go. In the distance he heard again the beckoning cry of the hawk.

13
Ruminations

IN THE DAYS THAT IMMEDIATELY FOLLOWED Nainoa's and my flight as a hawk, I wrote down everything I could recall about it. At about this time I began to teach an evening class in anthropology for the University of Hawai'i's West Hawai'i branch in Kealakekua. This course helped ground me in my intellect and kept me focused in ordinary, everyday reality. My students were ethnically diverse, a cross-section of the community. Through my biweekly interactions with them, I reentered my profession after my hiatus as a farmer, glad to be working as an anthropologist once again.

Near the end of the first semester, I was lecturing on religion from the anthropological perspective and decided to discuss aspects of traditional Hawaiian mysticism. I felt some ambivalence about doing this because several Hawaiians of Polynesian descent were in the class, and I was concerned that they might regard discussing information once regarded as the sole property of the *kahuna* shamans to be trespassing into their culture. To the local people I was still an outsider—a mainland *haole* (white person) who would always be a mainland *haole*, no matter how long I lived in the islands.

Before I left for class on the evening I was to give this lecture, I had an early supper with my family at home, then got my lecture notes together. As I left through the front door and headed for my car, I felt a peculiar tension in the air. Beyond and above the stone in the rock garden, the sun loomed close to the horizon, and yellow light streamed across my property, creating a tropical mosaic of brilliant greens set off by deep shadows. The trees, plants, flowers, and grass sparkled with moisture from the afternoon's rain, and thousands of tiny suns reflected back at me from everywhere. The many points of dynamic, brilliant light reminded me of the phosphenes of my altered states, and as my subconscious *ku* responded to this strongly suggestive visual effect, I felt an inner shift. I went into a light trance state, similar to my visionary experiences but not as total or intense. The sensations vibrated at a very low frequency, allowing me to continue to function normally in every regard although my perceptions of everything around me had altered significantly, expanding and spreading out horizontally, so that I "merged" to some degree with my surroundings. Looking around my small farm holding, I was able to *feel* the landscape. I admired the gray-green texture of the bark of the banyan tree beside the house and the beginnings of its buttressed roots, and I felt the wind rustling through its great clouds of viridian leaves as it grew. I could hear its rootlets pushing through the crumbly lava substrate and sense its benign, neutral, dreamlike consciousness as its roots imbibed water and its leaves absorbed the light.

In the magic of this moment, I turned to the stone in the rock garden. I should ask its permission to discuss *kahuna* knowledge with others, I realized. I went over to it, set down my briefcase, and placed both hands on its wet surface. Clearing my mind of other thoughts, I greeted the spirit in the stone, then formally asked permission to share the knowledge I had acquired from my teachers both in ordinary reality and in nonordinary reality. I asked the stone for its blessing in my endeavors—and for *mana*, so that I might speak well and truthfully and persuasively.

In offering my intense gratitude for the beautiful island paradise in which I lived, in recognizing the vitality of the living beings around me, and in asking for the stone's guidance, I was essentially praying. I was trying to connect with my most essential nature and with that of all other beings. Something vivid flowed into my consciousness in that moment. Through the stone I suddenly felt strong connections between me and the rest of creation. I felt at one with the mountain and the ocean, with the wind and the beach, with the land and the trees—and with Nainoa.

Abruptly, my hair rose and my skin prickled into goosebumps. The strange awareness in the stone touched my mind. I felt something beyond its mere presence—I felt a mind-shape, an utterly remote form of consciousness, profoundly different from a human mind but a form of consciousness nevertheless. The term *awareness* perhaps conveys it best. In those brief moments, I could feel quite clearly that this awareness was focused upon me. The rough, wet boulder suddenly became warm, and its heat penetrated rapidly into my hands, through my arms, and into my chest and stomach. Startled, I let go of the stone. My hands tingled. The sensations of power had vibrated up a notch and were much stronger. It was as if the stone had bestowed on me a gift of energy by which I could speak for it and the rest of the natural world.

Reassured and even eager, I picked up my briefcase and got into my car.

That evening, something decidedly unusual occurred. After a half hour of straight academic discussion about cross-cultural religious beliefs and ideology, a rumble of thunder came from the south as I broached the topic of mystical power. Thunderstorms are rare in the islands because of the mediating influence of the surrounding ocean, which I mentioned to the class.

As I continued my talk, I was interrupted again . . . and then again by louder and louder rumbles. The thunder was coming closer . . . the storm was advancing down the volcano. I continued lecturing, and the thunder cracked again, this time with a flash of lightning. The sun had set by now, and darkness was falling, so the effect was dramatic.

I deviated from my planned script and began to talk about the mythic lightning man, called Jondar in southern Africa and Namarkun by some of the Aboriginal Australians. Rock paintings of this supernatural being are remarkably similar in these two widely separated geographic areas. I described how the lightning man was portrayed as a fearsome entity with a long, spindly body and hornlike extensions projecting from its head, and long, zigzag arms and legs that produced thunder by clashing together stone axes tied to its elbows and knees. In Australia Namarkun is depicted with a long arc of lightning bent around itself like a great, phosphenic horseshoe.

I talked about Thor and his magic hammer from northern European mythology, Zeus and his thunderbolt from classical Greece, and Shango and his double axe of the Yorubas of West Africa. I mentioned that Kanekehili, the Hawaiian thunder god, was an aspect of Kane, the leading deity among the great gods of Hawai'i for whom scholars had listed up to seventy names. More lightning flashed and thunder crashed in response. Nainoa's name for the lightning man had been Makua'uwila. I asked the Hawaiians in the class if that name was known to them. It wasn't, and I guessed the name would come into use in a future time.

The storm was now almost upon us. The wall of noise was advancing nearer, and big drops of rain were pelting the cars in the parking lot. It continued to intensify, the tropical rainfall becoming almost deafening. I wondered if I could continue lecturing. An older student in her sixties, who had lived all her life in the islands, volunteered above the din that she had never seen a storm like it in Kona before.

A brilliant flash followed immediately by ear-splitting thunder lit up the room. Attempting some humor to ease our tension, I related that African people say that Jondar the lightning man is always showing off. One student said somewhat flippantly, "Let's invite Jondar to come in really close and see what he does."

As the collective attention of all thirty individuals focused on this thought, the lightning struck in the parking lot right outside the classrooms. The crash of thunder was instantaneous. The lights flickered and went out, plunging the classroom into darkness apart from the lurid glow of the lightning, which snaked all over the ground outside hissing and sputtering for the longest five seconds I could remember. When the lights came slowly on once more, the smell of ozone permeated the air.

Startled in spite of myself, I said, "Well, that was close enough—and what's more, I can't lecture with all this thunder and lightning." Trying to recover some calm, I turned to the night sky, raised my voice, and projected it out the window. "And I would be very grateful if the lightning man would take all this *mana* back up the mountain so that I can continue the class."

To everyone's astonishment, including my own, the storm subsided. Within five minutes the last rumbles were retreating into the distance—up Mauna Loa, back from where it had come! The rain ceased, and the night became absolutely silent. I concluded the lecture, and everyone left looking somewhat dazed.

As I drove home down the wet country highway in the dark, I felt almost as if there had been some connection between me and the storm. Although my scientific nature dismissed the speculation immediately as absurd, later that evening, the question continued to gnaw at me as I lay in bed, trying to get to sleep. I realized at a deep level that I was dealing with stuff I knew next to nothing about. Had I been careless? *Had* there been some association between myself, my topic, and the lightning? Could there actually have been spirits involved? And if there were, would they have allowed someone to be hurt by my carelessness?

I retreated from these speculations into a consideration of Nainoa's spiritual beliefs. He knew about Gautama Buddha and was aware of Jesus of Nazareth as Iesu Kristo, the "white master." While I did not yet have a clear idea of what this term meant to him, neither Buddhism nor Christianity existed as an organized religion in the Hawaiian settlements of his time. These religions had not survived the collapse of Western civilization—at least, not in Hawai'i.

Nainoa's knowledge of the demise of civilization was limited to what had occurred in the islands—events that had apparently been recorded by the descendants of the survivors many generations after the process was complete. He did not know specifically *when* it had happened or *what* had happened. He had three major pieces of information, however: The sea level had risen; the islands had been abruptly isolated from the rest of the world; and most of the human population living in the islands had perished, presumably from the combined effects of social chaos and starvation.

I lay very still in the darkness and tried to imagine what would happen if the islands were suddenly and completely isolated from the outside world. Hawai'i is the most remote of all the world's island groups—considerably more than 2,500 miles of open ocean lie between Honolulu and anywhere else. I devised the following scenario:

The collapse of Western civilization would cause all imports of food and fuel to cease abruptly. Supplies of both would dwindle within days, rendering useless all motorized transports dependent on gasoline, from cars and trucks to boats and aircraft. Public utilities—water and electricity—would be lost, as would all medical services and supplies and all communication systems dependent upon electricity. Most critically, there would be ever-greater shortages of food and water in all the communities, whose populations would be on foot.

Access to food and water would be the ultimate factors making survival possible. Hoarding would only delay the inevitable. Only those people still capable of deriving all of their sustenance from the land and ocean would survive. Only those with knowledge of the traditional Polynesian strategies of survival would pull through—some ranchers, some farmers, and some fishermen perhaps—but only those able to adapt, and quickly.

The rest of human society's jobs and occupations—the politicians, the business people, the bankers, the lawyers, the realtors, the merchants—would instantly lose meaning and value. Only food, and those with the knowledge, skills, and ability to produce it, would have worth. Only those able to derive their sustenance in the traditional ways, without machinery or gasoline-powered craft, would survive—a very sobering thought.

I considered this scenario with growing unease. There would have to be an instant reversion to the traditional Hawaiian system of dividing the land into self-sufficient slices of landscape called *ahupua'a*. Each of these ran from the mountain to the ocean and included a fishing community on the coast and a farming community inland. Historically, their boundaries were determined by the presence of arable soil, suitable canoe landings, and the availability of fresh uncontaminated water. Reversion into this ancient biodynamic pattern would have to be accomplished immediately, or else all would perish—all.

Most of the islands' contemporary population, I knew, holds little regard for the well-being of the land and the water. Developers continue to throw up densely planned communities with the backing of politicians and bankers. In the process former farmlands are converted into expensive subdivisions inhabited by people who have not the slightest idea of how to produce food. As a result, the lion's share of everything purchased and consumed in the islands is imported. Hawai'i is very much part of the Western world, and its population is completely dependent upon the world market economy. Even the local fishermen use gasoline-powered craft.

Hawai'i also has serious environmental problems. Chemical residues from pesticides, herbicides, and fertilizers are now found in the critical aquifer of fresh water that lies under each island. Agricultural and environmental pests have been ignorantly and irresponsibly introduced to the islands, with calamitous results for endemic species of plants and animals as well as for export crops themselves. Even if a transition back to ancient Polynesian methods of survival became necessary, could it be accomplished?

Yet Nainoa's people had made it. Some had survived civilization's crash and repopulated the islands, and their descendants eventually had sailed all the way to the California coast to rediscover the lost continent of America, five thousand years in the future.

After the crash high technology apparently would be lost in its entirety. Without the power to run them, all machines—from automobiles and computers to jumbo jets and CT scans—would be junked. Their metal parts could be made into things that would have value—fishhooks, harpoons, knives, nails, wagon or boat fittings—but the machines themselves, like anything that did not directly contribute to food production and survival, would be immediately discarded. How much of the current population would survive? Ten percent? One percent? A tenth of a percent?

When the crunch came, the human species would once again be subject to the impersonal judgment of natural selection. The laws of nature would be ruthless and the genetic bottleneck extreme, but Hawai'i's ethnic diversity would be in its favor. The populations remaining on the different islands would be small, but they would possess the genetic variability necessary for survival. And in the process, a new race of Hawaiians would come into being, one to which all of Hawai'i's current ethnic and cultural groups would contribute.

The people Nainoa knew as friends and "colleagues" were all uniformly dark-skinned, with strongly expressed features. Their noses varied somewhat, but most had broad cheekbones, wide mouths with full lips, and "almond-shaped" eyes. There had been no racially distinct individuals of purely European, African, or Asiatic ancestry. Hair color was somewhat variable, but there were no blondes, although blue eyes did crop up.

The various religions and religious sects in the islands today would probably be discarded virtually overnight as priests and parishioners died. As the survivors refocused on the ocean and the land as sources of life, religion would become reoriented toward what was most important—the natural world and its supernatural aspects. Ancient shamanic methods of living with and understanding nature would survive or be rediscovered, because they would be immediately appropriate—and because they worked.

Shaken by this apocalyptic vision, I got out of bed and made a large mug of Darjeeling tea, then went out onto the lanai to sit under the stars. The night was quiet, and as the waning moon cast its ghostly light over the shadowed landscape, the warm tropical air was soft. I located the Big Dipper, which Nainoa called Na Hiku, and followed the curve of the handle toward the south to find Arcturus, known to Hawaiians as Hokule'a, the star of gladness, for which the famous voyaging canoe is named.

Nainoa's visionary spirit flight in the form of the hawk resembled many experiences in the ethnographic literature of becoming-one-with a power animal. Flying with a spirit bird is a universal experience, common to shamans the world over. The large alpine lake over which Nainoa flew could be Lake Tahoe, and the eastern escarpment of the Sierra Nevada had looked very familiar from the air, yet the contemporary high deserts of the Great Basin beyond appeared to have changed radically, becoming grass-lands and savanna-woodlands not unlike those in Africa today. An environ-mental shift of this degree implied that the entire world must have undergone a dramatic climatic change. The wooded grasslands reflected increases in both rainfall and ambient temperature. Judging from the flora and fauna, the world was once again largely tropical-warm, as it had been for much of its evolutionary past.

Was I living at the end of the golden age of Western civilization? Were the predictors of imminent environmental catastrophe correct? Would I be there when it happened?

My thoughts returned to Nainoa's concept of the standing stone as a symbol for the spiritual aspect of the self. Monoliths are found all over the world, and they are everywhere the subject of mystery and speculation. Although much has been written about them, their original functions remain unknown, lost with the passing of those who erected them so long ago—as long ago as 3000 B.C.

Perhaps the best-known standing stones were arranged in circles by prehistoric megalithic peoples of Europe. More than nine hundred such circles can be found in England and Ireland alone, the most famous at Avebury and Stonehenge. Some of these circles were arranged so precisely that they may have been used as solar timepieces by megalithic agricultural societies, for which accurate timing of plantings and harvests must have been critical in a short growing season. Other groups of standing stones, such as those arranged in long rows at Carnak in northern France, had functions that are less clear. Nowhere have I read that they might have been symbols for the spiritual self, although this not being my area of expertise, I might have missed it.

In old Hawai'i, however, the standing stone was a symbol associated with the deity Kane. In his outer aspect Kane was the leading creator *akua* and one of four greater "deities" of the Hawaiian pantheon. In his inner aspect Kane was felt by many to have represented the dual-natured god-self or higher self of each person, the *kane'wahine* or *aumakua.*

Down through the darkness on the coast, a small cluster of lights marked the location of a partially restored Hawaiian archaeological site known as the Pu'uhonua o Honaunau, the Place of Refuge at Honaunau. Traditionally, it had been an important religious center with a strong healing focus, where priests of the sanctuary cleansed law breakers of their sins. Today it is a national park, visited daily by busloads of tourists.

Within the inner sanctuary bounded by a massive stone wall are the remains of several *heiau* platforms. Before one of these lies a huge monolith that rests on its side. Jerry Shimoda, the park's superintendent, informed me that the giant stone was brought to the Pu'uhonua from elsewhere, but by whom and for what, nobody knows. Legend relates that it was a favorite of a local high chief named Keoua, hence its name—the Keoua stone. I thought about the curious relationship that was growing between myself and the stone near my front door and wondered if it could have been the other way around. Perhaps Chief Keoua was the favorite of the monolith. . . .

Throughout the islands other well-known stones are said to be inhabited by spirits or are known to be receptacles of supernatural power. Those at Wahiawa, on Oahu, are said to have healing power. Birthing stones, *pohaku hanau,* stand where high-ranking chiefesses gave birth to future *ali'i.* Several minimally carved stone faces reside today in the Bishop Museum in Honolulu. Others stand where they always have. Traditionally, almost all *pohakus* were named, and all were highly revered.

Since monoliths are found in such different parts of the world, they may have been symbols derived from shamanic knowledge that was once universally understood, expressing an ancient idea that was rediscovered over and over throughout the world's cultures at a certain stage of psychosymbolic development. It was tempting to speculate that crystals, too, represent small monoliths, portable symbols that the subconscious *ku* recognizes and is drawn toward.

Remarkably, Nainoa had understood the concept of the "collective unconscious" articulated by the visionary thinker Carl Jung among many others. In Nainoa's belief system, each person is a physically manifested part of a greater composite human spirit that contains the collective wisdom of the human species. Theoretically, each person has access to this knowledge through their spiritual aspect. If this was true, I pondered, why can we not discover a cure for AIDS or invent nuclear fusion through this collective wisdom? Why didn't the megalithic builders of Stonehenge conceive of the DNA molecule? It is conceivable that human society must attain a certain level of knowledge and awareness as a foundation from which to ask the right questions, and in the right way. The concept of the DNA molecule would have had little meaning in the cultural context of the megalithic, for example, so why would they have asked?

From an evolutionary perspective, the mystical concepts of Ho'omana made sense. Since the physical plane of earthly existence is considered a level of action and the spiritual realm a level of information, knowledge might not take form "there" until it has come into being "here." Within this framework the spiritual dimensions and their inhabitants come into being in response to what happens on the physical plane of existence rather than the reverse. Growth, change, and diversification happen "here" in ordinary reality, rather than "there," in nonordinary reality. This line of thought implies that we are the originators of our own spiritual "god-selves"—that we are the creators of our personal *aumakua* aspect and, through it, of the collective human spirit as well.

If everything in nature has a spiritual aspect (and most shamans hold that it does), the same process would apply to everything in the objective world of the physical universe. Every manifested thing would come into being, then change and diversify, here on the plane of action, while each nonmaterial *aumakua* aspect would shapeshift in response. It would exist as a reflection projected "through the looking glass" into the spiritual levels of reality.

There is a cyclic aspect to this mystical relationship, into which the concept of reincarnation fits nicely. All living beings eventually die; then the individual exists solely as *aumakua* between death and the next rebirth. One's spiritual aspect thus functions as both the repository and the source of who and what will be reintroduced into the next round of life on the physical level of earthly existence. Seen from this perspective, we humans are indeed "created in the image of god"—but the "god" is not some alternately wrathful and beneficent creator god of Judeo-Christian-Islamic tradition. It is the individual, personal god-self, the *aumakua*, through which the greater collective human spirit can be accessed.

The *aumakua* thus both creates the newly reincarnated self and evolves in response to that self's actions, thoughts, emotions, and accomplishments here on the physical plane. Creation is not a one-sided affair but rather a dual-natured co-creative process that has been going on for immense amounts of time everywhere within the phenomenal universe of extant forms, from atoms and molecules to stars and galaxies.

I stared out into the night sky. How could I gain access to the informational matrix in nonordinary reality? Hawaiian mystics believe that access is gained not through the intellect but through the *ku*, through the deeper subconscious levels of the mind, where the *nierika* is located. No matter how many books one has read on the subject, or how pure one's intention, one's *ku* must act as an ally in the endeavor. But how did a "left-brain" person like myself get my *ku* to cooperate? Perhaps the key lay in achieving the particular altered state that Michael Harner calls the shamanic state of consciousness.

Harner[1] describes this state as one of expanded awareness in which the shamanic practitioner "sees" with what Australian Aboriginals call the "strong eye"—a heightened manner of perception enabled and maintained by drumbeat frequencies (or rattling) in the theta-wave EEG frequency range of four to seven cycles per second. Harner tends to avoid the word *trance* because Western cultural conceptions often imply that trance is a nonconscious state. While in the shamanic state of consciousness, the practitioner is usually aware of both ordinary and nonordinary reality simultaneously and is able to fully recall what was seen and heard in the visionary realm.

Charles Tart, a professor of psychology at the University of California at Davis, has put forth a general theory describing the way in which altered states may be induced, breaking the process down into three stages.[2] In the first stage one's everyday state of consciousness is destabilized by disrupting forces—intense sensory stimulation from drumming, rattling, music, chanting, dancing, or physiological-psychological disruption from sleep deprivation, hunger, sweat lodge experiences, or psychedelic drugs, to name a few. In the second stage the specific altered state of consciousness—the destination—is "patterned" by one's intentions, expectations, psychological and physiological condition, and the environmental setting. In the third stage one's consciousness restabilizes within the new state, remaining "there" until one desires to return to normal brain-mind patterns of activity "here."

Tart and others have discovered that the ability to achieve altered states of consciousness is a learnable skill. Although it may be difficult at first, subsequent practice makes the process easier until the destabilizing force (drumming, rattling, or mind-altering substances) is no longer necessary. The subconscious *ku* can be programmed, implying that one can eventually enter the visionary state by means of intentionality alone.

My excitement about my experiences was tempered by caution. My academic colleagues had given a vitriolic reception to Carlos Castaneda's well-known books about his apprenticeship with a Yaqui Indian sorcerer. Castaneda's work was steeped in controversy almost from the start, and most professional anthropologists believe he had made up a story and foisted it on the world as the real thing. To the anthropological establishment, the fact that his books became immensely popular and made a lot of money was the kiss of death. One of my professors at Berkeley ranted against Castaneda's work, calling it cultural anthropology's equivalent of the Piltdown man hoax. Perhaps this tirade was due to the professor's never having experienced an altered state. Harner says that individuals who have the most difficulty in achieving the shamanic state of consciousness tend to be in highly structured, "left-brain" professions. My academic colleagues would probably share my own inner professor's skepticism about my experiences. Most anthropologists have highly trained intellects that become ever more narrowly focused on their specialty areas. Many are completely unaware of the nature of their subconscious and how it functions.

Albert Einstein, it is said, went sailing to relax after intellectually wrestling with a problem that he couldn't quite solve. During his sail a bolt of intuition suddenly showed him the solution. From the Ho'omana perspective, Einstein's solution probably originated from his *aumakua*, came in through his *ku*, and was received by his *lono* intellect. The *ku*, which is gratified by any pleasurable physical activity, must have been delighted at being outdoors, in dynamic association with nature. Under these circumstances Einstein's *ku* responded to his need for information, rewarded him in turn with a momentary expanded state, made contact with his *aumakua*, which is in touch with the collective informational matrix, and the problem's solution was revealed.

I could also now see why Nainoa might think that the cross represented the human *aumakua* in nonordinary reality. Other ancient cultures also use it as a spiritual symbol. At the American Museum of Natural History in New York, for instance, I have seen crosses embroidered on the breast and knees of a Chukchi shaman's costume. Ethnographic data obtained when the outfit was acquired in Siberia in the 1800s revealed the crosses to be birds, symbolic abstractions of the shaman's spirit flight into nonordinary reality.[3]

Even the Neanderthal people may have used the cross as a symbol. A small round stone engraved crudely but definitely with a cross—from the site of Tata in Hungary[4]—has been dated at fifty thousand years before the present. It is one of the earliest examples of symbolic expression in human evolution. It may mean that the Neanderthals had shamans or that they used the cross as a symbol for an abstract concept. Like the stone monolith, the cross found its way out of the human mind and into the art of most of the world's prehistoric cultures.

Viewed from this perspective, the image of Jesus on the cross acquires an entirely new, expanded meaning: a composite symbol of both the spiritual teacher and his *aumakua* aspect. On the one hand the image shows suffering on the physical plane to be an avenue of transformation. On the other, it shows the physical aspect of humanity merging into its spiritual form at death.

Through my experiences I was achieving an expanded understanding of reality. A *kahuna* shaman might say that my personal *aumakua* was instructing me. I wondered if my *aumakua* and Nainoa's *aumakua* could in fact be the same entity. If they were, he and I would both be "first-level" physical manifestations of the same spirit self-source. In such a case our immortal spiritual aspect could be the connection through which our encounters were occurring. The two of us seemed to exist simultaneously in ordinary reality but in different slices of time, each making contact with the other periodically, possibly by crossing over the *aka* threads connecting us through the second level of reality to our shared *aumakua* in the third. In addition, both of us appeared to be protected by the same animal *aumakua* as companion and guardian—the leopard man or tiger man. There was also the stone. . . .

It was now very late, and dawn was not far off. I had finished my tea, and so I drifted silently through the house to wash my cup in the kitchen. Then I checked on my small daughters and climbed back into bed beside Jill. The tropical night was warm, and she had thrown most of the covers off, sprawling nude in the soft light. Life was now very different from our initial courtship. Now we were rarely alone, being "married householders with children." Our life together was full, yet in the midst of the many responsibilities that having children had thrust on us, our lovemaking still nourished us, renewing the bond, restoring the balance. . . .

Suddenly, my *ku* wanted to make love with her, and her *ku*, feeling the strength of this emotion through her dreaming, through the *aka* threads that connected us, stirred in response. . . . We made love in the dark before dawn, flowing together, sleepily laughing, kissing, touching—and I disappeared into the flash of her dark eyes as I felt my love for her at its most magnificent intensity.

Then we drifted toward sleep, journeying together toward the middle world of dream. Just as I was slipping off, I inexplicably recalled the huts that Nainoa had seen beside the lake in the valley. I wondered about them now, even though I was tired and wanted to sleep.

In spite of my desire to sleep, my *ku*, stimulated by lovemaking, opened the doorway. The exquisite sensations of power flowed across the interface and surged into me. My chest expanded as I drew it in, gasping for breath. The roaring hiss filled my ears. The phosphenes appeared against the darkness, streaming into the distance through the curious arc. Abruptly, I had a sense of going, of passage, of great speed.

I crossed the zone of silence quickly, almost before I knew it. It was easier now. The sensations subsided, and I opened my eyes. I was staring down from the mountains through the haze of the dry season into the valley far below.

14
Seventh Journey
The Forest's Edge

I T WAS EARLY AFTERNOON, AND NAINOA WAS STANDING
upon the summit of a mountain, feeling both elated
and troubled. He was looking at the same landscape
he had already seen through the eyes of the hawk, although the dry season's haze concealed whether there
were huts on the lake's far side.

The southern face of the strange scarred mountain
soared into the sky to his left. His spirit lifted as he
realized that he had successfully crossed the great range—
and that he was the first Hawaiian to do so, the first. His
skin prickled into goosebumps, and his blood sparkled
with light. Impulsively, he jumped to his feet and shouted
with joy. As his cry echoed off the mountains, he knew
that nothing in his life would ever quite match this moment.

In the midst of his exultation, he suddenly sensed a
presence. Was it the tiger man? He recalled him as he had
last seen him—a transparent wraith all spots and eyes.
But looking around, he saw nothing out of the ordinary.

It didn't really feel like the tiger man anyway. He became completely still, alone on the ridge, yet the sense of another presence remained. Who or what was there?

The sense of another presence persisted through the afternoon as he descended the mountain, through the thick forest of the lower slopes. He surprised a group of monkeys and dispatched one with an arrow as the survivors fled through the trees with howls of disapproval. He tied the dead monkey's tail to its head and hoisted the animal to his shoulder, so that it hung under his arm like a bag.

He made an early camp near a ravine, where he could hear the roar of distant waterfalls. He gathered wood, built a fire, and singed the hair off the monkey. Slightly unsettled at how human the charring form appeared, he offered a formal apology to the monkey's spirit, thanking it for the food it would provide. Then he cut it into quarters and cooked it slowly over the fire. After he ate, he tied the remainder of the meat into leafy bundles, which he hung in a tree. Later, he slept fitfully, dreaming of monkeys, still sensing the presence of another.

The air was clearer the following morning, and he marveled again at the accuracy of his visionary flight. As he continued his descent, the feeling of presence grew stronger. Was he being stalked? He found a suitable tree from which to survey his surroundings, pulled himself up into its lower branches, arranged his weapons, and settled in to watch. Quieting his mind, silent and motionless, he watched for movement and saw none—but he still perceived the presence. Perhaps it was a spirit. The air was very still, and the thinning forest was quiet. He decided to move on, but kept his senses alert.

When Nainoa finally reached the foot of the mountains, he also emerged from the forest's edge into the grasslands. Here the sky was huge. His uneasiness returned as a shadow passed over him. Many vultures were gliding on the hot air currents above the valley. He felt exposed and vulnerable. Perhaps the vultures were *ouli*, an omen. As a hawk, he had seen lions here—perhaps death awaited him out in the dry grass, watching him with pale eyes.

At the trees' edge the land dipped gently to the east. A sea of grass stretched to the lake, which shimmered in the midday heat. The open expanses were dotted with animals in great numbers, and the glare was intense. Far in the distance rose rounded gray-blue hills, forming the eastern wall of the valley. The lake's far shore was obscured.

Nainoa decided to proceed north, to meet the stream as it emerged from the mountains. A dark line of forest fringed its path to the lake, beckoning him. He climbed the shoulder of a tall termite mound and looked out across the tussocks of gray-green grass, observing the grazing herbivores. They would have been far less relaxed if any big cats were nearby. To save time, he decided to cut diagonally across the grass to the riverine forest.

Since it was almost time to retrace his journey and return to the settlements, he felt an urgency in his mission now. He strung his bow and took several arrows from the quiver. The monkey meat would not last forever. He set off across the grassland toward the line of trees, using the animal trails that wound among the tussocks. The herd animals regarded him watchfully. Many of them appeared to be long-horned wild cattle. Smaller goatlike animals, with ridged, swept-back horns, stayed closer to the forest edge. They did not let him get within bowshot and departed swiftly at his approach.

Nainoa reached the riverine forest, which was thick with thorny shrubs and bushes, and continued along its margin until he came to a large opening. The shade under the trees in the thorny tunnel was comparatively dark. Many of the animals were drifting back toward the woodland to escape the heat of the day. It was considerably warmer in this valley than in the mountains. He moved carefully into the tunnel toward the shade.

A sudden movement of air in his direction was all the warning he got. With a rush of sound, a bull slammed into him, catching him full in the chest. Its long horns passed under his arms, which reflexively wrapped around and grasped the animal's neck. The bull lifted its head with a bellow of rage and charged free of the thorny brush out onto the open grassland, carrying Nainoa along.

The impact had knocked the wind out of him, but Nainoa remained clamped to the beast's face as his traumatized chest tried to suck in air. The bull hooked its head hard from side to side. As Nainoa began to lose consciousness, he was thrown to the ground and landed on his back among the thigh-high tussocks of grass, stunned.

The bull charged immediately. Desperately, Nainoa tried to roll sideways under the overhang of the tussocks. He partially succeeded—the horns missed him as the beast's charge carried it past, but its hoof and the full weight of its body came down on his left thigh. An instant of extreme pain was followed by numbness as the leg became useless.

In a last desperate move, Nainoa rolled as much of himself as he could under the overhanging grasses. If the bull couldn't see him, he would have a chance. Gasping for breath, his heart pounding, his ribs and shoulders aching, he tried to be still. He held his breath as the beast rushed by on the other side of the tussock, its hooves shaking the ground. As he watched through the darkening haze of dust and pain, it turned and gored his raincape, reducing it to tatters in moments. Then the bull stopped and looked around. Not seeing Nainoa, it abruptly turned and trotted back through the tunnel of brush into the shade of the riverine forest.

Nainoa lay sweating and gasping for breath. Dry leaves and dirt stuck to his shuddering body. His mouth felt very dry. Light-headedness and nausea pervaded him. Closing his eyes, he fainted.

His consciousness returned only by degrees. Breathing was now agony. Chagrined, he tried to move his leg, but beneath its numbness was deep pain. The herd had probably gone into the shade to rest from the heat of the day, and he had walked right into them. In the distance now, the bull bawled, the cows' answers receding as it drove them out onto the grassland.

Risking movement, Nainoa rolled out from under the tussock. Although the pain in his leg and his ribs was overwhelming, he managed to sit against the grass tussock and brush leaves and earth from his face and mouth. His thigh was swelling—a plate-sized bruise was forming where the bull had stepped on him. Even though feeling was returning to his foot, with it came an increasing pain in the thigh.

The heat was extreme, and his thirst was intense. Looking around, he saw some of his possessions scattered in the grass. His net bags had survived, and fortunately his water bottle had been spared. It was almost full, and he drank greedily. His spear, bow and arrow quiver, sticks, and one of his sandals were missing. Moving his leg with great care, he pressed the heel gently against an opposing tussock. The pain was immediate, nauseating him—the leg was probably fractured.

Nainoa sat still, recovering from the shock, trying to conserve his strength. After some time he began to crawl carefully in ever-expanding circles until he had retrieved all his lost possessions except the sandal. The leg was now swollen and discolored, the pain hideous. Still, even though he could not tell how bad the break was, the leg did not seem misaligned, and the skin was intact. Among his medicines he had some powdered root of a plant called *koali*, which he mixed with a little water and some salt. He spread the paste liberally over the bruise. Then he used his spare *malo* to strap his injured leg carefully to his digging stick as a splint. Recovering the spear, he used it as a crutch. When he tried to heave himself upright, he almost passed out again from the pain. Some of his ribs felt cracked too.

It was nearly evening. He still was terribly thirsty, and he knew that his survival depended on reaching the stream within the trees. He listened for the cows but could no longer hear them. Keeping his leg as immobile as possible, he crawled slowly toward the tunnel once more, a foot at a time. After fifty feet the pain in his leg gained in intensity, and he stopped to dig into his supply of medicines again. He extracted some powdered bark of *ohaloa* root and took it with water. Resuming his torturous crawl, he came on the missing sandal in the thorny tunnel.

He crawled and rested, crawled and rested, drinking frequently but sparingly from his water bottle. He moved his bags of possessions along carefully, taking long detours to avoid dense thickets of thorny brambles. He found and cut some slender saplings to improve his splint. By dusk, he was beneath one of the larger trees that was shedding its bark in long woody strips. Climbing was out of the question, so he made a small fire using the fallen bark and deadwood and settled himself as best he could against the base of a needled tree, with its soothing, pungent smell.

The forest came alive with the sound of birds as they settled for the night in the bush around him. He unwrapped his injured leg and felt it carefully. Perhaps the bone was only cracked rather than fractured. He mixed and drank some more *ohaloa*, waited for it to take effect, and maneuvered himself over to a clump of saplings. Still sitting, he carefully wedged his foot securely between two saplings. Then taking a deep breath, he leaned back to stretch the leg and allow the fractured bone to reset itself correctly. The pain was overwhelming, and he passed out.

When he came to in the darkness, the fire was out. He used the fireplow to restart it, then rewrapped his leg, splinting it with the saplings. His ribs ached ferociously, and he could breathe only in shallow breaths, using his belly muscles. He did not feel like eating.

Nainoa fed the fire and considered his options. His leg would take time to heal. It was now highly unlikely that he could return to the settlements before the onset of the rains. For better or worse, he would be on this side of the mountains for at least a year.

He sprawled back against the tree in the darkness, keeping his mind and his spear between him and whatever should come in the night. The sounds of frogs indicated that the stream was to the north. He would be there in the morning.

As he lay in the darkness feeding the fire, despair overcame him momentarily. Would he survive? He was alone, severely injured, unable to walk, and at least a month's journey from whatever remained of his own settlement. Eventually, he drifted into sleep, then woke, then slept again as the pain waxed or waned. Lying in the darkness, he waited for the light, feeding the fire, enduring the pain. The vultures he had seen earlier in the day had indeed been an omen.

The pain was constant; his body one large ache, his leg throbbing. Just before dawn, as he was drifting off to sleep again, a peculiar sound came over the noise of the stream. Perhaps it was the wind coming down from the mountains, but the night air seemed still. He peered into the darkness but saw nothing unusual. Puzzled, he closed his eyes and tried to relax his battered frame. Above the rushing sound was a high-pitched whine that increased and decreased, began and ended, as if something were continually moving past him to his left.

He opened his eyes again, but the night was as it had been. As his mind became active, he noticed, the noise decreased. When he closed his eyes and tried to relax once more, he let his consciousness flow along the sound. It was still there, definitely to his left. Suddenly flashes of light assailed his closed eyelids, and the sensations of power appeared. Simultaneously, a strange vibration arose in his lower back and buttocks, while another sound matched the vibration, a low, repetitive *tuk-a-tuk-a-tuk-a-tuk-a-tuk-a-tuk-a-tuk. . . .*

The continuous sounds became louder as the power sensations increased. Nainoa felt himself to be sitting on some kind of chair that was absorbing and transmitting the staccato rhythm to his body from below. His leg ached, and he shifted position slightly to lessen the discomfort. In the process, his right foot pressed down on something, and he felt a surge of forward movement.

Startled, he opened his eyes. He was indeed sitting in a chair and looking out the windows of an extremely small room that was moving with incredible speed along a road. His intellect snapped on as he struggled with his perceptions, trying to reconcile what he knew to be real with what he was seeing around him. His hands were resting on a wheel attached to a post that emerged from the wall of the room. His skin was very pale. Realization dawned: He was in a machine—and it was moving.

He looked out through the windows that surrounded him. Similar machines were everywhere, and all were speeding in the same direction along the road. Glancing again at his pale hands, Nainoa knew that he had regained contact with the American. A surge of emotion caused "him" to grip the wheel. Small movements of this wheel resulted in the machine moving to the left or right, he noticed. Amid his inner turmoil, "his" body seemed to know precisely what it was doing. He decided not to interfere in any way with the American's handling of the machine. In some incomprehensible fashion, he was in the American's body while "he" was still in residence there too. Where was "he," and what was this machine called? Within his mind, a word appeared—*car.*

A new roar of sound approached on his left as a huge, rectangular boxlike machine flew by on many, many wheels. The wind it created in passing buffeted the car. Fearful, Nainoa glanced to the right and saw another machine passing him on that side as well. He concentrated on steering the car so as not to strike the others. Lines on the greater road surface seemed to delineate paths. "His" car was proceeding along one of these paths, and all the other cars were doing the same thing. His fears began to ease with the realization that the American was controlling the car. He relaxed somewhat and began to look quickly around, recording details.

The American was strapped into a chair next to another chair on his right. A sheet of folded paper with odd black and red lines on it lay on the other chair. Parts of it were blue, but mostly it was white with pale green areas. It was covered with tiny words—a map. He was about to reach for it eagerly when another rush of sound passed him again, and his eyes snapped back to the road. Nainoa perceived he had to become passive and relinquish control of the American's attention so that he could steer the car. He settled down to watch.

Below the large window in front of him, he noticed smaller dark windows, some of which had numbers arranged in a circle within them. In one, he saw a thin stick moving slightly between the numbers 60 and 70. Nainoa wondered suddenly why he could not feel the wind. Reaching out, he touched the hard, transparent material that covered the window, registering with amazement that it appeared to be made of a single sheet of clear glass. Surveying the machine's interior, he marveled at what he saw. A long rectangle of reflective glass that was attached to the car's ceiling caught his attention. Studying the images within it, he realized he could see what was occurring behind the car—another marvel.

He shifted position slightly so that he could look directly into the reflective object. Once again he saw the familiar face of the American, the face that had reflected back at him from the large wall of glass of the house in Hawai'i. A scar bisected the left eyebrow. Nainoa saw the dark eyes narrow speculatively, thoughtfully, and wondered if "he" could feel his presence.

The American shifted uncomfortably. His legs and back ached, Nainoa realized, with the discomfort of one who has been sitting absolutely still for a long time. "He" had apparently been traveling in this manner all day, and "his" back and legs were cramped by the unaccustomed immobility.

Nainoa realized that he was "hearing" the man's thoughts, receiving them in some unknown fashion. As he absorbed this amazing bit of information, he looked beyond the road's edge at a hill covered with extensive orchards. On the road's other half, to his left, more machines moved in the opposite direction. The scale of the great road boggled his mind. He tried to count the number of machines traveling on its surface— and failed.

An immense dry landscape stretched in all directions beyond the orchards. Mountains were far in the distance. There was no evidence of the ocean. In fact, the American did not seem to be in Hawai'i now. Nainoa formed a question in his thoughts, and as if in response to his inquiry, a word appeared in his mind—*California.*

Nainoa was shocked. There was simply too much to take in, and his mind began to withdraw. The vision was dissolving as the pain in his own leg reasserted itself as primary. Realizing that he was losing the contact, he desperately tried to calm his mind and emotions. But darkness descended on him. He tried to relax, to let his awareness travel on the roaring rush of sound. Long moments passed, and then the sound increased once again. Tentatively, he opened his eyes.

Again, astonishment swept through him. Just moments before, the time of day had seemed to be early afternoon. Now it was close to sunset. The American was still in control of the car, and "his" legs and back still ached. The road was now elevated off the ground on a huge bridge above an immense settlement. It was choked with machines in long continuous rows, with brilliant red lights in back and brighter white lights in front. Crossroads below stretched away into the distance, also filled with machines. Off to his right, enormous buildings also had lights.

The size of the settlement exceeded by magnitudes that of the ruins in the forest. In the distance a cluster of geometric buildings soared into the sky, reflecting light from their polished metal and glass surfaces, glittering with rows of lights. The amount of metal alone was unbelievable.

"So this was what their *sitis* were like," he thought. To the west, several flying machines with blinking lights were slowly descending toward some unknown place. The speed of the cars had slowed markedly, allowing him to observe the landscape. To his left, far beyond the edges of the settlement, he saw water, its surface reflecting the low sun in a blinding sheet of light. Beyond the water, dark masses of long mountainous ridges framed a bay that ran north and south. Perhaps it was part of the inland sea, he thought excitedly.

Directly ahead stood a familiar mountain beyond the bay. It was Long Mountain, Nainoa realized, the peak that marked one of the major outlets of the inland sea to the ocean. He had seen it many times during excursions on Chief Kaneohe's double-hulled canoe. There could be no mistaking its distinctive shape. His mind reeled. He was seeing the inland sea's outlet as it had been before the Fall.

Silhouetted against the setting sun to the south of the mountain, bridges crossed the bay on immense towers. Like the buildings, they were lined with lights. Across the bay was yet another *siti* with uncountable numbers of buildings soaring into the sky. He gauged the distance. Their size was beyond belief. He was overwhelmed. The entirety of what he was seeing implied vast numbers of people—an enormous population. Perhaps this was why their civilization had collapsed.

The cars around him had almost come to a complete stop. Nainoa sensed the American's growing impatience. This must be the *siti* that the navigators had assumed they would find when they made landfall. He formed a question, and a response from the American's mind appeared in his consciousness—*San Francisco.*

"So it had existed after all," Nainoa thought as his eyes drank in the forest of lighted forms. The histories had completely and utterly failed in their attempts to describe American *sitis*. But where was it in his time? Where were its remains?

Nainoa observed the surrounding land-forms in the fading light, beginning with Long Mountain. The Americans' land was much more extensive, and the bay was considerably smaller. The sea level must indeed have risen. All that he was seeing was covered by water in his era.

Nainoa's concentration wavered as his aching leg throbbed. He felt his contact with the other man slip sideways as his attention shifted. Quite suddenly, the great roads covered with machines, the *sitis*, the lights and bridges—all became transparent. The vision faded, and the lights swirled like sand settling in water and disappeared.

Nainoa was lying once again beneath the shedding-bark trees as dawn broke. The strain of his experiences burst within him—and as the first tentative bird calls drifted through the trees, he wept.

15
The Place of Refuge

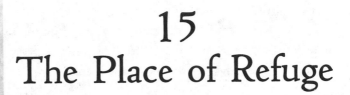

WHEN I RETURNED FROM NAINOA'S ENCOUNTER with the bull, it took me almost an entire day to recover from the emotional strain. I had experienced what happened to Nainoa as though it were happening to me. Being attacked by a longhorn, having my leg broken and my ribs cracked, then having to crawl for the rest of the day while suffering from pain and thirst completely exhausted me psychologically.

Because I could "receive" Nainoa's cognitive and emotional processes, I was able to measure my own response to this experience against his. Of the two of us, I must admit that I was probably the one less able to deal with the pain. Yet I was thrilled that Nainoa had managed to "cross-visit" with me once again and see my world through my eyes. His visit seems to have taken place during one of my all-day drives from southern California up to the San Francisco Bay Area, where he and I got stalled in traffic on the Nimitz Freeway in Oakland. I had made many such trips, and it could have happened during any of them, except for one thing. I wore a beard the entire time that I lived in California. When Nainoa looked into the rearview mirror of my car, I was beardless. I didn't know what to make of this. I had shaved off my facial foliage when I moved to Hawai'i and hadn't made any trans-California runs since. I wondered if Nainoa had visited with me in a time segment of my life that hadn't taken place yet.[1]

Nainoa's amazement at the amount of metal on the cars and buildings both intrigued and worried me. Metals were first discovered several thousand years before the present, during the Neolithic period, when low-grade ores of copper, tin, and iron existed at the earth's surface, readily and easily obtainable for the experimentation that led to the Bronze Age and later to the Iron Age. Today, however, metals must be mined from deep in the earth's crust, and high technology is needed to find and extract the ores. Metal-finding and metal-making processes are now completely dependent upon many interlinked scientific disciplines. But the machine-age technology of Western civilization was completely lost to Nainoa's age, and the Hawaiian settlers had no knowledge of where metals had come from. In Nainoa's time, iron was the rarest of metals—rarer than gold, silver, copper, or bronze, which, being more inert, could theoretically last forever. Five thousand years of tropical rain and humidity had oxidized even steel I-beams, reducing them to the brown stains that Nainoa saw at the overgrown archaeological site.

I came to an inescapable conclusion: Once our high technology is lost, it may never again be rediscovered. Without iron, machines and a machine-age technology will never again be possible. Without machines and machine-age technology, iron will never again be obtainable. Those who survive the collapse of Western civilization may live in a Neopaleolithic future forever. The "machine age" may happen but once, then never again. . . .

Nainoa's awareness of the rise in the sea level led me to investigate paleoclimatic shifts and sea level changes in the past. What I discovered led me to more conclusions with serious implications for humanity.

It is well documented that at the end of the Cretaceous era, approximately sixty-five million years ago, a major environmental shift of planetary proportions occurred. Before the shift, tropical ecosystems extended far to the north and south into what are today temperate and subarctic regions, and there were no polar ice caps at all. After the shift, the climate became temperate or cool; ice caps formed at the poles, and alpine glaciers expanded in the high mountain valleys. As the earth's water was converted into snow and ice, the sea level fell about 650 feet! Simultaneously, more than seventy percent of all living species, including the dinosaurs, became extinct.

The evidence is now compelling that the collision of an extraterrestrial object with the planet's surface partially contributed to this catastrophe. A meteorite or cometary body, estimated to have been six to ten miles in diameter, had its primary impact in the Gulf of Mexico north of the Yucatán peninsula, causing an explosion of immense proportions, while a second strike occurred in the northwestern Pacific. These blasts could have filled the earth's atmosphere with dust, creating a dense cloud cover that may have been intensified by smoke from extensive forest fires. These clouds may have cut off the sun's rays, plunging the entire planet into continuous frigid darkness for weeks or even months, causing the paleoclimatic shift and mass extinctions.

Many such climatic shifts have occurred in the earth's long history, usually accompanied by massive extinctions of flora and fauna. The sea level reached another extreme low point about eighteen thousand years ago, during the coldest part of the great ice ages of the Pleistocene, when much of the world's water was once again locked up in vast continental ice sheets and domes of great elevation. At the end of the last major glaciation—about 11,500 years ago—the climate shifted again, and the world became temperate warm. The sea level rose again in response to the melting ice and snow cover—by about three hundred feet.

The total volume of water on the earth's surface has remained relatively constant through time. Today, roughly the same volume of water exists as at the end of the Cretaceous. Alpine glaciers, polar snowfields, ice shelves, and ice caps of considerable thickness and extent could still contribute another three hundred feet to the sea level if a warming climatic shift melted them.

Several multinational groups of scientists are currently studying ice cores extracted from the Greenland ice sheet. Their initial studies reveal that the terminal Pleistocene's final cold spell, called the Younger Dryas, was accompanied by an extremely rapid shift into milder, more temperate conditions. Preliminary analysis confirmed that the ice retreated quickly to the north in less than two decades. During this time and for the next thirty years, the overall regional temperature warmed by a substantial seven degrees centigrade.

More detailed analyses of the ice cores have since demonstrated that modern conditions replaced glacial ones even faster than had previously been thought. Evidence for this was uncovered while scientists were measuring variations in the electrical conductivity of the cores—a technique that gives estimates of the relative amounts of acids and bases trapped within the ice layers along the length of the core. A drop in conductivity indicates the presence of neutralizing bases—the result of the windy, dry conditions of cold periods in the Northern Hemisphere. During the warmer, wetter periods preserved within the ice layers, the acidity and conductivity rise.

These data now reveal that the climate at the end of the last ice age shifted from glacial cold to temperate warm in less than five years and that similar rapid climatic shifts took place several times during the last forty thousand years. The implications of this are disturbing.

The three-hundred-foot rise in sea level may have happened quickly, rather than over the course of hundreds of years. If the climate warmed as rapidly as the earlier studies suggest (in fifty years), and if the ice and snow cover melted rapidly in response (in two decades), it is possible that the sea level rose at the rate of six feet per year for fifty years, or fifteen feet per year for twenty—or something somewhere in between. The newer data suggest that the climate shifted in just a few years and that the sea level rose even faster.

Computer models that are currently being used to estimate how quickly the increasing greenhouse gases will heat the planet may be inadequate because of our lack of knowledge about extremely rapid climatic fluctuations, which were all prehistoric and therefore beyond our own experience. But the geological evidence is that they occur from time to time, and scientists have given them a name—Dansgaard-Oeschger events. The scientific community has been forced to concede that a similar dramatic climatic shift could lie just around the greenhouse corner.

The subject is controversial, and I know that if ten scientists were asked to comment on it, they'd give at least eleven different opinions. Many would contend that the causes of the rapid climatic changes at the end of the Pleistocene's final cold spell are unclear. Others would say that the data are inconclusive and that we simply cannot use them to predict what will or will not happen. Still many others would maintain that what did occur provides a point-blank warning for what may very well happen in the near future. Many suspect that a global climatic warming trend has already begun.

A study by a team of ten Canadian researchers that appeared in the November 16, 1990, issue of *Science* has documented a profound disruption to the ecosystems in northwestern Ontario. This disruption has been directly attributed to a rise in the mean annual temperature of that region in the twenty-year period between the mid-1960s and the mid-1980s—an increase of three and a half degrees Fahrenheit. The warmer temperatures have made forest fires and droughts more frequent, have substantially reduced soil moisture, and have disrupted the ability of the northern boreal forests to renew themselves. This, in turn, has decreased the flow of water into the region's freshwater lakes, changing their chemistry and temperature and killing the aquatic fauna. The fisheries of that region have been profoundly damaged.

The Canadian scientists predict that if humanity continues to emit heat-trapping chemicals into the atmosphere at the current rate, a further warming of at least two degrees can be expected by the year 2025 and at least five and a half degrees by the end of the next century—a total increase of nine degrees. The average global temperature is known to be about nine degrees higher now than it was during the last ice age. Are the alpine and polar ice caps showing any response?

The scientific literature reveals that the snow cover of the Northern Hemisphere does indeed seem to be shrinking. It is presently at its lowest expanse since scientists began making satellite observations in 1972. Snow cover affects the atmospheric temperature by reflecting sunlight and enhancing cold conditions, but when the ground is clear, more solar energy is absorbed by the earth's surface, which in turn warms the air. A study conducted by a couple of climatologists named Robinson and Dewey, published in one of the October 1990 issues of *Geophysical Research Letters*, found that the snow cover in 1988 and 1989 was at its lowest level in the eighteen-year study period, eight to ten percent below the annual average within their ten-million-square-mile study area.

The high mountain glaciers in various regions of the earth have also shown signs of accelerated climatic change in recent decades. Alpine glaciers outside the polar regions are extremely sensitive to changing conditions, and many believe they may provide an early warning of abnormal climatic warming. In Africa, for example, the glaciers on Mount Kenya shrank by forty percent between 1963 and 1987, and in Peru one glacier from the Quelccaya Ice Cap has receded up the mountain at a rate of fourteen meters per year since 1984, nearly triple the rate recorded between 1963 and 1978. Evidence from the central Asian ice caps reveals a similar story. Recent oxygen isotope studies on ice cores from three sites in China and Kirghizia show an enrichment of heavy oxygen, revealing a warming trend in these regions over the last fifty years. At one site, the warming exceeds any recorded during the last twelve thousand years. Taken together, these data hint that the current global warming has now exceeded the normal range of climatic variation. They indicate that the current trend is no mere natural fluctuation that will soon reverse itself.

The alpine glacier loss may also stem from increasing water vapor in the atmosphere, a change that suggests rising ocean temperatures. A recent study confirms that the oceans are indeed changing: The May 2, 1994, issue of *Nature* contains an article on the results of taking deep-sea temperatures from a well-studied area along Columbus's original route across the Atlantic. The area is of interest because deep oceanic temperatures were taken at specific sites and depths along its length twice before, in 1957 and in 1981. A resurvey of these sites in 1992 revealed that the waters between 800 and 2,500 meters in depth have consistently warmed over the past thirty-five years and that the warming since 1957 has been remarkably uniform across the east-west extent of the northern Atlantic. The trend is broadly consistent with model predictions of climatic change due to increased carbon dioxide in the atmosphere. But what is disturbing is that the observed warming (accompanied by salinity changes) is occurring in the oceanic interior, not at the surface, as the models predicted. This suggests that the oceans are responding to the current warming trend.

How the ice sheets of Antarctica are responding is unclear. The snowfall is less there, so Antarctic ice lacks the annual layering that allows scientists to date the Greenland ice cores so precisely. But a recent reanalysis of the oxygen isotopes in air bubbles trapped in a core taken by Russian drillers twenty years ago has shown that the climatic oscillations of the Northern Hemisphere were accompanied by responses in the Southern; the oscillations were thus global rather than regional in their extent.

As if in confirmation, an iceberg the size of Rhode Island broke off from the immense Ross Ice Shelf in Antarctica in the late 1980s. Some scientists have expressed concern that the entire ice shelf may do the same. If this should happen, the world's sea level could rise immediately by six to eighteen feet.

Something is clearly going on. What if the greenhouse warming advocates are right? What if the sea level does indeed rise by three hundred feet?

The probable scenario is not difficult to imagine. As human populations continue to grow in ever-increasing numbers, the resultant greenhouse gases will continue to be produced in ever-increasing concentrations. Slowly but inexorably the atmosphere and the seas will warm until they reach a critical threshold. At some point, the snow cover and the polar ice will begin to melt, and each high tide will get perceptibly higher, while former low tide levels will never be quite reached.

An initial rise of several inches the first year will be disturbing. Real estate values of expensive coastal homes will immediately plummet, and the coastal cities will brace for the worst. A rise of several feet the next year will bring chaos as the world's low-lying coastal cities and agricultural and residential areas become flooded, forcing billions of people to relocate and causing incalculable agricultural losses. Worldwide famine will begin.

A subsequent annual sea level rise of between six and fifteen feet—and another the year after that, and the year after that—will quickly and completely inundate the world's ports, including all those involved in the onloading and offloading of oil.

And that will most likely be it. The entire world transportation system, dependent on the oil industry, will collapse, and with it, Western civilization.

All of the world's people who live in urban and suburban areas are completely dependent on the long-range transportation of everything they consume, from food and medicine to gas and electricity. They will be completely without these products. Lacking either local or long-distance transportation or communication, they will be completely isolated. Within weeks or months, vast areas of the earth's surface will be completely depopulated as their huge populations literally starve *in situ*—as the sea continues to rise, and to rise. . . .

There will be some who last for a while—small isolated groups of hardy survivalists—but they will tend to disappear after a few generations because of the lack of genetic diversity within their relatively small breeding populations and because of the possible concentration of genetic lethals. It will be a genetic bottleneck of immense proportions as the urbanites starve and the small groups of survivors succumb to the hazards of inbreeding.

And who will ultimately survive? Will it be the so-called "primitives," the few remaining traditional tribal people left out there in the bush? And if so, how many?

The impact of the West on tribal cultures is well documented. There are now few places on the globe where people are not dependent to some degree on imported goods, be they flour and sugar, or gasoline and computers. Many anthropologists who did fieldwork in the 1960s within traditional, self-sufficient communities now return to these communities to find their old informants commuting to work in factories and cities on the backs of motorcycles.

When I did fieldwork in the 1970s in southern Ethiopia, this part of the world was so remote that I frequently met African tribesmen who had never seen white people before. Yet even then the Ethiopian government was providing flour to feed formerly self-sufficient pastoralists and part-time farmers. Even then the traditional way of life was being altered as former nomads set up semipermanent settlements around the police posts and Christian missions, the new sources of their food and livelihood.

The only people who survive the collapse will be those who are still producing all of their own food and other necessities, whether by herding and horticulture, or by fishing and hunting-gathering. These people are still involved in a close and balanced relationship to their immediate environment and are relatively isolated from, and thus largely independent of, Western civilization. Only those will survive, and a few others who are able to make the shift back into their former traditional lifeway strategies—quickly.

Nainoa's world was the world as it will be five thousand years after the crash and subsequent rebalancing. I thought about him lying injured and alone and felt deep concern. He was crippled and unable to hunt or climb trees to safety. How serious were his injuries? Was he bleeding internally? Would he survive the hazards of infection? Would a large cat or a pack of wild dogs make a meal of him?

I felt a growing sense of responsibility. I was certain that it was my presence that Nainoa had detected as he descended from the mountains.

Had I distracted him, dividing his attention and allowing him to be injured? I had left him in pretty bad shape and wished fervently to help him —but how?

Something else is important here: I was familiar with the valley where Nainoa was injured. I knew with certainty where he was.

A string of memories assailed me, recollections from my adolescence. During the late 1950s, I spent several summers on a ranch in Washoe Valley, in western Nevada. My parents had just been divorced, and in the aftermath Gus and Jeanne Bundy, the ranch's owners, became my spiritual father and mother. Gus was a Renaissance man, an artist-photographer and poet who had lived in the Orient and was well-read in literature and Eastern philosophy. He was a powerful role model for fifteen-year-old me.

At my house in Kona, Gus's influence was everywhere. The walls were covered with masks, prints, paintings and photographs, and many, many books—on art and poetry, on anthropology and Eastern thought, on literature and science. Sculptures and aging cameras rested on horizontal surfaces. Bonsai and rock forms graced the garden. I had become who and what I was in response to him. Gus had initiated me.

I was certain that Nainoa was convalescing in the Washoe Valley of the future, not too far from where the Bundys' ranch once stood, below the massive scarred bulk of Slide Mountain. I was absolutely sure of it. As I thought about him, my wish to help him intensified. Although I knew where he was, I could hardly pick up the phone and dial the emergency operator in western Nevada. I knew that accomplished shamans could effect long-distance healings, however, by working through the psychic realm of second-level reality. I decided to try to use some information about *kahuna* healing techniques that I had learned from Serge King.

Kahunas, King had told me, are adept at using mental techniques to create objective events in ordinary reality. Three factors are involved: an aspect of the imagination called *laulele,* the mystical power the Hawaiians call *mana,* and the psychic connections through the *aka* field.

Laulele, as King describes it, is imagination used consciously to establish a mental pattern or strategy, combined with strong will forces to accomplish that end. *Mana* is the energy whose abundance or scarcity determines the effectiveness of all psychic practices. *Aka* is the basic stuff of which everything in the universe is formed, even thoughts and inner imagery. *Kahunas* believe that *aka* can be formed and shaped by thoughts, that it can serve as a receptacle or conductor for *mana*, and that effects are manifested through the *aka* connections established between the *kahuna* and his objective.[2]

I was unsure of what I could do to help Nainoa, but I knew where to find high concentrations of *mana*. Late one afternoon, I took my family for a picnic supper down to the Pu'uhonua, the Place of Refuge on the coast.

A light rain began to fall as we drove slowly down Middle Keei Road, savoring the landscape. In spite of the rain, sunlight was streaming in from the west, and my *ku* sparkled, happy at the interplay of light and shadow. My residence in Hawai'i had become an enchanted time that I knew would eventually end; sooner or later, I would have to leave this island and return to my life as an anthropologist. I knew with bittersweet certainty that I would miss it greatly. The island was inside me now, transforming me from within. In my own way I was becoming Hawaiian.

I turned south onto Painted Church Road and surveyed the local inhabitants' homes. Some had catchment tanks for water and some grew their own food, but would it be enough to help them during the coming crisis? The escalating value of Hawaiian real estate had driven up the price of this land, and formerly substantial agricultural plots were now being subdivided into small residential lots on which the new owners grew only ornamentals. When Captain Cook arrived in the late eighteenth century, an agricultural zone under intense cultivation circled the island, producing the food on which the population depended. Perilously little land was producing food today.

We passed the Painted Church, so named for its colorful murals within, and saw the pure white life-size statue of Jesus of Nazareth at the entrance to the driveway. Someone had hung a *lei* of flowers around the neck of the image; the vibrant colors contrasted with the cool white stone. Nainoa had called him Kahaku'keokeo, the "white master." Had this name derived from historic descriptions of his images or from the memory of his foreign origin?

We reached the road leading to the Pu'uhonua. The tourists were gone for the day, and the parking lot was empty. I took the crushed-coral service road, which led through an impressive grove of coconut palms and *noni* trees growing directly out of the coral sand and black lava substrate. It was not raining here and was considerably warmer. The light was soft and the shadows long, and we all became silent as the car passed slowly through the trees. The leafy green and gold tapestry would be a perfect habitat for the leopard man, and impulsively I sent him greetings, inviting him to come and share the company, to enjoy the locale—and to help me contact and aid Nainoa.

We slowly passed the great black wall of fitted lava blocks that delineates the sacred area, then drove along the coral track to some picnic tables near the shore under the palms. A large Hawaiian clan had spread out nearby, waiting for their fishermen to return. Some locals still adhered to their old ways and relationship with the marine environment, and to those people the ocean still provided. Our two families exchanged friendly smiles as we spread our evening's repast on a table under the trees.

The children headed for the tide pools among the lava flows at the ocean's edge, followed by Jill in a flowing muumuu, with her long black hair. I followed, systematically searching for artifacts across the sand. One of the park rangers had told me of finding a small stone adze blade here, and I had been looking for one ever since. When I neared the temple site several hundred yards to the north, I stood still and formed images of Nainoa in my mind, focusing on my deep concern for his well-being.

Jill and the children returned with a bucket filled with seawater, hermit crabs, and shrimp. The Hawaiian family nearby was cooking meat over a fire, and waves of delicious smells filled the air, accompanied by frequent outbursts of laughter at comments beyond our hearing. It was comforting to know that the Hawaiians would regain control of the world that had been wrested from them by invading foreign cultures. Traditionally, they had lived in balance and harmony with their environment. Some of their party returned from the tideline with *opihi*—limpets—and I felt reassured that many still had that knowledge, or parts of it. The Hawaiians of the future would probably be somewhat more racially mixed, and as one of the children ran over to present my daughters with some cookies, I noted that she had blue eyes. I smiled to myself at the realization that the process of transformation had already begun.

We finished our meal and put away the leftovers in the car. The sun had not yet touched the horizon, and I suggested we walk to the Pu'uhonua. At sunset, among the palms and silent stones of this place at the edge of the ocean, feelings of peace and tranquillity are very strong. The sanctuary has been a holy place for a long time and radiates *mana*.

While Jill and the children looked for shells in the tide pools, I went to the wall of the sanctuary. I asked permission, then entered the sacred area, where I listened to the wind rattle the palms. Nobody else was in the Pu'uhonua, and I absently picked up two stones and clacked them together as I walked. I had never done this before, and in retrospect I don't know why I did it that evening, but whenever I find myself in a place in nature and wish to get the spirits' attention, I do it to this day.

I walked slowly past the silent stone platforms of the *heiaus* within the empty sanctuary and focused my intentions in the fading light. I thought of Nainoa lying injured beyond the Sierra far away in the future, and I sent him good wishes through the threads of *aka* that connected us. I continued to walk, clicking the stones together regularly, calling to the spirits of the place, requesting their aid.

I walked around the large *heiau* platform called Ale'ale'a. It was built before A.D. 1550, and its surface originally supported thatched buildings and carved wooden images. The huge monolith called the Keoua stone was my goal. It lies on the rock substrate in front of the *heiau*'s north side. I approached the reclining giant and placed my hands on it to see if anything might occur, but I felt nothing. I hesitated, then asked permission and climbed up to lie on it on my back.

I concentrated on the stone and cleared my mind of all thoughts. Then I visualized the monolith filling with *mana*, becoming the fulcrum for the power of this place. I continued to build this energy, attempting to feel it, then formed a mental image of Nainoa in the riverine forest. I sent him healing energy through the *aka* field. Again, I asked the spirits of the place for assistance and concentrated fiercely on the injured man. On impulse, I tried to visualize some faceless and formless inhabitants in the huts Nainoa had seen near the lake coming to his aid. I watched and waited, but I could not induce the altered state.

Eventually, Jill and the children approached. I rose from the stone, feeling some disappointment. Perhaps because I didn't have a relationship with this stone, as I did with the *pohaku* in my rock garden, it could not help me.

We left the sanctuary and returned to our picnic site. The Hawaiians waved as we got into the car, and then we drove back through the grove of palms in the dusk. I asked the leopard man to help Nainoa—and strangely, I felt something answer immediately. It was a feeling, nothing more, but as I glanced out the window, I imagined I saw the spotted therianthrope running beside the car.

We drove back up the mountain as another gorgeous Kona sunset unfolded into night. I remembered reading somewhere that dusk was the time that the *ali'i*, the chiefly class, received *mana* directly from the *akua*. I tried to imagine myself receiving *mana*, and I did feel as if an external warmth were permeating my body.

Much later that night, after fitful, vivid, waking dreams, I suddenly felt the approach of the sensations of power. They flirted with me at first, coming and going, coming and going, until I finally relaxed my body fully and said, "Okay, let's have it."

Then they rushed into me. As I gasped for breath and as the phosphenes danced in the dark, my last thoughts were of the great stone lying before the *heiau*. I felt it again under my back as I passed outward . . . outward through the sparkling darkness . . . outward through the zone of silence —and then the shift occurred.

16
Eighth Journey
The Lady and the Tiger

W HEN I JOINED NAINOA, THE FIRST LIGHT OF
dawn was appearing in the eastern sky. He
had just awakened in his hammock tied between two trees at ground level. Ten days had elapsed
since he had established camp alongside the shallow rocky
stream. He had improved the design of his splint and
fashioned a crutch that allowed him to hobble upright,
one step at a time. The ache in his leg was bearable now,
so long as he was careful not to put any weight on it. The
pain in his ribs was still there, but it had not gotten any
worse. He had moved his camp twice and was currently
occupying a wide stony ledge over a deep pool that he was
systematically depopulating of fish with his arrows.

He had been thinking of me at the moment of my
arrival—and about his ancestors, considering as I had so
often the various causes for our connection.

In the settlements around the inland sea, kinship was
central to identity. The villagers spent a lot of time dis-

cussing the merits and shortcomings of their ancestors. To have no ancestry, no esteemed forebears, was socially unacceptable. One then had no status. In spite of this, Nainoa had strived to achieve recognition and had succeeded to a degree. Perhaps Chief Kaneohe had given him this mission as a way of allowing him to achieve even more standing. The thought of the chief's honoring him and their last meeting helped sustain him in his injury. Perhaps his deeds would help him surpass his lack of honored ancestors.

Even one's life-force was passed on from one's ancestors. Keala, the old woman in the kitchen, had told him that the life-essence, *keola'ika'ika*, was an aspect of the supernatural power dispersed throughout the universe. When this power was highly concentrated in living things, it saturated them with life-force. The old woman had described each living being's life-essence as a spark of a larger fire that could weave itself in and out of lineages through time, taking different forms, expressing itself endlessly until it had experienced all possible manifestations, from the lowly worms to the gods themselves.

Keala had said, "The life-force is a process rather than something material, and yet everything in the universe, material and nonmaterial, is ultimately an aspect of it. A pattern exists within the web of life, and the life-force can inbreed or outbreed to achieve the design. In this sense, the life-force has its own direction, its own volition. Each living thing is part of the great pattern, *ano'holo'oko'a*, and each being is thus filled with *kumu*, with purpose and direction, even if that purpose is unknown to the individual person—or worm."

Nagai had confirmed this worldview during one of their trips into the forest. "It is the nature of the life-force to diversify," he had said, taking in everything around them with a sweep of his arm. "Each thing has both an ordinary bodily aspect here in the phenomenal world and an *aumakua* aspect in the spirit world. As these spiritual aspects change and grow in response to what occurs during the endless cycles of birth, life, death, and rebirth on the physical plane, so the pattern also changes and grows. In this way, the nonordinary levels of reality are formed in response to what transpires here in ordinary reality."

Nagai had looked very seriously at Nainoa as he continued, "This is why intentions are so important. Your goals provide the destination, as well as the framework for your experiences. Those who continually manipulate others or events to acquire material wealth and power are more focused within the dark side of their nature. When such people die and exist solely as *aumakua*, their spirits are not beneficent, peaceful, or at ease. They are hungry, anxious spirits, and when they remanifest in the ordinary world, they resume the same kind of character.

"This is why evil exists in the world. It is simply part of the pattern. Everything is dual in nature, and 'not-good' is simply the other half of 'good.' Each of us contains within ourselves the capacity for both. When we come into the world, the shape of our personality reveals what is prominent in our spirit aspect. As we pass through life, the choices we make affect both ourselves and that which exists around us. These effects reflect back into the spirit world, which changes in response. Part of our task as we grow is to overcome the dark side of our natures in favor of the light. As we do this, the great pattern shifts in that direction as well.

"In this way," Nagai had concluded, "each of us travels through time in many lives, until we achieve our destiny within the great pattern. When we have become fully formed and fully aware, we humans will become something else. This is our destiny, and each of us must achieve this in our own individual way. This is our true work, our real reason for being."

Nainoa had often wondered whether there was a creator god in the spirit world whose will directed the process. Nagai had told him that no one knew for certain if such a creator existed, and that in his opinion no one ever would because Io, the great void from which all expressed forms issued, was too remote for human minds to understand. Perhaps the pattern itself was the creator, since each thing was an aspect of it.

Nainoa's thoughts turned to the American. The concept of *aumakua* suggested that both he and the American could be manifestations of the same spiritual source—that the American might be himself living a former life in a former place in time. Perhaps this was what it meant to be part of a lineage.

Nainoa's thoughts now returned to everyday concerns. His hunting had not been very successful. He had picked a good location from which to ambush game, but potential prey were keeping their distance. Perhaps the huts he had seen in his vision and the bull's hostility indicated that these animals had been hunted by humans.

Suddenly, the birds around him became unnaturally quiet. Alarmed, he looked around and froze as he saw the tiger at the same moment it saw him. It was across the pool, a large striped cat of the most feared kind. Surprised in the act of drinking, it was upwind and had probably been unaware of Nainoa until his slight movement had revealed his presence. He felt a surge of fear as he looked deep into its amber eyes. Its belly was distended, and there was blood on its face and chest. It had fed recently.

His spear, knife, and bow were all within reach. He would have to use the spear. He would have no chance to string and use the bow when the tiger decided to come for him.

As the huge carnivore stared at Nainoa impassively, the blankness of its gaze did not reassure him. He felt the tension generated by the great cat's presence, yet despite his fear he marveled at its terrible beauty.

Nainoa slowly shifted and prepared to reach for his spear as the tiger watched him with its vacant, detached expression. It shifted its own position slightly, and its muscles began to flow under the striped skin, the great claws emerging from their sheaths to grip the ledge. Nainoa understood with great clarity what it would do.

Very slowly, he reached for the leather-wrapped shaft of his spear. If the tiger rushed him, he would have only an instant to shift his body out of the hammock, grasp the spear, and plant its butt securely against the tree. His only chance would be to let the tiger's own weight impale itself on his spear —and there would be only one opportunity to place the point into the correct spot.

But what if it did not charge? What if it simply walked up to him? He eased his other hand onto the spear and waited.

The tiger remained still and continued to watch him. Nainoa gazed at a spot several yards to the tiger's left, so that he could observe it with his peripheral vision without staring directly at it. Perhaps it would go away. An idea took shape.

Nainoa cleared his mind and formed a single intention: a strong directive for the tiger to leave him. He appealed directly to his personal *aumakua* self, requesting that it make contact with the *aumakua* of the tiger, to encourage it to go. As he held these thoughts strongly focused within his mind, he imagined himself filling with power and felt the emotional charge growing within. Gooseflesh formed on his arms and legs as the *mana* started to flow. He continued to direct his intention upon the tiger, and out of the corner of his eye he saw its claws retract.

The tiger's gaze shifted downstream in a flicker of movement that almost made Nainoa bolt from the hammock—he arrested the impulse just in time. Its huge face showed no expression, but its ears moved slightly, as if it were listening to something beyond his range of hearing. As its attention moved from Nainoa, he felt a wave of release.

The sun's first rays suddenly fell over them, dividing the world into sectors of light and shadow, and in that instant, as if a spell had been broken, the tiger disappeared.

Nainoa blinked, uncertain. He stared at the forest's edge across the stream but saw no movement. The tiger had vanished into the pattern of light and shadow under the trees beyond the water's edge. Except for the water drops on the stone, it might not have really been there at all. Nainoa knew that something had alerted the big cat, and he fervently hoped it was not another tiger. Easing himself out of the hammock, he used his crutch to get into a sitting position on a large stone, his back against a tree. He strung his bow and extracted four of his largest copper-tipped arrows from the quiver.

His feelings of vulnerability and dread grew by the moment. The tiger, knowing of his presence, could return whenever it chose, even in the dead of night, to make a meal of him. He would have to move his camp, the sooner the better. Nainoa considered the ordeal that this would entail with his crippled leg, and he wondered which way to go—to the lake, or back into the forest?

The forest beckoned. He needed to find a tree to climb, even in his injured state. Slowly and carefully, he arranged his belongings, watching the trees around him and keeping the spear in one hand at all times.

He was seated on the stone again and had just finished adjusting the strap of his splinted leg when he detected movement downstream. Motionless, he gripped the spear and prepared for the tiger's charge. Instead, two large dogs ambled slowly out of the shadows of the forest onto the raised levee above the stream. They were within bowshot. Fearing they belonged to a pack, Nainoa decided to dispatch both before they alerted the rest to his presence. Abruptly they froze, stiff-legged, staring intently upstream, sniffing the air. Had they smelled him or the tiger? As he notched an arrow, they saw him, and their hair slowly stood up. It was not a promising situation.

He drew the bow and was about to let the first arrow fly, when a second movement caught his attention. There behind the dogs, a pale human face appeared among the leaves, regarding him with a flat, penetrating stare. Nainoa's resolve faltered, so unexpected was the encounter. As two more dogs appeared in the shadows, however, he recovered quickly and estimated the odds. Then he saw the eyes flicker over his form and suddenly perceived himself as this person must see him—dirty and unkempt, his clothing stained and travel-worn, his leg in a splint. He probably looked rather desperate, arrested in the act of drawing an arrow. Nainoa came to a decision. It was definitely time for diplomacy.

He slowly divested himself of his weapons, placing the bow and the spear within reach of the stone on which he sat. At that moment the dogs began their rush, and he realized he had made an error in judgment—a serious one.

As he snatched up the spear, the person softly hissed, and the dogs stopped, uncertain. Another hiss followed, and with some reluctance the dogs sat down. As their pale eyes regarded him balefully, he reflected that he had never seen dogs quite like these before. Like his former canine companions in the canyon, they had long legs and faces and short gray and black fur on their lean frames. But unlike those guides, these had tails that were curled up in back, and they looked considerably bulkier. They panted in the warmth of the day.

His attention returned to the face in the leaves. The eyes were long, gray verging on blue, the cheeks broad, and the chin small, giving the face a graceful oval shape with a strong nose and mouth. He looked back to the eyes that regarded him evenly, giving nothing away. He came to another decision.

Slowly, carefully, using his crutch for support, he stood up. The eyes widened, and a low growl from one of the dogs was abruptly truncated by another soft hiss. Nainoa placed his hands together before his chest and gave a short, graceful bow. Another growl was followed by another hiss. He straightened up and assumed what he hoped was a benign expression and waited for whatever might happen next.

Long moments passed, and then the person moved, coming forward out of the cover of the trees. Nainoa drew in his breath. Standing before him was a tall angular woman, as wild-looking and lean as her canine companions. Nainoa studied her with growing amazement, as she continued to watch him. Her skin was paler than his own. The brevity of her clothing revealed arms and legs that were long and well-muscled. She was wearing a strange combination of apron and skirt made of leather. The skirt hung down in back almost to her knees, and the V-shaped apron hung down in front, leaving her legs bare to her waist on the sides. Skirt and apron alike were edged with many rows of ornamental beads—it was probably their weight that kept the garment from blowing up in the wind. Long strings of polished beads were draped around her waist, made of wood, ivory, bone, and metal. On her wide feet were leather sandals of an odd design whose straps were decorated with more beads.

She was naked above the waist; her stomach was flat and her small high breasts had dark prominent nipples. Around her neck hung more strings of polished beads, with many bright metal disks he recognized as artifacts from the past called *moni* by the Hawaiians. From her necklaces hung several flat tongues of bone or ivory incised with designs. Graduated metal rings pierced each of her ears, one behind the other from the lobe to about halfway up the rims on both sides, and she wore about ten thin metal bracelets on each wrist. In addition, several metal rings adorned her fingers, some of which had blue stones or glass set into them. In one hand she held a long stick with a bend in it.

Her thick black hair was gathered into a plume that cascaded from the top of her head to halfway down her back, held in place with what appeared to be a metal clasp and a thick peg of ivory. Slung under one arm was a large leather bag that hung to her hip. Under her other arm hung an antler-handled knife in a leather sheath. She had strapped a conical woven basket, open at the top, across her back. In it was another container of some sort and a bundle of sticks.

Nainoa suddenly realized that he was gaping at her and attempted to regain a semblance of dignity. He glanced at her dogs, all of whose tongues were lolling out as they watched him. They and the woman looked as if they could run long distances without tiring on those long legs. The five of them made an indomitable group.

It was hard to guess her age. She was not a young girl, nor was she an old woman. The lips of her wide mouth were slightly stained, perhaps from eating wild fruit. Her breasts did not betray whether she had borne children. A sudden hollowness in his stomach told him that he was attracted to her. Within himself, he retreated from these feelings, smiling at her instead, opening his hands in a gesture of welcome.

She did not move or return the smile but continued to observe him without expression, as the tiger had. Was she a spirit? With a slow gesture, he pointed to himself and said his name. She said nothing. Her composure showed an inner balance and strength. Perhaps she was of chiefly rank among her people. She obviously felt very much in charge of the situation. If she chose to set her dogs on him, they could probably kill him with ease. Her long leanness, pale skin, and black hair reminded him of someone, but who? He searched his mind and realized that she looked like the American's woman.

He tried again to communicate, raising his open hand to his chest and saying his name. Again, she gave no response but seemed to come to a decision. Abruptly, soundlessly, she turned and disappeared into the trees. After a moment's hesitation the dogs followed.

He called after her a little desperately, but she did not reappear. He sat down on the stone, excited but saddened at her departure, questions racing through his mind. Perhaps she was part of the group who had built the huts. Had he found the lost descendants of the Americans? Would she return with help? She had already helped him by scaring away the tiger. That made him feel a little easier, and he hoped she would return to her settlement and bring help. But what if her people were warriors and treated him as a captive? He had no desire to become a slave in the commoner class once again. He decided he had better make a strong first appearance.

He hobbled down to the pool, stripped off his *malo* and washed it, then laid it out on the rock ledge to dry in the sun. He washed himself and his hair too, combing, rebraiding, and tying it back with a length of dyed cotton cord. When the *malo* was dry, he tucked the end of it under his chin and retied it carefully, then arranged his belongings. What if the woman did not return? Should he still move camp, as he had planned? The tiger was still a danger. Should he wait for the woman to reappear?

Something stirred in his memory. It was a story, a riddle from antiquity, of a lady and a tiger. They were behind two closed doors, and the hero of the story had to choose which to open. Behind one was life, behind the other, death.

"And how am I to choose?" he thought.

Near midday, a flock of small birds rose suddenly out of the foliage upstream and winged off toward the south. Nainoa clearly had company—but which was it, the lady or the tiger?

He arranged his cloak around his shoulders and sat, leaning on his spear, propping his leg so that he might rise gracefully to greet whoever or

whatever might come. A small supply of fish, which he had dried slowly over the fire during the last few days, was wrapped in leafy bundles. He was ready to travel.

To his relief, the dogs appeared, panting in the heat. There were more of them this time, and they were followed by the woman, who was carrying several long poles bound together in a heavy bundle with leather straps. She deposited the poles at her feet and observed him once again from a safe distance.

Deciding on his preplanned course of action, Nainoa rose gracefully to his feet, using his spear to assist, and gave a short bow before making a brief speech of welcome. He spoke in Old English:

"Dear lady, and hopefully my benefactress, I have come through the forest and across the mountains from the great ocean to the west seeking information about the fate of the American people and their civilization. Perhaps you have the knowledge I seek?"

Nainoa paused. Her face did not change expression, nor did she reply. Long moments passed. He decided to try again with a simpler introduction. He placed his hand on his chest and said his name once more. She remained silent. Nainoa was about to try again when someone gave a discreet cough immediately behind him and to his right.

His head snapped around. Just out of arm's reach, an older man with pale skin like the woman's was squatting in a relaxed pose at the base of a tree. Nainoa realized that his startled response had shattered his dignified demeanor. The older man had noticed this too, and humor flickered briefly across his face. Nainoa felt chagrined that he had been flanked so easily. These people must be good hunters.

Recovering his poise, he propped himself between his spear and his crutch to study the man. He was in early old age, his thick gray hair braided into plaits that hung to his waist. His lean, well-muscled frame had wide, powerful shoulders, his cheekbones were high, his nose strong, and his face heavily lined. It was the face of someone who had spent his life outdoors, and he reminded Nainoa of Nagai.

The man had a sparse white beard around his mouth and chin, and like the woman he was virtually naked except for a short leather *malo* wrapped around his hips. Heavy bracelets of metal encircled his wrists, and braided leather thongs, intertwined with the fur of some animal, were wrapped around his muscular upper arms above the elbows and around his legs just below the knees. Three large feathers were fastened in his hair, and the skin of his upper arms bore several rows of curious chevron-shaped tattoos or scars. Among the beads on his necklace hung the canine teeth of a tiger and many tongues of bone or ivory, also incised with designs.

A short, unstrung, oddly designed bow and a quiver of arrows hung across his back. He held a long knobbed cudgel loosely in one hand; in the other, a flat stick with a noselike projection on the end of it and two short spears with crude metal points. He too had a knife under one arm, and a long water bottle with grasses woven around it like a basket was slung under the other.

The older man smiled up at Nainoa, revealing a mouthful of big white teeth. With exaggerated pantomime, he stretched his arms and back, cracking his joints, and slowly stood up. Nainoa was at least a foot and a half taller than the older man. Was he a commoner within his society?

Nainoa returned the smile, placed his hand on his chest, and again uttered his own name several times. Then he directed what he hoped was a look of inquiry at the other. The older man's look became formal, and placing his broad hand on his own chest under the tiger teeth, he said a single word:

"Gwil-yom."

Nainoa smiled and nodded, repeating the word. With gestures and strong looks of inquiry he tried to ask if that was in fact his name. The man repeated it in turn several times, pointing to himself and smiling. It sounded slightly different each time, like *Gwil-yem* or *Kweel-yom* or *Gwee-yom*, but it was very similar to William, an old American name recorded in the histories. Nainoa said the name William with another exaggerated look of inquiry. The older man smiled broadly in response and repeated the word, nodding vigorously.

Nainoa glanced at the woman but decided it might be impolite to ask her name. In his own society, one did not point at a woman who might be another man's wife and ask her name, so he turned and pointed to the mountains and repeated the speech he had given to the woman. William watched him politely and smiled when he'd finished, looked thoughtful, then turned. Compressing his lips together, he extended his mouth slightly, using it to point to the northeast in a spare but effective gesture. He then uttered what could have been a short formal speech of reply. Nainoa did not understand a single word, but it was the first human voice besides his own that he had heard since leaving the settlement, and he felt so grateful that he beamed in response, giving an exaggerated shrug to indicate his inability to understand. William smiled and nodded as if he too understood.

Nainoa reflected with considerable emotion that he was developing a relationship with descendants of Americans and that it seemed to be going well. Overwhelmed, he sat down heavily.

William turned slightly and said something to the woman. His tone conveyed respect and request rather than authority and command. She stooped gracefully, picked up the bundle of long poles, and approached. The dogs came as well, and with caution they sniffed him and his belongings, lingering attentively around his bundles of dried fish. Obviously trained, they did not urinate against anything, nor did they take any of the fish. At a sharp hiss from the woman, they grew still.

Working together, William and the woman unwrapped the leather strapping from around the poles, and soon they had harnessed the dogs together, each slightly behind the one in front. They fastened the poles into the harness with their distal ends resting on the ground and wove wide leather straps through the whole thing, creating a crude sling seat.

William then approached Nainoa, looked meaningfully at his splinted leg, and gestured that he should sit on the poles. Without waiting for his assent, the older man put a broad shoulder under his arm and helped him hobble over to where the dogs waited. Before he sat, Nainoa added his woven hammock to the seat, making it more comfortable.

At this point, William turned and said something to the woman, who was adjusting the harness on the dogs. Something approaching an expression crossed her face for the first time. She straightened and looked at Nainoa with a blatantly appraising look. William laughed and then began to gather Nainoa's belongings, some of which he slung around his own shoulders.

William studied Nainoa's spear with great interest, lingering over the iron point before handing it to him. Nainoa's bow was of equal interest. He drew an arrow from Nainoa's quiver and appraised its straightness and design, his long eyes widening as he studied the copper point. Replacing it, he handed both bow and quiver to Nainoa with a smile.

Last, he helped Nainoa get more comfortable on the poles and adjusted the woven straps so that his injured leg was supported. Judging from the careful attention being paid to his well-being, Nainoa was definitely not being treated as a captive.

The dogs waited patiently, bearing his weight. Then, at a soft hiss from the woman, they began to walk, pulling the pole-drag behind them. In this way they drew Nainoa through the woods and out onto the open grassland to the north.

William walked ahead through the shimmering heat of the early afternoon, choosing the easiest way through the tussocks. The poles dragged on the ground and the dogs farted continuously, but for Nainoa it was better than trying to walk. He was relatively comfortable, although the jolting pained his ribs and leg. The strength of the dogs was impressive, he reflected, but travel would still have been much easier in a cart. Did these people have knowledge of the wheel? From time to time his benefactors lifted the ends of the poles to clear difficult obstacles or holes, and Nainoa was struck by their caring attitude toward him.

The woman moved with considerable grace on her long legs, and when she stooped to help William lift the poles, her muscles rippled under her pale skin. A series of small tattoos, a curved line of dots, stretched from one cheekbone to the other across the bridge of her nose. As she walked, her leather skirt softly rustled and her metal ornaments jingled dully. She had a warm, spicy smell—of woodsmoke, leather, and something else. As she stooped to lift one of the poles, her breasts swayed, and sweat sparkled in the dark hair in her armpits.

Sexual feelings again stirred within him. William had not missed Nainoa's observations of the woman, and he said something to her with a sudden laugh. Then, the older man turned to him. Pointing at the woman with his lips, he offered what Nainoa took to be her name:

"Kenojelak."

Nainoa looked at her and repeated the word, syllable by syllable—"Ken-o-je-lak." She nodded solemnly in return. William grinned again and said something to her, followed by his strange, soft laugh—"Heeeeeee." He seemed to be teasing her. She looked away, but her mouth twitched with the hint of a smile.

They proceeded north across the grassland toward the base of the scarred mountain. William and Kenojelak scanned the land as they walked. Occasionally, they stopped to allow the dogs to rest, and William helped Nainoa off the pole-drag.

They made one such stop on a high place, from which Nainoa looked out at the lake shimmering in the light. Its edge was partially obscured by fringing forest. The dry gray and yellow grassland encircled it, extending to the foot of the wooded hills beyond. In the far distance a small herd of elephants emerged from the trees to head toward the lake. Nainoa pointed in their direction and uttered the Hawaiian word for them—*"Elepane."*

William looked at him quizzically. An idea formed. . . . Nainoa pointed at them again and said their name in Old English—*"Elephant."* William smiled, held his arm up to his nose in imitation, and said, *"Gin-gagodalek."* As Nainoa strained to assimilate the long word, he repeated it more slowly: *"Gin-ga-go-da-lek."*

Nainoa still looked puzzled. William laughed and broke the word into two. He offered the word *gingak* or *gingag* and pointed to his own nose. Then he used a word that sounded like *dagiok* or *dakiog* and spread his hands apart to indicate length. Then he put the two together in a slightly altered form —*gingagodalek*—and pointed at the elephants with his lips. Nainoa took the word to mean "long-noses," an appropriate term.

William then gestured at the elephants, looked pointedly at Nainoa's spear, and said something to Kenojelak that included the word *gingagodalek.* Kenojelak said nothing but glanced at him again. William laughed his strange, high laugh: "Heeeeeee."

Nainoa had never before encountered anyone who spoke a foreign language. He offered a silent prayer of gratitude to his adoptive father who had encouraged him to study both Old English and Classic Hawaiian. Through his studies he had learned that these languages had changed through time, slowly transforming into the language that was now spoken in the settlements.

Yet these two people had said nothing that he could understand. If they were in fact descended from the ancestral Americans, there should be some evidence of it in their language. How many Old English words did their vocabulary contain?

Nainoa pointed to his own nose and said, "Nose." William looked interested but betrayed no recognition. Nainoa repeated the gesture and said, *"Gingak."* William nodded vigorously, and Nainoa was rewarded by seeing Kenojelak smile for the first time. Tipping her head back slightly, her blue-gray eyes flashed, and her wide mouth was filled with big white teeth. He noted a faint resemblance between her and William. Perhaps she was his daughter.

Late in the afternoon they approached the edge of the woodlands below the high, scarred mountain. As the land rose gently, rocks outcropped among the trees. The stream, bracketed by its fringing forest, emerged from its ravine out onto the grassland to the south.

With a swift, sudden movement, Kenojelak snatched a long stick from her basket and braced its curved end against something in the tall grass beyond his sight. A high-pitched whirring sound filled the air. With the same easy flow of movement, she extracted a knobbed cudgel from the basket with her other hand and delivered a single short chopping blow, whereupon the sound stopped.

Kenojelak grinned at William and used the hooked stick to lift a long thick snake from the grass. He took it from her and weighed it appraisingly, making what sounded like appreciative comments. Drawing his knife, he cut the snake's head off, gutted it, then carefully dug a small hole with his stick, placing the snake's entrails within. The short blade of his knife was made of black flaked stone, not metal. William tied the snake's head to a nearby bush well off the ground, then uttered what was perhaps a short prayer and filled in the hole.

Nainoa pointed to the thick reptile's body, and William brought it over. The heavy scales of the skin displayed broad geometric patterns, and the tail ended in a series of bizarre segments. It was what the hunters of his settlement called *kanaheka'nakeke*, the rattle serpent. They were very poisonous, and this one was distinctly different from those found in the great forest. William, noticing his interest in it, said a single word, *"Serpon."*

Nainoa started, since the word was very close to the Old English *serpent.* Perhaps these people were Americans after all. Nainoa pronounced the word *serpent* several times for William, who nodded vigorously and replied, *"Serpon, serpon."* Smiling broadly, the older man shook its tail, causing it to give off its distinctive rattling sound, and said, *"Serpontasonnet."* Then, seeing Nainoa's look of inquiry, he repeated it more slowly. Nainoa repeated the term several times until William indicated he had it right.

They put the snake into Kenojelak's basket and continued north along the woods' edge until plumes of smoke were visible, rising from the trees farther up. The ground now became too broken for the easy passage of the pole-drag. Kenojelak stopped the dogs, and William helped him off to sit on a stone. The older man gave a shrill whistle, which was answered immediately by another coming from the general direction of the smoke, and soon three young men emerged from the cover of the trees. Two of them closely resembled William. The third's hair was much lighter, almost the color of dry grass. Like William, they were short and minimally clad. They seemed courteous and smiled broadly at him as they looked him over with barely concealed curiosity.

William spoke to them, presumably relating the story of Nainoa's discovery. The four men examined his splinted leg with obvious concern, and with gesture and pantomime Nainoa attempted to convey how the accident had occurred. He used the Hawaiian term *pipi kane* but got no reaction and instead offered the Old English word *bull.* He still got no reaction. Using his fingers to simulate horns, he imitated the bellow of the bull and the mooing of the cows.

This time there was instant response, and all four men said the word *toktuvak* with excitement. When Nainoa looked puzzled, William repeated the word and then offered two more terms—*lutoro* and *lavash.*

There followed a lengthy discussion of which Nainoa understood not a word. Kenojelak finally interrupted their deliberations with a gesture of impatience. They looked at her with surprise and then at him—and then went into action, unharnessing the dogs, who departed toward the distant stream to drink. The men used the poles to carry him over the rougher, rising ground, while William and Kenojelak carried his belongings.

In this way Nainoa was brought at last to their camp among the trees at the foot of the mountain. He looked around and wondered if these people could really be descended from the once-great Americans.

The camp was situated on a high place that overlooked the valley to the east. Spread out through the trees were a series of low brushy mounds with leather hides thrown over them, among which about a dozen people were standing stock-still watching their approach. A considerable number of dogs rushed toward them and milled excitedly around the men carrying him.

The brushy mounds were huts constructed of saplings and branches, whose butt ends rested on the ground and whose terminals were bent in toward the center. Interwoven through this framework were more branches and vines, with hides roofing the top. Each hut had a low arched doorway but no windows. They were without doubt the crudest dwellings Nainoa had ever seen.

Meat was drying on racks over low fires. Several women were scraping fat from the inside of a large hide staked out on the ground. An old woman and a young girl detached themselves from this group and walked toward them. The woman's white hair was in long braids that framed a heavily lined face. She was clothed very much like Kenojelak, except that she had many more strings of beads around her neck and waist. Her breasts hung like flat leather slabs on her bony chest, yet despite her age she looked very strong. The young girl was similarly clothed, but her hair was arranged in a long unbraided plume like Kenojelak's, and her breasts were just beginning to show. Kenojelak handed the girl the burdens she was carrying without a word.

All eyes were on Nainoa as he was helped to sit on a broad, flat rock next to a large fire-pit ringed with stones. Nearby was a massive bulbous-trunked tree of the kind he had seen in his vision, its trunk studded with thorns and its stubby leafless limbs loaded with robust green seedpods. The people were absolutely silent, and Nainoa felt momentarily uncertain. At that moment a fight broke out among the dogs. Several well-aimed kicks from those standing nearest terminated the brawl and order was restored. Then the entire group gathered around the newcomer to gaze at him in silence. Unused to company after being so long alone in the forest, Nainoa felt uneasy under this intense scrutiny.

As a group, they had pale skin and "long eyes." Most had dark hair and brown eyes, but several had lighter hair or blue eyes. One woman had hair the color of fire. All were considerably shorter than he; Kenojelak appeared to be the tallest person among them. Were they all commoners—a hunting party perhaps? But where were their nobility? He saw none among them. Where were their chiefs?

The older woman spoke to William. The older man glanced at Nainoa and replied in his soft voice at some length. His speech, liberally inter-spersed with gestures, gradually rose in volume so that all present could hear. Nainoa heard the word *toktuvak* and assumed his accident was being recounted. William's gesticulations portrayed the dogs pulling Nainoa across the grassland, the elephants, and Kenojelak killing the snake. William concluded by saying something that caused his face to crack open with delight, and all listening responded in kind with that odd soft laugh—"Heeeeeee."

The tension was broken; the release was palpable. The entire group looked at him with barely repressed amusement, then glanced over at Kenojelak. William made another comment, to which all responded again with laughter.

Nainoa smiled, and all who met his glance smiled in response. He felt encouraged. He glanced at Kenojelak, who had skinned the snake with a single deft pull and was cutting it into sections. Her knife was of the same design as William's: a short, flat blade of black volcanic glass, pressure-flaked to form a sharp edge and hafted in a handle made of antler. As she squatted, knife in hand, Nainoa was again struck by her wild appearance, so different from a Hawaiian woman's.

The crowd did not miss his brief contemplation of her, and another comment brought another laugh. He peered around slowly and counted twenty-seven people in all, of whom twelve were males. William and the old woman appeared to be the eldest. There were nine children of varying ages; the rest were adults or adolescents. Nainoa came to a decision, and grasping his crutch, he stood up.

An audible murmur broke the group's silence, and those nearest him withdrew slightly, their faces expressing astonishment at his height. He towered over them. Even Kenojelak stopped what she was doing and stared.

Perhaps these people were fugitives, he thought, who had left their settlement to escape retribution for some broken *kapu* and were living in the wild. Then, as he surveyed their faces, he wondered if they had a chiefly class at all.

It seemed a good time for diplomacy, and so he hobbled over to his belongings. He extracted the bundles of dried fish from his net bags and presented them to William, who received the modest gift of food with dignified formality. Nainoa then pointed to the fish and named it, using the general Hawaiian term *ia*. No response. He offered the word *fish* in Old English, adding gestures to mimic its swimming. He had everyone's full attention.

He repeated the word *fish* several times, intensifying his pantomime of a fish swimming. William smiled and said something to the assembled people. Then, repeating Nainoa's swimming gestures, he said the word *puason* or *bwason*, much to everyone's delight. William then pointed at the fish in his hands and gave a second term, *opulayak*, perhaps the name for the specific kind of fish in question.

Nainoa repeated these words several times and then with the end of his crutch drew a crude fish in the earth at his feet. William and his people appeared absolutely delighted with this, and a lengthy dialogue ensued. William pointed to Nainoa's basic fish symbol and called it *puason*. Then he squatted and used his finger to modify the drawing in subtle ways to become the species of fish Nainoa had dispatched in the stream. Standing up, he proclaimed it *opulayak*.

Everyone crowded around to see it, and in the ensuing excitement the dogs obliterated the drawing. Nainoa smiled at William, pointed to the dried fish in his hands, and said, "*Opulayak.*" William smiled and nodded, then qualified it by knocking on the dried fish with his knuckle and offering a new word—*zek* or *sek*. He repeated it several times, then said another word, *bitzek* or *pitsek*.

Nainoa assumed this implied dry fish and said, "*Zek,*" knocking on the hard slab of fish with his own knuckle. Everyone beamed at him good-naturedly. It was a good beginning. Nainoa then pointed to the fish and pantomimed the act of eating and gave the Hawaiian word *ai*. Then he repeated the gestures and used the Old English term *food*.

William caught on immediately and said, "*Ailemon.*" Then he spoke to the old woman, who shook her head slightly, pointed to her own mouth, and said the word *naki*. William used a sparse gesture that captured the act and said another, longer word, *nagigzak* or *nakikzak*.

The old woman curtly terminated the conversation, whereupon the group began to disperse, reapplying themselves to whatever they had been doing when he arrived. Another series of sharp words sent the younger women scurrying, and very shortly they began to prepare the evening meal. Perhaps his words about eating had been taken as a request.

Nainoa looked over at Kenojelak, pointed at the cut-up snake, and used what he thought was the term for food, *naki*. She rewarded him with another smile. Then, using gestures and words, he repeated the terms for *snake, fish, food,* and *elephants,* much to the delight of all within earshot.

Nainoa then named a variety of things that he pointed at: his net bags, his spear, his bow, his arrows, and so forth. For each item, William gave the equivalent name in his own language. Nainoa heard no English words among them. He learned that the older woman's name was Kovak and that the young girl's name was Karul. In this way, he began to learn their language.

On that first evening, sitting around the communal fire, Nainoa learned much about these people. They cooked, for example, using a method he had never before seen.

A row of wide, shallow holes in the ground circled the large fire-pit. The women fitted greased leather hides into the holes, tamping them down with a stone to fit the contour. They held their edges in place with a ring of stones and filled them with water from tightly woven fiber containers. Using bent sticks, they took heated stones from the fire-pit and dropped them hissing and popping into the water, which was rapidly brought to a boil as more stones were added. The women then placed the fractured long bones, backbone, and tail vertebrae of a recently killed animal into the water, to boil them for their fat. Heated stones were continually added to keep the "soup" cooking, and the cool ones were extracted. After a time, pieces of meat sliced from the supply hanging on the racks were added to the boiling stock. The rattle serpent went in last.

After a while the women fished out the chunks of meat and skewered them on palm-leaf ribs, which had been inserted vertically into the ground downwind of the fire. In this way the meat was first boiled and then slowly smoked. Their word for meat cooked in this fashion was *bonazi* or *ponasi.* After they took the meat out of the stew, they removed the bones and added some vegetable foods—some small wild squashes, wild onions, and mushrooms.

Nainoa noted that the women also added salt and wondered where they

got it. He called William's attention to it and named it, using the Hawaiian word *pa'akai*, to which William responded with his own word *dareok* or *tariog*. Then, watching the older man carefully, Nainoa gave the Old English term *salt*. William brightened and nodded vigorously, offering the word *sel*, repeating it several times. The match was close, and Nainoa counted it as a victory. He had two words now, *serpon* and *sel*, that were possibly connected to Old English.

Only women were involved in preparing the food. When the meal was ready, the people brought wooden food bowls out from the huts. Nainoa extracted his own food bowl from one of his net bags, which caused some stir as its simple lines and symmetry of craftsmanship were openly admired. Their bowls were works of comparable beauty. Many were inlaid with carved pieces of ivory or bone depicting abstract animal forms.

The entire community ate together. Perhaps communal dining was an old American custom. Nainoa remembered an ancient story from the histories about a Hawaiian chiefess who had lived during the period of contact and who had been influenced by the Americans to eat at the same table with her son. According to the legend, this act had produced dire consequences for the Hawaiian people, who had nearly been exterminated by the spirits in retribution for the broken *kapu*. Nobody knew for certain if this myth was based on a true story, but it was thought to be the source of the custom of men and women eating separately.

His hosts talked animatedly throughout the meal, tossing pieces of conversation around in the same manner that they tossed food scraps to their dogs, which drooled with silent intensity around the edges of the firelight. Nainoa caught William's attention, pointed to the dogs, and said the Old English word *dog*. William responded with the word *kinmet* or *ginmek* and pantomimed a dog scratching itself with its back leg, to the vast amusement of those assembled.

As the meal ended, William said something to Kenojelak, who turned and looked at Nainoa for several heartbeats before responding. Nainoa again found himself the center of the silent collective attention of the entire group—and again it was slightly unsettling. He felt that something was expected of him, but he had no idea what, so he got to his feet and gave a repeat version of his earlier speech to Kenojelak—a much longer one, liberally interspersed with gestures, pantomime, and words in Old English.

All, including the assembled pack of dogs, were attentive throughout his performance. When he stopped talking, they were silent for a while as if appraising what he had just said. Then, a long discussion among them ensued, confirming his suspicion that they had understood nothing of what he said. But judging from the gestures that they used, it was clear that they had understood at least one thing—that he had come from the mountains to the west.

William talked for some time while those assembled listened, men and women alike contributing occasional monosyllabic sounds. Then the older woman spoke at some length, gesturing to the west and to the north and up to the sky, and again all listened respectfully. Then Kenojelak stood and spoke in her soft dry voice. As he sat listening carefully, Nainoa was again aware of how tall she was compared with the others. The young woman spoke in a dignified and slightly reserved manner with graceful gestures. She did not express herself like a commoner.

She pointed to the west and then to the south, using her lips and head to indicate direction, and spoke again at some length. When she was finished, she paused—and then looked at Nainoa and said something to the assembled group that caused her to burst out laughing.

The entire gathering joined her laughter. Nainoa felt slightly annoyed, not having understood the joke but guessing that he was the butt of it. Then Kenojelak said something else, and again all erupted into joyous gaiety. She smiled at him. Her merriment was infectious, and his irritation dissolved as he found himself grinning back. This brought more sustained laughter from the group, and suddenly he felt very good indeed.

The old woman Kovak then volunteered something, and they all laughed again. The resemblance between William and Kenojelak added strength to his idea that she was his daughter, not his wife. This idea was reinforced considerably when Kenojelak's laughter subsided, and again she looked at him appraisingly.

He glanced at William and raised his eyebrows inquisitively. William laughed and said something to Kenojelak, who responded by throwing a stone at his side. William collapsed in midlaugh, clutching his side in mock agony, then howled with mirth in the midst of his farce.

In this way the evening progressed in great good humor. The younger girls and boys giggled but said nothing. The infants slept in their mothers' arms. The dogs waited at the edge of the firelight, watching the humans, waiting for more handouts. Eventually the fire was allowed to die down, and William indicated by gesture and word that Nainoa was to sleep in one of the huts. He took Nainoa's possessions and placed them within, leaning his spear against the hut's wall outside. Then he returned to help him hobble over.

On the way the two men paused to relieve themselves just outside the firelight. As he stood urinating in the company of this strange man, he felt a growing camaraderie between them. In the darkness beyond the firelight, he saw something that caught his interest. Indicating to William that he wished to look at it, he hobbled over and found a section of stonework protruding from the ground.

Parts of two walls, the remains of a small fireplace, and part of a chimney were all that were left. Rounded river cobbles had been used, bonded together with a hard mortar that was lighter in color than the stones. He pointed to the stonework and made a gesture of inquiry to William, who shrugged and said, *"Mayzovigako . . . tuneget . . . tuneget."* Then, the older man gestured out into the darkness in many different directions as if to indicate the unseen presence of more such artifacts. After a long pause, the older man said, *"Layzonzeen."*

Nainoa had no idea what this meant, but he guessed that William's people were not responsible for the building. He peered around in the darkness but could see little else, and so he proceeded to the hut with his host.

The two sleeping areas within were composed of piles of animal furs placed right on the ground. William directed him to one, and he took the other. Nainoa carefully arranged the furs so that his injured leg was supported and fell asleep almost immediately. The day had been exceptionally full.

As he drifted off, he wished William good night in Old English. William's teeth flashed in the darkness as he raised himself on one elbow and responded, *"Zai mo."*

17
Reflections

ZAI MO, I STARED AT THOSE ENIGMATIC LAST WORDS written on the yellow pad before me and sighed. Hunter-gatherers, I thought. The descendant-survivors of Western civilization were living as hunter-gatherers.

I had seen no evidence of either agriculture or pottery. The only metal objects William's people possessed were their decorative beads, bracelets, and crudely fashioned arrow points. They had no iron. Their only domesticated animals were dogs, their only vehicle the pole-drag. The descendants of the North American people were living in a Stone Age future. My shock and sadness at learning this was profound.

Several months passed between this contact and the next. One afternoon late in the fall, I was sitting in relaxed meditation in my studio, listening to the wind rattle the palms. On my desk was a large art book of paintings by Aboriginal Australians. I opened it and randomly began to survey the dotted abstractions of psychic maps and images of places and things perceived in "the Dreamtime." Although the paintings had the same lines and spots of light I usually perceived at the beginning and end of my altered states, these were more tightly arranged, perhaps because of the limited size of the piece of tree bark on which they were painted. I wondered if they were images of the *aka* field or guide maps to help initiates find their way to their ancestral places in the spirit world.

The traditional Aboriginal Australians had a deep mystical sense of contact with their land. They believed that when their physical bodies died, their personal spiritual essence merged with the collective spiritual essence of their land. When the time came for them to be reincarnated into the physical world, they reemerged from that same spiritual source. Thus, the Aboriginals were always part of a larger spiritual whole, one that was intensely alive and aware. This is why it was (and is) unthinkable for them to leave their land, especially if ordered to do so because of some Caucasian Australian businessman-politician's relocation scheme. This is why it was (and is) sacrilege to bulldoze their land to create a road or development project. For the Aboriginals, everything in their land, from the merest ant to the mightiest cliff face, is holy. When the ordinary aspect of their terrestrial estate is altered, so is its nonordinary aspect.

This understanding was remarkably similar to Nagai's, which caused me to wonder if it had once been universal among tribal people. This knowledge, this intimate connection with nature and the spiritual dimensions of reality, seemed to have been lost during the ascent of Western civilization.

The doves in the banyan tree beside the house reminded me of the deep connection I felt with nature here on the "big island." I had also felt this in Africa, an intimate relationship, I was becoming convinced, that could well be the main causative factor through which the "experience" was being manifested. I suspected my ongoing contact with Nainoa was occurring through the collective spiritual essence or "energy field" of the island. I also had come to believe that this amazing phenomenon was facilitated through the assistance of two helping spirits—the leopard man and the "stone that travels."

I rose from my deliberations and walked outside to where the stone sat among the beach boulders in the rock garden. My children, without any prompting from me, had begun to call it the "rock man." I focused my attention fully upon it and created a strong desire to regain contact with Nainoa. The stone's impassive face stared at me in silence as I held the intention with one-pointed concentration. For long moments, nothing out of the ordinary occurred. Then the tall, buttress-rooted *wi*-apple tree next to the carport dropped a fruit on the iron roof, breaking my concentration with a crash. I returned to my thoughts, which were now of Nainoa's new village.

Who were the people whom Nainoa had found? Some of their words were recognizably French. The way in which William pronounced his own name was very close to *Guillaume*, as were the alternate words he had used for the bull, *le taureau*, and cow, *la vache*. When he was gesturing toward the ruined stonework wall, he had said something that resembled the French words for "the ancestors" or "the ancients"—*les anciens*. But what about the rest?

Linguistics is not my field; nor do I have an exact memory for dialogue. I had jotted down some words that I remembered phonetically, but I had no idea what they meant or what language they represented. William and his people did not closely resemble contemporary Amerindians; nor did they look like people of Euro-American, Latino-American, Asian-American, or African-American stock. Their facial features, skin tone, and body build suggested that they were a new hybrid "race" descended from Amerindian and Caucasian ancestors. Their French-sounding words suggested that they originated in the French-speaking areas of Canada. The names of the women—Kenojelak, Kovak, and Karul—sounded Eskimo. What would people of mixed Eskimo-Amerindian-Caucasian descent be doing in what was once western Nevada? And what had happened to the original inhabitants of that part of the world?

Nainoa's preoccupations with the fate of the Americans had now become my own. I resolved to revisit Berkeley to see if one of my old professors had an Eskimo dictionary.

· · ·

I reachieved contact the next morning just before dawn, although it was midday in Nainoa's world when I "arrived." Nainoa was walking with Kenojelak and her pack of dogs across a wide grassy plain toward a distant line of trees. As he paused to survey his surroundings, I saw that he was still in Washoe Valley, below the massif of Slide Mountain. The grass, which had been dry during the previous visit, was now long and green. The rainy season had obviously begun.

Nainoa's memories revealed to me that he had already been with William and his people for several months. Within moments of my "arrival," Nainoa became aware of my presence. I could not mistake it, although his attention was almost immediately distracted by Kenojelak, who made a remark about the lushness of the grass. Even though her words were alien to me, I understood their gist because Nainoa did.

They walked through the grass as I looked out through his eyes at their world.

18
Ninth Journey
The Ennu

THE FRACTURE IN NAINOA'S LEG HAD HEALED enough
that he could walk again, although he was using
a cane that William had made for him, with a
natural bend for the handle.

As he walked with Kenojelak, Nainoa thought about
the strange feeling he had just had, the uneasy certainty
that he was being watched. This was the first time he had
felt it since he had joined William's people several
months ago, and he wondered anew what "it" was. Distracted, he thought back to his first days with these people.

The first thing he had learned about them was that
they were a friendly, easygoing, cheerful folk who tended
to laugh at life's vicissitudes. They had treated him as an
honored guest, caring for him in both obvious and subtle
ways, providing him with food and shelter and above all
with company—good company.

He had acquired a working understanding of their
language during his convalescence because his hosts had

displayed no driving interest in learning his. He made very slow progress at first, but as he listened to them, he repeated this word and that, trying to establish the context and meaning of conversations. He was not sure when he had crossed the critical threshold. At one point, it was all still pantomime and gesture, and then he began to be able to talk to them and understand them.

He was struck by how different their language was from his own. It was highly descriptive, and "things" could be changed into "actions" by adding a word ending that implied process. Possession was indicated in the same way. There were many, many word endings that produced long complex utterances in which there was no separation between the "subject" and "other." One of the first words he learned was *bitsek*, which meant dried fish. If one said *bitselevog*, it implied that "he" had dried the fish, while *bitseliak* was "my" or "your" or "his" dried fish.

William's people called themselves *ennuduinag* or *ennug*, depending on the context. *Ennug* or *ennuyug* literally translated as "a human being who is alive," as opposed to *ennuvinag*, one who was dead. The term *ennuduinag* included all humans, both male and female, although there were several other terms as well, including *layzom* for men and *layfom* for women. To himself, Nainoa had come to think of William's people as the Ennu.

Nainoa spied some horses in the far distance. The Old English word *horse* was unknown to them, but they had several terms of their own. *Ganagodalek* was one, which literally meant "long-legs." A term whose meaning was less clear was *lushuvag*. Still another, *ginmiyuag*, implied that horses were large dogs. Nainoa still wasn't sure what distinctions impelled the Ennu to use one term over another. *Omayag* was the general term for "animal." Translated, it literally meant "it is living" and was derived from the root word *oma*, which meant "alive" or "life." Nainoa had long lists of such words and word endings stored in his mind now. His memorization training as a historian had borne unexpected fruit.[1]

The second thing he learned about the Ennu was that their diet consisted almost entirely of meat and fish that were broiled, roasted, boiled, or eaten raw. They were hunters with no knowledge of agriculture. They gathered some vegetable food from their surrounding environment, but very little. Aside from the nuts of a certain tree, of which they were very fond, they gathered only mushrooms, wild onions, and occasionally seasonal berries and fruits. They gathered honey whenever they happened to find a hive.

As Nainoa watched the horses in the distance, he reflected that an incredible abundance of animal food was available to the Ennu. These dry grassy woodlands and open plains were filled with game, from elephants to rodents, serpents and insect larvae. The Ennu ate them all. So much animal food was available that they had to hunt only every third or fourth day to obtain enough meat for the next three or four days, although they tended to gather all the time.

When his ability to speak their language had progressed to the point that he could communicate to some degree, he had asked William why the Ennu did not farm or keep animals. The older man did not comprehend these notions, and during several days of frequently interrupted discussion, Nainoa attempted to describe agriculture and animal husbandry to the Ennu community. They had been very polite and very interested in what he had to say, but they failed to grasp the reasons for doing such things. The idea of accumulating food surpluses as a hedge against famine meant nothing to them; nor did living in one place in a settled community.

The land provided everything they needed, and when the local game and resources dwindled, they simply packed up, abandoned their crude huts, and moved camp to a new location. They were nomadic, and upon arriving at their next camp, men and women constructed new huts in only an afternoon's work. They had little in the way of material possessions beyond their weapons, tools, clothing, personal adornments, food bowls, carrying baskets, animal pelts, and leather hides. When they broke camp, these things were either carried by their owners or transported by the dogs on pole-drags.

As Kenojelak began to hum a strange tune, Nainoa reflected that the Ennu sang a great deal, usually with a curious nasal twang that produced what to his ears were rather harsh, shrill melodies. Their songs were about animals and hunting, love and revenge, success and misfortune. They entertained their children and recounted stories through song. Some songs were composed for special events, while others were said to be very old. They sang while they worked, while they danced and played games, and they sang simply to pass the time.

The Ennu had no knowledge of the wheel, nor of ceramics or glassmaking, although they used a fine-grained earth they called *urgilug* to form toy animals for their children, as well as small lamps in which they burned animal fat for light. Their metal was limited to "soft metal" objects found at places "where the ancients had lived," which they reworked into personal ornaments and crude projectile points. They had no iron and were amazed at the hardness of Nainoa's knife and spear.

Their basic tool kit consisted almost entirely of flaked stone points, scrapers, and blades that were resharpened from time to time. They made knives from glassy volcanic stone or from glass shards that were traded from group to group. Deer antler hammers were used for stone-flaking: The pointed tines acted as punches for striking long, thin blades from larger stone cores and for retouching blade edges.

Nainoa had demonstrated his own skill at stone-flaking during his early days with the Ennu. The men had shown their own in return. It had been a very friendly interaction, largely independent of language, demonstrating personal skills and exchanging designs.

The Ennu gathered sap from various trees, creating a resinous all-purpose glue for hafting projectile points and knife blades and fletching their arrows. From leather hides and woven grasses they made long balls of string, from which they fashioned snares and nets for catching whole flocks of birds or schools of fish. They made containers from wood, and their basketry, for which they used woody vines, slender branches, grasses, or anything else that took their fancy, was particularly fine.

The Ennu made bows from the springy upper branches of trees. The average bow was short and "recurved" from lamination with sinews from the legs of deer and other herd animals. The sinews were first soaked in hot water, then chewed and applied wet to the front of the bow's wooden belly with a kind of glue made from the roots of a plant. The sinews were laid on the bow in long strips, extending beyond the ends of the shaft to form rigid notches designed to receive the bowstring. When dry, the sinews contracted, giving the unstrung bow its reverse bend. Like Hawaiian hunters, the Ennu usually tied fur around part of their sinew bowstrings to silence the twang.

The Ennu had no chiefly class and no commoners—no class structure at all, no leaders, political organizations, governing board, or organized priesthood. Men appeared to have no authority over women. Decisions about moving camp and the direction of travel all seemed to be made by consensus of the entire community. The men would get together and talk it over. The women would also discuss the issue among themselves. All would share their ideas on the subject over the evening meal.

From long discussions with William and his family, Nainoa had learned that the Ennu lived in many small groups or bands of between fifteen and fifty people that were spread out to the east, north, and south over vast landscapes filled with game. These were highly mobile groups of extended families, whose core was a man, a woman, and their children.

Women seemed to bear only two or three children in their lifetimes, probably due to prolonged breastfeeding and many spontaneous miscarriages. The daily life of the Ennu was arduous, and women underwent extreme physical exertion during travel and during the butchering of large animal carcasses and conveying the meat to camp. Two of the women in William's band had recently suffered miscarriages.

Perhaps because of this low birth rate, it was not uncommon for a man to have two or three wives, usually in different bands, and some of the women also had more than one husband. In both cases, the man would visit with the wife, staying for various lengths of time in different bands. Nainoa had not yet determined how they worked out the fine points of these extended relationships, which were further complicated by the custom of cousins addressing each other as "brother" or "sister," and by uncles and aunts treating their nephews and nieces as their own children. Parents also commonly addressed their own children as "grandfather" or "grandmother," or sometimes as "father" or "mother."

William's band included a small number of children, who were highly valued and virtually never disciplined. The older members, too, were highly valued for their knowledge of customs and history, their abilities as arbitrators in disputes, and their capacity as storytellers.

The Ennu had a rich oral tradition and told stories all the time, especially during the long evenings. It was not unusual for a tale of exceptional length to take up every evening for weeks to be told in its entirety. In a small band in which relationships were often intense, stories helped disperse accumulating tensions and head off disputes. Both William and his wife, Kovak, excelled at storytelling, so the harmony within their extended family was good.

Since the Ennu had so much free time, they talked incessantly about everything and everyone. As Nainoa's knowledge of their language grew, so did his store of gossip about individuals within the group. He learned much about the people in the other groups within their hunting territory. Heated disputes and clashes of personality occasionally broke out. When unresolved, larger bands frequently split into smaller groups.

The Ennu had no system of centralized authority, either within their bands or between them. The only hierarchy that existed was within the family. Fathers and mothers had authority over their children, and the grandparents over the parents, but the elders functioned more as counselors than as leaders. They had a well-developed sense of ethics and strongly discouraged troublemaking either by social ridicule and teasing, or by songs about mythic individuals who met undesirable fates as a result of their disruptive behavior. More serious social problems such as violence or murder did sometimes arise, although the violent person usually came to a bad end, either because of the wronged people's revenge or because he was exiled.

One of William's distant cousins had always been a troublemaker, even as a child. His life had been one fight and attack after another, and disciplining him had always been futile. He eventually took another man's wife by force while the husband was away on a hunt. The band in which he lived had debated the matter, and one day soon thereafter he had been killed in a hunting accident. This had caused trouble with the dead man's immediate kin, and that particular band had then divided into two separate groups to allow emotions to cool. William had assured Nainoa that such instances were rarely ongoing problems. "There is always someone like that around," he said, "and they must always be dealt with, sometimes in this way, sometimes in that."

Then the old Ennu had fixed Nainoa with an intense look and said, "Nainoapak, you and I look to the light because that is our nature. But there is also darkness within us. We experience that darkness as we pass through life, and in doing so we learn what it is that we are not. It is in this way that we discover what it is that we are."

William had then laughed with delight and with the joy of being alive: "Heeeeeee."

The Ennu called him Nainoapak. At first, Nainoa had theorized that this ending was a term of respect, but as his grasp and knowledge of the many word endings increased, he realized that *pak* referred to his size—he was a giant beside them.

William possessed exceptional *mana*. He had a relaxed, humorous way of expressing himself that made him a master at arbitrating disputes. He was also a skilled hunter, and his influence extended itself over his entire group —and beyond.

One day, Kovak informed Nainoa matter-of-factly that William had had many wives, and that he presently had one in another band with whom he stayed sometimes when visiting relatives. William overheard her and responded with a remark that Nainoa missed in translation, but those nearby stopped what they were doing and looked up in gleeful anticipation. Kovak replied with a verbal thrust that got everyone within earshot laughing with that strange soft "Heeeeeee." William retorted with another remark and those assembled roared with laughter, and so it had gone, back and forth.

Kovak put an end to it by informing Nainoa in a loud whisper that her husband was known far and wide as William the Conqueror—William *Luvankar*—not because of his prowess as a hunter or abilities as a craftsman, but because women found him irresistible. Although William had been the target of Kovak's barbed comments, they had somehow enhanced his status —and hers too.

One day early in his stay, William had squatted down next to Nainoa and pulled out a leather bag with a drawstring. From this he had poured out a handful of metal artifacts.

There were many curious, flat, serrated blades with holes through their spatulate ends. There were also many pieces of *moni*, most of which were made of several thin layers of silver and copper that appeared to have been hammered together, but many of the small ones were all copper and some of the larger ones were all silver. All were badly corroded, so that the surface detail was almost obliterated.

One of the middle-size disks was less worn than the others. Nainoa spat on it and cleaned its surface carefully. On one side could be seen the head of a man in profile, and on the other, a bird with outstretched wings. William had pointed to the bird and said, *"Nokdoroling"*—the eagle. It appeared to be holding something in its claws, but it was impossible to determine what. Remains of words could be discerned running around the edge of the metal disk, but corrosion had rendered them illegible. Nainoa had seen better-preserved ones in the settlements and guessed that the words on this one were the same. As he stared intently at the disk, he muttered, "United States of America."

William immediately picked up on the word *America* and repeated it, saying, *"Amerik . . . Amerik,"* extending his arms, pointing at the horizon all around them in a circular manner. Nainoa had simply repeated the word and William's pantomime. The older man had smiled in response and nodded vigorously. Nainoa had then pointed to the old hunter and asked, "American?" To this, William had simply laughed uproariously, shaking his head forcefully and proclaiming himself Ennu.

Turning the disk over, Nainoa pointed to the head rendered there in shallow relief and looked at William expectantly. The older man simply shrugged and said nothing. Above the head could just be seen the remains of a word—*Liberty*. Nainoa knew this was an Old English word that meant freedom, but freedom from what?

Over the millennia, Hawaiian scholars had debated the significance of this word on the American *moni*. Many thought it to mean freedom from some oppressive *kapu* system of social laws. Others felt that it meant freedom from an evil governor or ruling family. Still others saw the bird as a symbol for one's spirit-self and claimed that it meant the freedom achieved at death when one existed only as spirit.

Nainoa looked carefully at William's other disks, but all were illegible. As he gave them back to the older man, he named them, using the Hawaiian word *moni*. The older man's face had lit up in response, and he had offered a similar word, *monay*, repeating it several times and nodding. The match was close. He asked William where he had gotten the *monay*, to which the older man responded by looking to the south and pointing with his lips.

When Nainoa's knowledge of the Ennu language had progressed to the point where he and William could actually converse, one of the first things he had learned, much to his amusement, was that the Ennu had thought he was one of the "lost Americans." His iron spear and knife had lent support to this theory because Ennu stories and myths recorded the existence of a "strong metal" associated with the Americans. No such strong metal had ever been found in the "places of the ancients" where the Ennu dug for metal artifacts and glass shards. They had doubted the existence of this metal until they had found him.

Many evenings of discussion, supplemented by gesture and pantomime, had taken place around the fire. Nainoa had struggled with the language to offer a rough summary of Hawaiian history. He related what was known about the Americans and the Time of Contact. He had spoken about the Fall and the thousand-year period of isolation, during which the islands had been cut off from the rest of the world. He told the Ennu about the first attempts at transoceanic voyaging and how the first contacts had been made with other island groups out on the vast watery world. He described the several expeditions to America that had never returned, and he gave an account of his own ancestors' voyage to the American continent 130 years before. He offered a brief history of the settlements around the inland sea and explained his own interest in the history of the Americans and the collapse of their civilization. When he concluded by observing that he had thought the Ennu to be the descendants of the lost Americans, all were very amused.

He then recounted his journey through the forest and the mountains up until the time Kenojelak had found him. He did not tell them about his mystic experiences, however, having decided that this information could be shared only with certain individuals. He did not yet know who.

The Ennu, fascinated, revealed their own story in return. Like that of the Hawaiians, it was preserved both in historical accounts and in myths and legends. Nainoa listened, rapt, as their long story unfolded over a period of many nights.

The Ennu had not always lived here on these grassy plains but were fairly recent arrivals who had come originally from the far north and east—from the mythic, white, treeless lands of the *ziku*.

No one among the Ennu knew exactly what the *ziku* was, but legend recounted that it had come from the sky and that it had covered the land and the waters like thick dust for much of the year. It was known that the *ziku* was white and cold and that its touch could cause water to become hard as metal. The Ennu of the *ziku* had hunted and fished from a great lake of endless extent and lived in huts made from the cold white *ziku* because there were no trees or bushes.

Much to Nainoa's amazement, the Ennu had many stories of mythic encounters with the *Amerik'ken* and with another people they called the *Ganad'dien*. Both of these peoples were said to be very tall and have pale skin and round blue eyes. They were outsiders who had apparently visited the Ennu in much the same manner as the Americans had visited the Hawaiians. Ennu stories abounded with tales of these foreigners and of the wonders they had brought with them, particularly their huge boats and hunting weapons that could kill animals at great distances solely with sound. Myths told that the foreigners, collectively called *odlonneg*, had boats that could carry them through the air and that they had been able to travel in these boats over great distances.

William's people even knew that the Americans claimed to have flown to the moon in their great ships. The Ennu did not find this legend particularly impressive. William said that he had been there himself and failed to see why the Americans had needed ships to go there. Nainoa asked him if he had gone there in his dreams, whereupon all the Ennu within earshot laughed heartily, and nothing more had been said.

The Ennu histories of encounters with the Americans bore an overall similarity to those of the Hawaiians. Many *odlonneg* had lived among the Ennu and had intermarried with them. But even more intriguing, the Ennu had a Great Flood myth. They called it the *olegdoaluk*, and it was supposed to have occurred in the very distant past at the same time that the *Amerik'kens* and *Canad'diens* had abruptly disappeared. This was also when the *ziku* had vanished. In many accounts the Flood coincided with a time of great chaos. The waters of the endless lake had risen quickly, covering the Ennu's lands. The air became very hot, and most of the Ennu had died.

The survivors had moved to higher land, where they lived and hunted for a long time. The Ennu ancestors had eventually migrated south, where they encountered forests for the first time. They had expected to find the *odlonneg* there because it was known that the outsiders had originally come from the south, but during their long migrations they encountered no other people.

They had lived in the forests for a long time, but neither the *ziku* nor the *odlonneg* ever returned. Some of the Ennu bands continued to move south and west through the forest until they came to the grasslands. Some had stayed, while others continued on. Some of the Ennu travelers who returned said that they had occasionally found ruins of *odlonneg* settlements, some of them quite large, but exactly how large was hard to tell. In this way, the Ennu had continued to move south and west, but they had never found any other people—until they found him.

As the Ennu told Nainoa this, all were staring at him. Kenojelak's discovery of the tall man called Nainoapak in the riverine forest would be repeated in their various legends and myths forever. Their names and his would be linked in their histories for all time, and this meant immortality of sorts—for all of them. As he watched their long eyes observing him in the firelight, he felt profoundly moved.

Nainoa liked these people very much. At the same time, he wondered if these Ennu were all that remained of the once-great American civilization. Compared with the Hawaiians, the Ennu would be considered less developed. Even the commoners back in his settlement had more material possessions than these hunter-gatherers. Yet William and his people possessed more freedom, which was not inconsiderable. Their society was fully egalitarian, free of the oppressive caste system at the core of Hawaiian society. Among the Ennu all were chiefs.

Nainoa watched Kenojelak stride through the grass as they walked. He had spent much of his time in the company of the women while the men were out hunting. They had encouraged his attempts to learn their language and had found his efforts vastly amusing, erupting frequently into gales of laughter over a mispronounced word. This had been irritating at first until he realized how basically easygoing and cheerful they were—and how easily amused. Their daily life was very strenuous, yet both men and women, young and old, behaved as lightheartedly as children when the occasion arose. They exhibited a keen sense of humor and expressed their happiness openly.

Being with the women on a daily basis, Nainoa had seen a fairly strict division of labor between the men and women. It was the men who hunted and killed big game—although the women distracted the animals or drove them into areas where the men were hiding. The women often "called" the animals, too, drawing them into position with their high, wavering voices.

The women did some small-game hunting of birds, monkeys, rabbits, rodents, snakes, tortoises, and so forth, as well as much of the fishing. Both men and women butchered the large-game kills and helped transport the meat and hides back to the camp.

The men made all the weapons, tools, food bowls, containers, and personal ornaments of wood, bone, ivory, or metal. They made a variety of scrapers, some of metal, others handsomely carved from ivory, that the women used to prepare hides for clothing, sandals, and bags. The men had a crude knowledge of metalworking and used a small bellows of wood and leather to heat found metal objects to the point where they became soft enough to work with stone hammers.

The women gathered water, firewood, and most of the vegetable foods, although the men contributed to some extent, especially with medicinal plants. The women did all the leatherworking and made all the clothing, including tanning the hides. They did all the weaving of basketry and rope, and made the string nets and snares with which they caught fish, birds, and animals. They prepared all the food and raised the small children, although the men participated to a far greater degree than among Nainoa's own people.

Since Nainoa's leg had mended to the point where he could manage short outings with his cane, this morning he had been invited to join the women on a foraging expedition. Because of his attraction to Kenojelak, he had accepted.

Once he had asked Kenojelak if she had any children. She had fallen silent and, after a long pause, told him gravely that she had no children. She had remained quiet for the rest of that day, and later he had asked Kovak about her.

The old woman told him that her daughter's husband had been killed in an accident the previous year and that Kenojelak had then left her husband's band and returned to her family. Kovak's eyes had twinkled at him as she observed offhandedly that it was hard to find a man for a woman as tall as Kenojelak. Then the old woman had bluntly said, "You two like each other. You would have tall children." Then with a smile: "They would grow to be strong hunters. You should give my daughter a child."

Slightly taken aback by Kovak's frankness, Nainoa had laughed and shrugged his shoulders. But at odd moments Kovak would catch him watching Kenojelak, and at such times she would look at him meaningfully. Nothing had happened between them, however, perhaps because they were never alone.

He glanced at Kenojelak now, and a hollow place suddenly appeared in his chest. The women's gathering baskets had been filled by midday, whereupon Kovak had suggested that he and Kenojelak obtain some monkey meat from the distant riverine forest. The older woman had chuckled as she emptied her daughter's basket into the others, and then sent the two of them on their way with a cheery smile.

In this way he found himself alone with Kenojelak for the first time since she had found him that day several months ago. As they walked, he reminded her of that day offhandedly. Kenojelak said nothing but glanced at him out of the corners of her long eyes with the hint of a smile.

Striding across the grassland with her dogs, she looked magnificent in a barbaric sort of way, with her long plume of black hair cascading from the crown of her head down her back. In Hawaiian society big women were most valued for their physical beauty. Yet Kenojelak's small high breasts and long legs gave her an exotic appeal. A curved throwing stick was hooked casually over one shoulder, ready to use should they suddenly flush small game or birds. She almost never missed.

Arriving at the trees fringing the stream, they moved into the shade. The dogs fanned out, maintaining complete silence. Nainoa strung his bow and drew several arrows from his quiver, as they worked their way up the wide, shallow watercourse through the trees, watching for monkeys. They continued in this way until the light breeze shifted, and the dogs suddenly stiffened. From the forest cover across the stream came the distinctive lowing of longhorn cattle, which the Ennu considered the most dangerous of all animals. Nainoa and Kenojelak proceeded cautiously, hoping to bypass them and continue.

All went well until the forest undergrowth became so dense they could barely see a few feet in front of them. Suddenly they realized that large animals were all around them in the bush. Nainoa quickly slung his bow over his shoulder and readied his spear as a crashing in the bush directly before them scattered the dogs. In silent alarm Kenojelak gestured, drawing him swiftly down into the cover of a recently fallen tree, whose many branches were still in leaf and could conceal them from whatever was approaching. This probably saved them, because no sooner were they hidden than a longhorn bull broke cover with a bellow and charged past the tree.

Nainoa threw his arm over Kenojelak as they flattened themselves on the ground and held their breath. Unmoving, they peered cautiously out through the leafy branches that surrounded them. William had told him that longhorns hated humans—this one had no doubt smelled them and knew they were there somewhere. The dogs went to work, harassing the bull as it trotted stiff-legged, searching for them among the thickets and bushes, its great hooves trampling through the brush within touching distance, shaking the earth with its passage. The bull's eyes were rolling, and its breath came in short indignant bursts of sound as the dogs feinted at it and scattered again. It showed no sign of leaving.

Nainoa decided that he would have to kill it with his largest metal-bladed hunting arrows. The first shot would have to be good, or they would be in grave danger. He watched the beast moving swiftly through the brush and considered the odds. It would be a very difficult shot.

Despite their precarious situation, Nainoa admired the bull's power. As it thundered by again, Nainoa felt his *mana* begin to flow in response, coursing through his body, heightening his senses. He risked a glance at Kenojelak, who seemed as captivated as he, her long eyes following the bull, her wide mouth slightly open. Her skin had prickled into goose bumps, and her left nipple was stiff. Feeling his gaze, she looked into his eyes.

Nainoa became acutely aware of the feel of her skin against his, of the hair in her armpit against the edge of his hand. The *mana* coursing through him abruptly transformed itself into a surge of sexual feeling.

Motionless, he continued to hold her and look into her eyes as the longhorn searched for them under the trees. Within the pungent odor of crushed leaves and trampled earth, Nainoa could smell her scent. He breathed her in, feeling the erotic pulses within him grow. A hand's length away, her blue-gray eyes held his and narrowed into a look that conveyed the intensity of what she too was feeling. He felt her breathing change and deepen. The blood started to hiss in his ears.

Something shifted, and the bull bellowed and charged past them. In the momentary hush that followed, the bull bawled again and they peered carefully out through the leaves. It had rushed up to one of its cows, and in its heightened emotional state, it abruptly mounted her.

The great penis emerged glistening into the air, weaving, searching. Kenojelak's breath caught as it found and sheathed itself in the cow's body. Nainoa felt her stiffen as they watched the huge animals engaged in the ancient pattern of life renewal—and then she turned, her eyes sparkling with delight as she brought her lips close to his ear.

"Obenkrazarbog," she whispered huskily. "It is spring."

She grinned widely at him before returning her attention to the spectacle before them. Within moments it was over, and the longhorn herded his female off across the stream, through the trees, and out onto the open grassland beyond the forest.

Kenojelak turned then and stared into his eyes with a smoky look. Bringing her lips close to his ear again, she whispered, "Nainoapak."

He slowly took her face between his hands and kissed her lightly, brushing her full lips with his. She stiffened and pulled back, and he realized that she had probably never been kissed before.

She looked deeply into his eyes with great gravity but said nothing as he gently took her face into his hands once again and slowly placed his lips upon hers. This time she did not pull away. Her mouth was warm and very soft. Without breaking the kiss, he gathered her into his arms and held her

long body against his. Her mouth opened slightly as her breath quickened and deepened, and a sudden spasm rippled through her as she learned to return the kiss.

She pulled back, remembering his healing leg, and ran her hand lightly down his thigh with a look of inquiry. He nodded and said, *"Bitziak*—it is fine."

She grinned her wide grin and gently pressed him back to the ground to lie on his back among the pungent crushed leaves. In a single long flow of movement, she removed her leather skirt, untied his *malo*, and took his stiffening maleness into her hands. Her pale eyes widened as she looked down at his erection, and with sudden humor she whispered, *"Bitziak!"*

Kenojelak's dogs burst in on them at that moment, and with much laughter they drove them off. As she crouched above him, throwing bark and wood fragments at her canine companions, he gently took her breasts into his hands, and her nipples stiffened in his palms. She looked down at him and, with a breathy laugh of pure delight, swung a long leg across him and rubbed herself against him . . . until at last, she took him slowly, slowly into her body. The sensation was exquisite. Nainoa felt it to his core.

Their lovemaking was frenzied, and he climaxed in moments, discharging the tension of their brush with death in an orgasm of great intensity. It had been a long time since he had had sex.

Kenojelak felt his release and laughed with delight, wrapping her long body around his, holding him tightly inside her. Recovering, he ran his hands lightly down her back, gently exploring her bottom and the intriguing connection of their bodies. He found her turgid crest of flesh in the thick dark thatch of her body hair pressed against him and touched her lightly, rhythmically, bringing a sudden gasp of pleasure and amazement from her. He continued gently to touch her there as her eyes widened and her breath came more and more quickly. She grinned at him and laughed again, her breath catching in her throat as his erection grew once more within her.

And lovemaking began again . . . again . . . slowly . . . slowly

. . . until he felt her orgasm approaching. Her long body began to ripple, to tremble against his. She was close—very close. Her taut nipples rubbed against his skin like soft fingertips as he continued to stroke her—to stroke her—and suddenly she brought her lips to his once more as she ground her hips against him. Her long body shuddered with the intensity of her orgasm as he held her against him—and then his own release surged forth once again . . . in response to her . . . in response . . . to her.

In the long lazy aftermath of their passion, they explored each other as lovers do, picking leaves from each other's hair, creating the space within which to say small unspoken things long thought of. Throughout, he kissed and caressed her as she looked into his eyes.

In the midst of their play, curious monkeys appeared in the trees above, and reaching out slowly, he took his bow and notched an arrow. With Kenojelak still lying full-length upon him, he shot straight up. The unfortunate monkey fell, transfixed, almost upon them. Again he shot, and again a monkey fell—and again. Kovak would get her monkey meat after all.

Eventually they went to the stream and bathed together. On the way, as Kenojelak strode naked through the forest, his seed streamed down the insides of her long, muscular thighs. Observing the obvious result of his passion, she gave him another measuring look and another wide grin.

As they washed each other, love came again in the middle of a pool. He invited her to recline against a slab of smooth, sun-warmed stone. After kissing her wet nipples until she shivered with the sensation, he buried his face in the luxuriant thatch below her flat belly and pleasured her with his lips and tongue until she stiffened and gasped, her thighs and hands gripping his head in the throes of her ecstasy.

She looked at him dreamily afterward, and noticing his swaying erection, she swiftly took him into her hands once again, looking with obvious approval at his turgid maleness. "*Bitziapag*—he behaves well," she said. Then she laughed with utter delight and, weighing his penis in her hands, whispered fiercely, "Nainoavangioaluk." The new ending to his name implied "of extraordinary size and power."

Her pale eyes narrowed suddenly. Grinning at him, she turned, assuming on hands and knees the position of the cow they had observed earlier, dipping her long back and presenting her widely spread bottom in obvious invitation.

He laughed with joy and mounted her from behind as she giggled with the delight of it. In that moment he took her into himself, into some deeply felt, secret place within his being, where he knew she would remain —forever.

In this way the afternoon passed, and Nainoa could not recall when he had been happier. They alternately played with each other like children and held each other as lovers until the light faded and they dressed once again.

Nainoa tied the monkeys' tails around their heads and slung one under each arm. Kenojelak took the third in her basket and whistled up the dogs, and they walked together out of the woods onto the grasslands holding hands.

As they headed back to camp, Nainoa reflected that his mind was oddly free of thoughts.

19
Anthropology
Meetings

I WAS IN A STATE OF INTENSE EMOTIONAL TURMOIL WHEN I returned from Nainoa's world, for I had been "there," merged with Nainoa, when he made love with Kenojelak. Jill was now sleeping beside me. Had I just been unfaithful to my wife? No, it was amusing even to consider such an incredible thing. How would Jill react to the story I had to tell her? It wasn't as though I were having a relationship outside of our marriage. And yet I was obsessed by my experiences with Nainoa, and through him I had just had a most unusual encounter. I had intimately experienced the heightened emotional state that Western culture describes as "being in love." I had "received" the imagery, thoughts, emotions, impressions, and physical sensations of lovemaking as though I were experiencing them myself.

A cognitive scientist would probably define what I had just experienced as a fantasy—an erotic dream whose source lay within my own subconscious mind. A traditional psychologist would have a heyday explaining this episode in terms of my own suppressed inner needs, wish fulfillments, repressed desires, and unfulfilled expectations of life. My subconscious, to be sure, was no doubt involved in my experiences, for the "doorway" to the interface through time and space had to be located there. My conscious awareness journeyed out of my physical body through my subconscious, or *ku*.

In many ways the subconscious seemed to be much more conscious than the conscious mind. My *ku* knew that I was interested in information about Nainoa's life and had continued to gather data from his memories, even while my conscious "director" had been wrapped up in Nainoa's love-making.

For instance, I had gained several of Nainoa's memories of Kenojelak while he was making love with her. The first was from a time when a number of Ennu adults had butchered a freshly killed horse. As they opened the belly, Kenojelak had been standing with several women on one side of the steaming carcass. Stone knife in hand, she had gore up to her elbows. She had sliced off a piece of fresh raw organ meat that looked like liver, still dripping blood, and was eating it with obvious relish—a real, honest-to-God savage.

In another memory Kenojelak had been playing a game with several other men and women. All were taking turns leaping high into the air, trying to kick some sort of ball suspended from a tree. Within this brief scene, I perceived the openness and joy with which she lived life and expressed her physicality. I saw part of the camp in the background as well, a random sprawl of crude huts with dogs sleeping, children playing, and women working. The flash of the Ennu woman's long thighs gave rise to another memory, this one my own—Kenojelak nude and in the throes of sexual passion.

With amazing clarity and vividness, I "received" Nainoa's strong feelings for this woman, her strong personality, her striking physical beauty, her incisive intelligence, and her great good humor. She was at the peak of her youth, with all its attendant vitality and abundant sexuality, and she was obviously held in high regard by those within her community. Kenojelak would be the perfect hunter-gatherer wife.

Having been with Nainoa in his lonely walk through the mountains, I was happy that he had found companionship now. I was somewhat embarrassed to have eavesdropped on his most intimate moments, but I was also grateful for the experience, since it seemed to me another confirmation that I was not dreaming or making these scenes up. They were simply too real. Nainoa might already have visited me at a similarly intimate time with my own wife. Until we learned how to contact each other and disengage from our mergings at will, I would have to deal with my sheepish feelings about my otherworldly "infidelity."

Shortly after this experience, in late November 1988, I flew to the mainland to attend the annual meeting of the American Anthropological Association, partly to get an update on my colleagues' research and partly to check the job market.

One evening over dinner in a hotel restaurant, a longtime friend and I were discussing his current research, an extremely specialized scientific project. I decided to see how he would react to the story of my altered-state experiences. Even though he would probably see me as just another anthropologist gone "troppo" in the islands, I decided to tell him anyway.

I waited until we had finished the first bottle of wine and then gave him a rough idea of what had been happening to me. My friend expressed amused concern and asked The Question almost immediately:

"How do you know this stuff isn't coming out of your creative imagination as mental projections and fantasies? How do you know you're not just making it all up?"

I responded, "The creative imagination is a function of the conscious mind, of the intellect. My intellect is not the source of these experiences. I can't make them happen consciously, although my conscious mind does form my intention to connect, to have the experience. I'm receiving this information through my subconscious, through what a *kahuna* would call my *ku*. Even my subconscious, my *ku*, perceives this other person and this other world as something separate from myself—as something separate from my intellect and my creative imagination."

This answer did not reassure my colleague. He looked distinctly uneasy and reached for his glass of wine. "But how can you know this? How can you be so sure? How do you *know* your so-called *ku* isn't making all this up?"

This, of course, was the crux of The Question. To understand and accept the truth of these experiences is to comprehend a basic truth about who and what we are as human beings. My friend and I are both products of Western culture and its scientific, reductionist view of the world. But these fantastic experiences and their intellectual and emotional challenges have taught me that emotional truths and mystical experiences have as much validity as the empirical truths that we can see in our everyday world. Many of the great scientific thinkers of Western history in fact came to some degree of acceptance of mystical, spiritual realities, yet these sides of them are dismissed as "gone mystic." Accepting the unity of spirit, the oneness of the universe, was a leap of faith for me, and I can sympathize with my scientist colleagues and their skepticism about mystical experiences when they have not had them themselves. But such experiences are common to all cultures, and I had come to believe that the capacity for having them is part of our human nature. By this point, after much anguishing and second-guessing, I had made up my mind. I told him so:

"I'm sure what I've seen is real because I ask my *ku*," I said. "The *ku* cannot make up anything. The subconscious only regurgitates what it already knows. The *ku* is not creative; it never lies. The conscious mind is our creative part. When I ask my *ku* if I am making this whole thing up with my creative imagination, the answer is immediate. It is not being created by my conscious mind, nor is it a product of my *ku*. It is coming in from outside of me. It is being perceived *through* my *ku* . . . through the noncreative aspect of myself."

My colleague took a long drink of his wine and shook his head with a smile. "But these episodes, as you call them, are not real. They are dreams. They are illusions. They must all be originating within your own mind."

I replied, "The *ku* does not distinguish between reality and illusion. It perceives both as real—both as equally 'true.' If the *ku* believes something is real, then it's real as far as the *ku* is concerned. So if they are illusions, my *ku* nonetheless believes they are real. On the other hand, if my conscious mind is not creating these experiences, and my subconscious is incapable of creating them, then where are they coming from? The imagery is not coming out of my memory, so it must be coming from outside myself, although the self is the vehicle through which it is received."

My colleague flagged down our waiter and ordered more wine as I continued, "I've been wrestling with trying to understand this for three years now, and I must admit I did have doubts for a long time. But I'm profoundly impressed at what the so-called 'subconscious' mind is capable of. I'm convinced that only with its cooperation am I able to achieve the altered state and transcend time as well as ordinary physical reality. I'm able to accomplish this merging with the awareness of this other man who lives in the future through my subconscious."

The wine arrived, but it failed to calm my friend, who became ever more agitated as I insisted on the truth of my story. I decided not to tell him I thought that Nainoa might be one of my descendants but retreated instead into a description of the altered state.

"My contact with this man tends to fall into two categories. On the one hand, I frequently 'plug in' when he is alone and in a reflective state. This is very productive because I 'receive' a lot through his own recollections. On the other hand, I also merge with him during dynamic encounters, when I experience his life and reactions and interactions as though they were happening directly to me."

I described being run down by a longhorn and Nainoa's sexual encounter with Kenojelak. The anthropologist's eyes went cloudy in response. He liked that idea, so I continued:

"I'm most curious about why I 'plugged in' to this man at that particular

time. Was it because of my own interest in the girl? Why didn't I merge with him during a hunt, or when I could observe Ennu customs in camp? There's so much I don't understand."

The wine finally hit and my colleague relaxed somewhat, but he still could not accept that my experiences were "real." As our conversation drifted slowly onto safer ground, I sensed a separation between us. In his perspective, I had become contaminated with New Age nonsense—or nonscience.

I drifted through the rest of the anthropology conference, listening to colleagues read their meticulously worded papers in the grim, geometric, fluorescent interiors of the hotel conference rooms. "Snipers" in the audience typed the presenters' research results into their laptop computers, pouncing on any errors or discrepancies in the data or method with which they could attack the presenter. The posturing of those in pursuit of scientific fame and glory seemed considerably more unreal and dreamlike than my visits with Nainoa. Observing the strained expressions on my fellow anthropologists' faces, I reflected that this was not a particularly good dream.

I was happy to see old friends again, and I felt much compassion that we were all getting older. I heard the troubles of some. But my nonordinary journeys had driven a wedge between us. I couldn't picture myself up there on the podium seriously discussing the customs of people who would live five thousand years from now. Should I tell the story of my journeys across time? How could I? Who among these serious behavioral scientists would even listen to such revelations?[1] I was tempted to write up these journeys disguised as science fiction, to save my own reputation as a "serious scientific investigator." But I couldn't deny my own experiences in this way. They had really happened to me, to a real person in real reality. And they were continuing to happen.

I returned to Kona in a strange state, feeling distanced from my chosen profession and disappointed by the certainty that my colleagues' reactions to my story would range from negative to hostile. I felt a real despair that my revelations would isolate me, that they would virtually kill me professionally. Fortunately, this sadness was balanced by a growing excitement that I had gone far beyond the borders of the known into an entirely new direction.

In the back of my mind lurked a hope. Surely there were others among five and a half billion human beings on earth who would be sympathetic to these experiences and who could also reach into the future. Perhaps even other trained scientists had had similar experiences, had transcended space and time to visit with their descendant-selves—or ancestral selves. In reading my account, perhaps other professionals would find the courage to come forward and reveal what they had seen.

Shortly after my return to Kona, I made another spontaneous journey. Nainoa was alone when I joined him, and in the moments following our contact, several things were immediately apparent.

First, he was no longer in Washoe Valley. Second, he was part of a group waiting in ambush for a herd of horses to drift closer to where the group was hidden. And third, Nainoa was aware of my presence the instant I arrived.

20
Tenth Journey
The Shaman's Teaching

IT APPEARED TO BE VERY EARLY MORNING, AND THE SKY was overcast. Nainoa was half lying, half sitting in a shallow dry wash in a grassy plain that stretched away to distant hills in all directions. He had gotten to this place under cover of darkness along with William and the other hunters, who had taken up positions among the scrubby trees and thickets closer to the lake. Many Ennu women and older children were hidden at intervals along the dry wash and behind low cairns of stones that had been constructed at various points on the plain to channel the herd toward the shallow water that formed a bay near the trees. All were waiting in silence, hoping the light wind would not shift and carry their scent to the horses.

Nainoa had been hunting with the men since his leg had healed, and he knew what to do. When the herd was close enough, he would stand up, and his solitary presence on the skyline would alert the stallion, which would then drive its females in the opposite direction. The hidden Ennu would "emerge from the ground," as they liked to say, scaring and moving the mares on toward the concealed men, who would kill one or more, depending on luck and skill. It was a dangerous game. The key was patience, timing, and concentration.

The herd of horses was still some distance away when Nainoa suddenly felt the familiar but unnameable presence. Someone or something was again watching him, and it was close—very close. Nainoa still had no idea who the "presence" was. It was not the tiger man, he knew, for he had not felt that spirit since leaving the mountains. Perhaps the tiger *aumakua* preferred wild places among the trees. Or perhaps Chief Kaneohe was sending him *mana*, or wondering what had become of his clerk. Or maybe it was someone else. Nainoa quietly watched the horses, but he also watched the "awareness" focused upon him. A strange thought suddenly appeared in his mind:

The American.

Nainoa very much wanted to renew his visionary connection with the American. But he had never before considered the possibility that the American might be able to connect with him, too. Could he have been doing so—and if so, for how long?

He felt like he had been struck in the stomach. Somehow he knew that visitations from the American were indeed possible, and that he could very well be here, within him, in the same manner that he had been "there."

Suddenly it was too much to think about, and it was not the right time. Nainoa withdrew from this radical idea and quieted his swirling emotions to concentrate on the horses. Too much was at stake to become lost in thought. Yet the presence remained, and an inner part of him watched it too.

He sat quietly studying the horses, thinking of hunting; *omayoziorag;* was one Ennu term for hunting. The Ennu hunters would try not to kill the male because if they did, the remaining females would disperse to other stallions' herds elsewhere. Horses occupied fairly small stable territories more or less year-round unless the male was displaced or killed, or drought forced them to move. The Ennu culled the females, working the same stable herds in the same areas.

On this side of the mountains, the long dry season lasted for more than half the year, during which most of the large herd animals moved into the woodlands to browse on shrubs and trees. Thus concentrated, the animals were easy for the hunters to locate. When the rains began, the herds migrated back out onto the more open savannas, scattering widely over the vast grassy plains to the east, north, and south.

"*Obengrabog*—it is summer," William had said to him just yesterday, and the animals were still scattered. In the spring the old hunter's band followed the animal migrations out onto the open grasslands, then back into the woodlands along the foot of the mountains in the fall. Along the way they camped where they pleased, utilizing the great lake's many bays and lagoons for fishing and hunting waterfowl. As the Ennu said often, life was good.

Nainoa watched the horses and wondered why they did not migrate like the other big hooved animals. The large herds tended to overgraze the grasses within their territories, which only caused them to move around a bit. More or less year-round, they seemed to stay within an area about a single day's journey across. Thus, the Ennu always knew where the horses were and where they could most easily be ambushed.

It would be far easier to lead Chief Kaneohe to the horses, Nainoa thought, than to return through the mountains and great forest with even one horse. Could he convince Chief Kaneohe to establish a new community on this side of the mountains? He had asked William why the Ennu had not domesticated the wild horses; the old hunter's response had been characteristic: Horses were good to eat, and there were endless numbers of them. Who would want to possess them?

Nainoa's thoughts turned to Kenojelak. As he recalled the day they had become lovers, he felt his blood rise. The Ennu didn't miss much, and when they had returned to camp that evening, the good-natured ribaldry had begun almost immediately. Nainoa and Kenojelak had gotten through it all with humor and had taken up residence together that night, without ceremony or exchange of gifts to mark the occasion. One morning after a particularly passionate night on their bed of furs, Kenojelak had placed one of her beaded necklaces around his neck and made him a leather *malo* in the Ennu style. She no longer wore her hair in a single plume but braided it in the fashion of the other "married" women.

The Ennu were clearly pleased with their union, and Kenojelak informed him proudly that he was now related to virtually everyone in the camp. Over the next few months William and the other men had presented him with small handmade tokens of their esteem: small carved objects of ivory or bone, perforated to be worn as pendants or charms. Some represented animals, while others were more abstract. Kenojelak had added these gifts, one at a time, to the necklace she gave him.

Nainoa glanced at it now and fingered William's gift, a vertical design as long as his finger, in ivory, somewhat humanoid in form, covered with a pattern of small shallow depressions stained dark. When William gave it to him, Nainoa had not been quite able to make out what it represented, and he asked the older man what it was. William had looked at him thoughtfully for a moment before smiling broadly and answering, *"Bushivak."* Then he squatted and drew an image in the dust with his finger: a spotted tiger standing on its hind legs like a man! Shock rolled through Nainoa. How had William known of his spirit friend? The old Ennu, perceiving the younger man's surprise, simply laughed with delight, and that was the end of it.

In return, Nainoa had made small objects to give the Ennu—fishhooks in the Hawaiian style. Starting with a roughly shaped plaque of ivory or bone, he would drill a hole in its center and then shape the hook around it. The Ennu seemed very impressed with these utilitarian presents, which also made handsome pendants. Generosity was important among the Ennu, and these gifts were tangible symbols of his new alliances.

One day, not long after he had moved in with Kenojelak, Nainoa was reminded of his vision of the legendary city of San Francisco. He asked William if he knew of any really big ruins where the ancients had lived. There was a large one to the north, the older man had replied, and a smaller one to the south. Shortly thereafter, they moved camp, and the two men stood on the hilltops to the south looking at a series of low mounds in the long valley below the forested wall of the mountains. William told him that the *monay* had come from there.

At Nainoa's request, they had spent a day investigating the site. Nainoa walked among the mounds eagerly, looking for evidence of the former inhabitants, but five thousand years of rain and wind had covered everything with a blanket of earth, trees, and grasses. Little could be seen on the surface, beyond broken pieces of masonry and stonework that protruded from the ground here and there. They looked for metal and glass but had found little, and William told him that to find such things one had to dig. Nainoa wondered what might be revealed if the overlying earth and vegetation were removed.

Game was plentiful, and they returned to camp with two wild goats slung over their shoulders and several braces of wild chickens. These ground birds, with spotted feathers and small, pointed horny helmets on top of their heads, lived in large flocks that roosted in low trees at night and foraged out on the grassy plains during the day. They were reluctant to fly and easy to kill with throwing sticks.

As they walked back to camp between the mounds, Nainoa wanted to ask William if he had seen spirits in such places, but his grasp of the Ennu language was not yet up to the task. Except for feeling the presence that day with Kenojelak, he had not had any mystic experiences since leaving the mountain forest and rejoining human society.

Nainoa's reverie was suddenly broken by the sound of the horses—they were almost upon him. The stallion was herding at least eighty mares, some of whom had colts, toward the lake, nervous that some of its rivals were trailing in the far distance. The time had come for Nainoa to close the trap.

Nainoa waited until the herd passed him and then stood up, bringing his spear forward and grasping it firmly. He had faced off these male horses before and knew what to expect. But this big gray stallion was canny.

When it saw him, it ran back and forth between the man and its mares, urging them into a run toward the lake in the opposite direction. Then it turned and headed right for him with a high thin scream of warning.

In only a few heartbeats, the ground on which Nainoa stood was trembling with its hoofbeats. It ran to within six feet of Nainoa and looked with its right eye into his face. At the last moment it veered slightly and cleared the dry wash easily with a graceful leap and a cry of rage. The ground shook as it landed. Without pausing, the wild horse began to run around Nainoa in a tight circle, jumping the shallow erosion channel again and again so that Nainoa had to keep turning and turning to face it. Nainoa whirled around—and around—becoming slightly dizzy as the horse, its eyes rolling, circled him more and more closely. This male was unusually aggressive, perhaps because its rivals were so near. Nainoa sensed uneasily that the horse was going to come for him and that he might have to kill it in self-defense.

The horse skidded to a stop at the edge of the ditch and regarded him balefully, menacingly. Nainoa leaped out of the wash, putting it between himself and the angry beast. The big gray's eyes rolled and its nostrils flared as it snorted violently and shook its head. With one eye, it checked on its mares. The females had paused halfway to the lake, uncertain. Nainoa cursed under his breath. Perhaps they had caught the scent of the Ennu hunters.

The stallion glared again at Nainoa, shook its head, snorted explosively, and reared at him. Nainoa readied his spear for the charge. The gray horse dropped its head and arched its neck, and its thick, black mane rose up as it gouged the earth with its front hooves, demonstrating its intentions.

Nainoa stood absolutely still. He had no wish to kill this animal. It would be contrary to the best interests not only of the herd but of the Ennu who hunted the herd. The stallion snorted and trembled with heightened emotion. Quite suddenly, Nainoa felt the great animal's power and was no longer afraid. The force flowed strongly into him as each looked into the other's eyes, and he formed within his mind the clear intention of meaning no harm.

The horse flexed its neck again and started to advance, whereupon Nainoa spoke to it in a level, soothing tone in Old Hawaiian, blessing the horse and his females and asking it to depart:

"E ho'omaikai keia po'e lio."

The horse stopped, uncertain. Again Nainoa spoke to it, using a formal, even intonation:

"Blessings on this group of horses. . . . I have no wish to harm you. We humans have need of only one or two of your extra females to feed the hungry people in our camp. We ask only for those. We will take only what we need, and we will celebrate and give thanks to their spirits. I appeal to you, great horse, through your *aumakua*—take your females now and depart with my good intentions and my blessing."

The horse stared at him as he repeated his request once more. Then it glanced toward its females and tossed its head. Turning to look at its rivals, it blew a last forceful snort and whirled to depart at great speed toward the lake. Nainoa watched it run. Unthinking, he let out a great shout into the sky—to follow the horse—to carry the horse onward.

When the stallion had passed, Kenojelak and the other women rose from the ground farther down the wash. Some of the older children leaped up onto their cairns of stones to encourage the entire herd to keep moving. It surged into thunderous motion, and the trap was set. The men's arrows quickly took two of the females.

The remaining horses raced eastward into the dawn, driven by the gray stallion along the lakeshore until they were out of sight and only a cloud of dust remained to mark their passage.

Nainoa drew in long breaths, recovering gradually from the close encounter as the *mana* drained slowly from his trembling muscles. One of the downed horses was thrashing and screaming, a shrill sound that one of the hunters abruptly silenced with a spear thrust. Composing himself, Nainoa walked

across the plain toward the men gathered around their kill. On the way Kenojelak joined him, first giving him a long look and then saying:

"Nainoavangioaluk, you seem to have a way with horses." She paused and grinned before adding, "And women."

He smiled. Reaching out, he drew her to his side and hugged her, running his fingertips lightly across her breasts. Then he turned her to face him, and her delighted laugh caught in her throat as he kissed her. There was noplace they could be alone on this empty plain, however, and so Nainoa released her, and the two continued toward the hunters, holding hands.

She suddenly turned and asked him, "What did you say to the horse?" Nainoa told her, translating it into the Ennu language as best he could. She was silent for long moments, then asked, "What is *aumakua?*"

Nainoa paused and composed the Ennu words carefully in his mind. "*Aumakua* is the immortal, spiritual aspect of each of us. It exists at all times in the realm of the spirits, and it can travel across time. Everything that exists has an *aumakua* in the spirit world. Horses too. So I was communicating with that horse through its spirit."

Kenojelak thought for a moment. "It may be what we call *dorniok,*" she said. "You must talk with William about these matters. He is *ungagok.*"

"What is *ungagok?*" Nainoa asked.

Kenojelak looked at him playfully out of the corners of her long blue-gray eyes. "Ask William—but not until after we bathe."

They approached the hunters and the freshly killed horses. One of the young girls had been sent to the camp to inform the rest of the Ennu of the hunt's success and to summon help for transporting the meat. Several others had been sent to the nearest hillside, to watch for any large cats or bears that might be inclined to share in the feast.

The larger mare had a spotted coat and had been brought down by William's *egimag,* his throwing spear, which had penetrated its heart. The smaller female was darkly colored and had been struck by several arrows, one of which hit high in the midsection, passing through the kidneys.

Nainoa recognized the arrow as belonging to Alonerg, one of the best shots, and gave him an appreciative nod. Another had struck high in the neck and bore Bier's distinctive marks. The wounded horse had been dispatched by a final thrust of Alonerg's spear.

Some teasing was going on as they walked up. Tagumi's arrows had missed entirely, and one of Alozua's had struck the spotted horse in the rump near the tail. William had made the best *koop*. He preferred to use a spear thrown with the aid of a *baton*, a stick with a small hook in the end of it like a nose. The spear and the stick were held together in the same hand, the end of the spear notched into the hook. The *baton* increased the length of William's arm, allowing him to hurl the *egimag* a long distance, forcefully and accurately. Nainoa glanced at William and said, "*Bitziak!*—well done!"

The old hunter laughed and made a self-deprecating comment about his age and his shaking hands, pantomiming decrepitude. All present laughed with him, releasing the tension of those who had not achieved a *koop*. The social challenge for the accomplished Ennu hunter was to excel at his craft without inciting the envy of others.

The hunters' mirth now escalated into expressions of general celebration. The hunt had gone well, and no one had been injured. The mood quieted somewhat when William turned to Nainoa and asked, "What did you say to the horse?"

Nainoa calculated the distance from the place of his encounter with the stallion to the spot where William had been hidden. There was nothing wrong with the older man's eyesight. All ears turned as Nainoa repeated what he had told Kenojelak. All the Ennu looked at him thoughtfully after he had finished.

After a moment of silence, William said a short prayer to the horses, asking for their forgiveness for ending their lives so abruptly. As Nainoa had, he explained that this act had been done only out of necessity to feed the hungry people of the camp and that all would feel gratitude as they ate the horsemeat. The Ennu would celebrate the horses that evening, he announced, and he asked their spirits to linger awhile, to hear the songs that would be sung in their honor. When the party was over, the horses' spirits would be free to depart, to roam into the spirit world, where he hoped they would find much sweet grass and a strong male to follow. He ended by wishing them safe passage.

All the hunters then shouted praise for the horses, wishing their spirits well: *"Ganagodalek! . . . Okshooni! . . . Okshooni!"*

As the oldest male hunter, William made the first cut, opening the spotted horse's belly with a single deft stroke of his stone knife. Then he deepened the incision and reached in, his arm disappearing almost to the shoulder, until he found and squeezed off the esophagus as it passed through the diaphragm and entered the stomach. With his knife hand, he made a quick cut and drew out the horse's entrails, freeing them from their connecting tissues and passing them to the others without spilling their contents. Reaching in once more, he grasped the intestine at its exit from the body and cut again, drawing out the remainder of the digestive tract. He then took his digging stick and dug a vertical pit in which to bury the steaming mass of offal they would squeeze from the entrails.

He repeated this operation with the second horse, and all fell to work. Nainoa began to skin the spotted horse with his long knife. They probably had enough meat to feed the entire camp for several days. The camp now consisted of more than a hundred people, since William's band had been joined by two others when they had arrived at the lake several days before. Nainoa's presence had made quite a stir among the two other bands, and over several evenings the Ennu had told stories about him and his origins. All had been intrigued by his height and size, by his possessions and weapons, and by the hardness of his iron spear and knife. The women had pressed Kenojelak for information as well and laughed bawdily at her responses.

Nainoa glanced at her now. She was working on the carcass on the other side of him, standing with her long legs well apart and her hands and forearms red with blood. As she extracted a fatty blob from the horse's body, a spray from a severed vessel spattered blood across her breasts and stomach. With a deft twist, she squeezed out a shiny, blue-veined kidney and took a bite before passing it to him. He smiled and passed the gleaming prize to her father. Nainoa still preferred his horsemeat cooked and had to endure her teasing laugh as everyone else ate.

What would the Hawaiians think of her? he wondered. But then, how could he take Kenojelak back with him to his own people? Surely she could not become a servant in a chief's household. The meaning of social hierarchy was completely outside her experience. How would she fare in a politically complex system based on privilege, in which men and women lived and ate in separate worlds for much of the time? The Ennu loved to surround themselves with as many kin as possible. How could he take her to a place where she knew no one and did not understand the language? What would that do to her spirit? For that matter, how could he himself return to being a servant, now that he had been a chief?

Nainoa smiled grimly. He knew that he could probably stay with the Ennu and live out the rest of his life with them. Yet deep within, he understood that he would not. The time would come for him to return to his world, to Chief Kaneohe and his people.

More of the Ennu arrived from camp, and within a short time the carcasses were converted into portable pieces for transport. The meat was cut in strips and hung on long poles for carrying. The long marrowbones were taken intact, as were the parts of the back and ribs to which meat was still attached. The skull and the hooves were carefully tied in a bundle with strips of hide and hung up in a tree near the lake.

Whenever the Ennu killed an animal, they always hung its bones in a tree. William had told him this was done because it had always been done, and because it would not be right to let their bones be dishonored by scavengers.

"All of our food and clothing comes from the animals we kill," he had said. "If their spirits are displeased with the way we treat their remains, they will not allow us to kill them anymore, and we will have poor hunting. The Ennu would starve, and we would all die. So we impress their spirits with our good intentions. We hang their mortal remains in trees just as we do our own."

The Ennu did not deal with spirits through any formalized religion; nor did they worship them. They simply had a profound respect for them—and a profound fear of them. To deal with their fear, they followed a system of *kapus* that helped keep the animals' spirits placated, so that the animals would continue to allow themselves to be killed and the Ennu would not suffer misfortune. They never cooked fish and meat together, for example, nor fish and fowl, nor meat and fowl. One should never bring things from the land or water or air into contact with each other, they believed. No one knew why this was so—it was done because their ancestors had done it before them. Another common *kapu* prohibited the wife of a hunter from making any clothing on the day her husband killed game. Nor could she have sex with him the day before a hunt.

William's short prayer to the horses' spirits would keep the horses' souls from harming the people and showed the profound respect they felt for all life. Nagai had taught Nainoa similar beliefs and practices.

When they arrived at the camp, a wooded hillside above the lake, all were delighted by the quantity of meat and by the amount of fat in it, which was unusual because of the sparseness of grass at this time of year. The hunters who had made the *koops* divided the meat between all the families, taking considerable time and care so that all among the three bands had roughly equal amounts. Each family took their share; some would be cooked immediately, some would be cut in strips and hung on racks over fires to dry slowly, out of reach of the dogs. All were talking animatedly about the details of the hunt, and Nainoa heard his own name mentioned frequently.

In the afternoon Nainoa and Kenojelak withdrew to a bathing place beyond the camp. They meandered slowly through the grassland toward the trees, which bracketed a substantial stream flowing into the lake. Kenojelak's pack of dogs accompanied them.

Most of the children from the camp were playing and swimming in the shallows of the lake with their mothers nearby. Several boys on the wide beach shouted excitedly as they played with a toy made from the flat shoulder blade of a horse. It had been drilled with several holes of varying size and was tied with a long cord to a handle made of a deer's lower leg bone, trimmed to a point. The boys swung the flat plate of bone high in the air and attempted to impale it as it fell on the pointed handle through one of its smallest holes.

Kenojelak noticed that Nainoa was preoccupied as they walked, but she said nothing. When they were alone among the willows and gum trees, she washed the dried blood from their clothing in the stream and draped it on bushes to dry. Then she washed herself. Nainoa watched her, and her beauty and grace took his breath away. She loosened her thick braids and shook her hair out, displaying her body in ways she knew would arouse him. Then she unbraided his hair and invited him to lie on his back on a slab of stone at the water's edge so that she could wash it. In doing so, she brushed her nipples against him until his mood lifted with his penis, and he laughingly took her into his arms and kissed her. They made long leisurely love and afterward slept for a while in each other's arms on the soft grasses in the shade of a tree.

The light had changed by the time he awoke. She was still holding him, watching him with her serious look. "Nainoapak," she said. "Do you have a wife among your people whom you miss?" The question surprised him, and he assured her that he did not.

"Is there a woman among your people who you wish to take as wife?" she persisted. He reassured her that there was none.

She regarded him seriously. "Today you have changed. Tell me what it is so that I may understand."

So he told her about his former life and about the structure of his society. He had talked of these things before, but he had never questioned them as he did today. Kenojelak watched him impassively as she listened, interrupting only occasionally to correct his pronunciation or clarify a thought with an alternative word ending.

He told her of his quest and duty to Chief Kaneohe, who wished to have horses and had sent him here to discover what lay beyond the mountains. He spoke of his place within his own society and of his duty to his people, who would value the knowledge he had acquired.

"So you see," he ended, "the time will come for me to return—to take back what I have learned to my people and to my chief. And when I think of this, it causes me sadness, for you will remain here with your people. I cannot take you from them. You would not be happy in my world."

Kenojelak remained silent for a while as he held her in his arms, and his heart ached as he thought of life without her. Then she sat up and looked at him. "Why not stay here with us?" she said. "Life is good. The land is full of game. The lake is full of fish. You like it here. I feel your happiness every day. Only today, when you thought of your people and your former life with them, only then did you become unhappy."

Nainoa looked at her solemn face. What she said was true. He was very happy here. He could stay—and yet part of him knew that he would have to return, for reasons that were not altogether clear to him. He would have to finish what he had begun. This cycle of his life would have to be completed before something else could commence. He told her this, and her eyes filled with tears that flowed silently down her cheeks, searing him with her sorrow.

"I do not understand why you must leave," she said, "but if you feel that you must, then you will go." For long moments he held her as she grieved, as her tears made warm spots on his skin. Inside he too felt as though he were losing something of inestimable value.

Kenojelak suddenly sat up and smiled at him through her tears. Her eyes began to sparkle with vitality and power once more as she looked into his eyes and said, "But you will return to me. I feel this very strongly. You will go back to your own people for a while and do there what it is you must do. And then you will remember your life with us, and you will think of your Ennu wife—and you will remember this."

She pushed him so that he fell over flat on his back and wrapped her long body around his. She ground her pelvis against him with a breathy laugh and kissed him as he had taught her—and he realized that she was right. He kissed her in return and held her closely, caressing her warm skin, feeling her beautiful body.

Later, she smiled languidly at him and said, "Now you can ask William about *ungagok*."

The light was fading as they dressed. Kenojelak filled her large, tightly woven water container and, with Nainoa's assistance, slung it on her back and adjusted the soft leather carrying straps up and over her forehead.

As they walked back to the camp, the land softened in the growing shadows, and Nainoa felt his connection with its spirit too. For the Ennu, even nonliving things, rocks and hills, had a spirit and a certain capacity for action. Each person, each animal, each tree and plant—each cliff face, mountain, and pebble—each cloud, rainbow, and thunderstorm—was considered to be *zakray*, to be holy, intelligent, and filled with mystical power and vitality. The Ennu believed each creature and thing had tasks unique to its being, which kept the universe functioning in life-enhancing ways, maintaining order and balance and keeping disorder within bounds. When any among the multitudinous forms failed to meet their obligations, all suffered. Humans in particular were required to live in ways that fostered order and balance. A person's every action, thought, intention, and feeling contributed either to the greater universal good or to its suffering. Nainoa felt keenly that he must be careful as he determined the actions he should take to complete his mission.

By the time Nainoa and Kenojelak returned to the camp, the celebration of the hunt and the reunion of the several bands were already under way. People were dancing, laughing, playing games, and gossiping. They were eating and singing and doing anything they had a mind to do. The mood was up. Life was good.

Kenojelak hung her water basket up in the tree next to their hut and joined her mother, who was cooking meat in front of her hut with a group of older women. Kovak greeted her daughter with a ribald comment that made Kenojelak blush. The others laughed and pointedly turned to give Nainoa appraising looks. Kenojelak ignored them, filled his food bowl with broiled meat, and handed it to him. He took the food, grinned at the women, and departed. Raucous laughter followed his retreat. The horsemeat had salt and herbs on it to make a delicious, spicy taste. He thanked the horse's spirit.

Half the camp was playing a game that the Hawaiians called *hukihuki*. Men of one band were pitted against those of another, both sides pulling mightily on a long woven rope, trying to haul their opponents across a muddy place. Everyone was straining and grunting, laughing and farting, all the while calling loudly to their women for reinforcements. They spotted Nainoa, and both sides implored him to join them. William protested loudly that Nainoapak, as his son-in-marriage, should pull on his team. The others offered him temporary loan of their wives or daughters if he would pull on their side. Much laughter and good humor accompanied their suggestive remarks, which became more and more elaborate as they strained and pulled.

Nainoa smiled. *Hukihuki* was a game at which Hawaiians excelled. He strolled up and down the line eating unconcernedly, offering free advice to both sides until he was finished. By this time, the rest of the camp had drifted over to see the outcome, so he handed his bowl to Kenojelak and joined William's team at their end of the rope.

Feeling the tension of the woven rope, Nainoa did something Nagai had taught him long ago. He consciously imagined himself filling with *mana*, forming a mental image of power entering his body through his head and coming to rest at his midsection. He closed his eyes and breathed deeply several times, pulling it in, and felt his *mana* begin to increase. A warm tingling rush flowed along his spine, and his arms and legs prickled into goose bumps. He continued to breathe, pulling it in—and when it reached a certain level of intensity, he focused it . . . and slowly pulled his extended family to victory.

The women unleashed a new barrage of ribald observations about his size and strength, shouting bawdy questions to Kenojelak, which she fielded with equally outrageous answers, much to everyone's immense enjoyment.

After the losing team had extracted themselves from the mud and gone off to the lake to clean up, Kenojelak got another bowl of spicy horsemeat, which she shared with Nainoa as they wandered through the camp. Mothers played what the Hawaiians called *hei*, cat's cradle, with their children. The Ennu had many, many designs for this game, each with a special name, each accompanied by its own stories or songs.

Some young girls ran up to them and sang an impromptu song about Nainoapak, the giant who had come from the forest, and about tall Kenojelak, who would bear him children. Kenojelak whispered in his ear that this was her wish too—that they would have tall sons who were strong and wise and who would be successful hunters like their father. Nainoa whispered back that perhaps they would have daughters of great wisdom, beauty, and sexual power like their mother. She laughed and pinched him playfully, her teeth flashing in the growing dusk.

Just before dark, someone brought out a large circular blanket. It had been fashioned from several large hides that had been sewn together, and many holes had been cut around the periphery. Everyone shouted for Kenojelak to get onto it. She did, and the men and women gripped its edges and pulled it taut, lifting her off the ground. They then rhythmically pulled the blanket, so that Kenojelak was tossed into the air and caught—tossed and caught. To loud shouts of encouragement, she flew higher and higher until she was ascending to over twenty feet, making graceful somersaults and turns in midair. Her long legs performed wild antics that became more and more outrageous—and erotic—until she had the whole camp hooting with laughter.

Nainoa laughed too, standing with William and his son Tagumi. The older man chuckled as his daughter performed a particularly spectacular leap, then turned and twinkled at Nainoa. "Come and get something to eat with us," he said. "To deal with these women, you need to keep your fire burning."

The three men walked back toward the center of the camp, where they received more food at Kovak's fire-pit. As they ate, Nainoa observed that the spirit of the horse they were consuming was certainly being properly celebrated. Both Ennu men agreed. The horse's soul, William added, would now tell all the other horse spirits of this *fut* and of how the humans had sung and danced and entertained it with music.

"The spirits of the animals love music," he said. "And having enjoyed our songs, the horses' souls will return to the spirit world and tell all the others. They will then allow us to kill them, so they too can get out of their skins and come to visit with us. Because of this, hunting will be good.

"If the people celebrate properly," he continued, "if they remember to observe correct hospitality when entertaining our deer or horse or elephant neighbors, then the animals' souls will be reborn again and again, and we will always have enough to eat."

Nainoa came to a decision and turned to look into the older man's eyes. "William," he asked, "how do the Ennu perceive the soul?"

William and Tagumi looked at him in silence, and then the older man gestured to the top of the hill above the camp. The gesture implied, "Let's find a quiet place to sit and talk."

William glanced at his son, who then went over to his own hut and reemerged carrying a large rolled-up hide. The three men then ascended the hill and spread the hide beneath a tree, from which they could see out over the entire camp and to the open countryside beyond.

Far away a lion roared—and roared again. William smiled. The *liobi*, he said, was letting all the others of its kind know where he was—that he was calling, "Here I am—here I am—here I am," so that other males would stay out of his way. As the moon cleared the hills beyond the lake, the three men sat in silence, watching the great ball of light grow round in the darkening sky.

Nainoa looked at William. "Among my people," he said, "the soul, *iho*, is one's personal, vital essence or awareness. It is distinct from the *aumakua*, the separate higher, spiritual level of the self. The *aumakua* lives in the spirit world. Everything in nature has one, but whether or not they have souls like those of humans, we don't know."

William thought for a while in silence. Then he said to Nainoa, "We also feel that everything has a vital, personal essence. For us, this essence has three aspects. First of all, there is that which we call *dorniok*. This is the personal spirit of each thing, both living and nonliving. This may be the same as what you call *aumakua*.

"There is also *onerniok*, the breath that fills living things with life. It is a second aspect of the soul. Only animals and humans possess an *onerniok*, and because of this we can interact with Zilatu, the spirit of the air. Because animals and humans have an *onerniok*, we have more power than do the plants and the rocks, which do not have an *onerniok*."

Nainoa struggled to understand. Then he suddenly got it and interjected excitedly, "What you call *onerniok* sounds like what we call the *ha*, the breath of life. We possess *ha* only when we are alive. When we die, we release our *ha*, our life-breath, which then returns to the universe, rejoining the life-force of which it is a part."

William nodded and smiled at Nainoa in the moonlight. "In addition to possessing *dorniok* and *onerniok*," he continued, "we humans are distinct from all other manifested beings in that each of us also has a name. We call this aspect of the self *odiok*, the name soul, and it possesses considerable power. The fact that we have *odiok* is the main reason that humans have more power than do animals or plants or stones. So you see, animals do indeed have souls, but not as we do. Animals have only two of these soul parts, plants and rocks have only one."

Nainoa digested this information slowly and then asked, "What happens to these aspects of the soul at death?"

William looked at the moon for long moments before replying. "When the body dies, it slowly dissolves back into the earth, but our soul aspects are released into the spirit world, to exist there until they are recombined and reborn as another human being. When a new child is growing within its mother's body, it is without spirit until it moves for the first time. This first movement marks the initial arrival of *dorniok*, which then comes and goes until it settles permanently into the growing child during the last moons of pregnancy. When the child is born, it receives *oneriok* when it draws its first breath of life-force from the spirit of the air. *Odiok* is given to the new child by those who name it."

William smiled in the moonlight and concluded, "The great cycle of life and death proceeds in this way, through an endless succession of physical bodies. It will never stop but will go on forever. Our wise elders and our spiritual helpers have revealed that each of us has lived countless past lives. In this sense each of us has existed before, as our own ancestor. We will be manifested again into uncountable lifetimes as our own descendants. In this way we will go on and on, living endless numbers of lives, continually growing, continually hunting and enjoying life, continually searching for answers about the mystery of our own existence. This is our destiny."

The three men remained silent for a while, staring up at the brilliant moon. Then Nainoa told William and Tagumi about his mystical experiences. He started with his confrontation with the immensely strong shadowy spirit *ke'aka* in the ruined *siti*. He spoke of his strange meeting with the tiger man and of his later encounter with the forest spirit, of his spectacular vision of the world tree that led to his breathtaking journey into a level of abstract patterns and symbols, and of his spirit flight with the hawk—a journey in which he saw the huts of the Ennu in the valley where they had finally found him.

Nainoa struggled because of his inability to name or describe in Ennu terms many of the things he had seen. William and Tagumi listened silently throughout.

Then he told them of his strange journeylike encounters with the American who lived in Hawai'i in the time before the Fall, of the amazing experience of having his own awareness detach from his physical body and travel through time and space to merge with that of another man. He described what he had seen and mentioned his growing suspicion that the American was also able to merge with him here, saying that he had felt the American's presence while watching the horses this morning. He speculated that the American might be one of his ancestral selves living a former life in a former time.

Nainoa's *mana* had steadily increased as he told William and Tagumi of his visions. When he finished, he was trembling with heightened feeling as he asked William, "How can I verify any of this? How is this contact with the American possible? What causes it to happen?"

William laid a hand lightly on his arm, and Nainoa felt himself calm. "There are some things we cannot know," the older man said. William's muscular arm then swept out to include the vast moonlit landscape all around them. "The ultimate nature of all this is beyond the power of our understanding."

Then he smiled warmly. "Some of us are able to spiritwalk and make direct contact with the spiritual realms and the beings who reside there. We can understand the nature of the experience in many different ways. These ways ultimately depend on how we each interpret our everyday lives. Our individual thoughts, beliefs, and attitudes make us perceive the spirits in our own way. Yet there are basic similarities. . . ." His voice drifted off.

Nainoa smiled and offered, "Reality is what we believe it to be."

"Yes," replied William. "*Lutok*—truly."

Nainoa thought for a while. "William—what is *ungagok*?"

In response, the older man gazed at Tagumi, who spoke for the first time:

"The *ungagok* is a living person who can voluntarily enter trance and walk with spirits," he said. "The *ungagok* can journey into the other worlds in order to deal with the spirits on behalf of the people. Spiritwalkers are people of exceptional ability who intercede directly with the powers of the universe. They are also known as the *bozdezpree*, the masters of spirits."

Nainoa thought about this. "There are such people among the Hawaiians as well," he offered, "and we also call them masters of spirits." Then he asked William, "I have need of such a person's abilities and knowledge. I must understand what I have experienced during my walk through the great forest and through the mountains. Are you a spiritwalker, William?"

Tagumi looked uncomfortable as he spoke once again. "You must understand, Nainoapak. The spirits are always about, and they despise spiritual arrogance. For a person to announce out loud that they are a spiritwalker would displease them greatly. It would be regarded as boasting, and so no *ungagok* worthy of the name would ever do so. It would be a quick way for even the greatest *ungagok* to lose his power. My father is acknowledged as *ungagok*, as spiritwalker among his people, and having heard of your experiences, I feel he would be pleased to talk with you about them."

William smiled at his son as Nainoa gathered his thoughts. "I never had any mystical experiences before this journey," Nainoa said, "although I have always been interested in the abilities and practices of the mystics among my people."

William responded thoughtfully. "You may have had what we call *dornamolinkayak*, mystic experiences, earlier in your life and simply been unaware of what they were. The spirit world can be considered not only a place but also a level of awareness. When the *ungagok* goes to meet with the spirits in their levels of reality, he shifts his level of awareness. Most children do this easily and naturally. Did you ever have spirit friends when you were a child—imaginary friends who played and talked with you?"

Long-forgotten imaginary friends had indeed accompanied Nainoa and nurtured him through his childhood: a forest friend, with whom he had daydream adventures; a magic tiger, which had always accompanied the two friends on their quests; a hawk, which had carried them through the air. As Nainoa remembered them now, he accepted that his visionary experiences had begun long ago.

"Those experiences were more like dreams," Nainoa began, struggling with Ennu syntax.

"It is somewhat like dreaming," William agreed. "When you sleep at night, you dream. Part of your soul leaves your body behind and has adventures. It meets old friends far away and finds spirits in strange, unreal places. Most people do this naturally when they are asleep. The *ungagok* does this with intention, when very much awake.

"Intentions are very important because they provide the framework and the destination. In order for the process to happen successfully, you have to have a destination, a strongly desired place that you want to go or a thing that you wish to accomplish or acquire. The intentions of the spiritwalker bring him into contact."

William paused as though he were listening to something only he could hear. "Sometimes human beings who wish to become *ungagok* will begin by deliberately seeking out the spirits," he continued. "These persons must be able to get the spirits to notice them and take mercy on them. They must get the spirits to agree to become their teachers. Sometimes such seekers of power are successful if the spirits deem them worthy."

William looked at Nainoa closely. "But sometimes people who are unaware of their destiny will stumble into it seemingly by accident. They may be comfortable and at ease with their life. They may be completely ignorant of what the spirits intend for them. And then one night, the spirits will send Ongamayo, the guardian, to visit them in order to see how they will react . . ."

Nainoa thought of the tall, dark *ke'aka* he had seen.

"And then," William went on, "the spirits will determine if the individual is ready. If the person reacts to the guardian with fear and terror, perceiving it as a demon and branding it as evil, that person is unready, and the doorway to the spirit world remains closed. People who react in this way are still of limited awareness. The evil they think they perceive in the guardian is actually the evil side of their own nature, reflected back at them." William glanced around uneasily. "And the great power to which the guardian has access can magnify this aspect of their personality into something truly formidable."

William smiled at Nainoa. "But those who are ready to embark upon their destiny will have a different reaction. Those who are ready to walk with the spirits will sense the guardian for what it is and will respond to it with interest and wonder, as you did. Ongamayo will perceive their receptivity and will test them—and if they pass the test, the gateway to the spirit world will then open to them.

"The spirits will then instruct the *ungagok*-to-be, allowing that person access to their realm across the zone of power. From what you have told me, you may be such a person, although you were unaware of it until the spirits gave you a glimpse of themselves and a taste of universal power— that which you call *mana*.

"You are being initiated, Nainoapak. You are being invited. Other *un-gagok* may be able to guide and reassure you to some extent. We may be able to clarify certain things and make some suggestions for you, but this is all we can do. The real teachers are the spirits themselves. Only they can convey true knowledge and power to the spiritwalker."

William paused and looked down at the sprawl of huts among the trees below. Talking certainly was thirsty work, he observed to no one in particular. Tagumi rose and silently descended to the camp. His father watched him and then went on.

"The primary task of the spiritwalker is to help others. The *ungagok* intercedes directly with the spirits on behalf of the people of his or her community. All *ungagok* have *dordok*—spirit helpers to assist them in their endeavors. These function as both protectors and teachers. You seem to have acquired at least one—the spirit you call the tiger man.

"The spirit of *bushivak*, the spotted tiger, is a most powerful ally and one of great ability. You acquired it as spirit helper through your friend Nagai. Perhaps *bushivak* was also a spirit helper for your ancestor. Perhaps you have had a good relationship with this entity within your lineage for a long time. This spirit has probably been at least partly responsible for bringing you and your ancestral-self together.

"I do not know the answers to these questions, but you do. The answers are all there inside yourself, and now you are beginning to awaken to that which is there. Your *dorniok*, or *aumakua*, knows all the answers to all the questions that you ever might think up. It will reveal many things to you if you know how to ask in just the right way. The first step lies in simply knowing that it exists. The rest then follows.

"Through the guardian that tested you, you have had what we call *kumonek*, the experiencing of the inner light of the brain and body. This inner light is imperceptible to most humans, but it is visible to the spirits. They are attracted to it and are thus drawn to the *ungagok* for whom some of them then become *dordok*, spirit helpers.

"In gaining your *kumonek*, you have begun to experience what we call spirit vision. You have been given a glimpse of the spirits and their hidden worlds. Life is going to be different for you because of this. You have been called, Nainoapak, and you cannot refuse the call. Once the spirits have chosen a person to become *ungagok*, the invitation cannot be denied. To do so is dangerous. There is a pattern within the mystery of life of which we are all a part, and the spirits have decided that the time has come for you to become that which you are destined to be.

"You must now learn to sharpen your ability to see and interact with the spirits. In time, this ability will deepen into a visionary capacity, in which you can summon them and see them at will. Then you will be able to accomplish much, and you will learn many things that are hidden from more ordinary people. But first you must learn to control the process.

"*Ogwayba*—the doorway. You have opened the doorway that lies within your mind. For most people, this door remains closed throughout their lives, and they are not even aware of its presence. Since you have now discovered it is there, you must develop your ability to open it and travel back and forth across the zone of power at will.

"You must appeal to the spirits to function as your *dordok*. You will need them to be there as your protectors and your teachers—to assist and protect you in your endeavors. Perhaps I can also help by showing you how to achieve that inner state in which you can perceive the spirits most easily."

The Ennu hunter fell silent and seemed to go into deep thought. When he looked at Nainoa again, his eyes were vacant. "When you have finally become a mature *ungagok*," he said in a monotone, "you may be able to see the spirits all the time, even in your ordinary waking state of mind. You will then be able to control many of them, thereby gaining access to their immense knowledge and power. As an awakened and accomplished spiritwalker, you will be able to benefit all those around you.

"But there is something else that you must understand. What the spiritwalker seeks when he or she journeys to the inner worlds is not just the spirits themselves. The *ungagok* seeks connection with the power of the universe, an ageless power. This power transcends even the spirits. This is what you felt in the presence of the guardian, and the spirits yield it only to those spiritwalkers deemed worthy.

"This is part of what it means to be *ungagok*."

They were silent for a long time, listening to the singing and drumming of the celebration. Tagumi returned with a container of drinking water and left again without making a sound.

William smiled. "Sometimes *ungagok* are recognized by special signs or by their behavior when they are children. But it is also common for a potential spiritwalker to be identified later in life, often by the sudden experiencing of unusual events such as yours. Sometimes a person may endure serious illness and come close to death. In the midst of their sickness, the spirits may assist them in curing themselves, and they may train the *ungagok*-to-be so that he or she can help others cure themselves in turn.

"Sometimes the initiation will begin with an inner experience of strange dreams and visions, but waking ones in which the dreamer is aware that he is dreaming and can act in and direct his dreams. The spirits will come to the *ungagok*-to-be through these visions, in order to offer instruction in the knowledge of things hidden from ordinary people.

"In my own case, I heard my name being called by a spirit. I followed it and spent the best part of a dry season alone out there." William gestured out into the vast distances revealed by the moonlight. "During this time of solitude, I gained my *kumonek* and was trained by my spirit teacher. Like you, I had no indication earlier in my life that I was to become a spiritwalker.

"Your solitude in the forest provided the spirits with a time when you would not be distracted by your ordinary life. The spirit that resides in your chief's stone seems to have intentions for you as well. You have said it comes from the lands of your ancestry. Perhaps it had a relationship with your ancestral-self."

Nainoa remembered the image of the American's face looking back at him from the wall of glass.

"Perhaps the spirit in the stone was responsible for initiating the contact between the two of you. If this is so, you have another powerful ally. The earth spirits have minds much like ours, but they are profoundly more

aware and are infinitely more knowledgeable. They do not have to think about anything. They simply know. They exist within the earth and inside rocks, through which they can move as though through empty space. The earth spirits may be thought of as the minds of the earth. The knowledge they possess is the collective wisdom of the universe.

"It is remarkable that you had a meeting with your chief's spirit stone on the eve of your departure. The earth spirits know that our human minds exist in a dreamlike state for much of the time. They know that for us to understand who and what we really are, we must first awaken. They perceive this quite clearly and call us to wake up. This call is like a force or power that can have a strong effect upon us, as it has had upon you. . . ."

William's words trailed off. An owl flew soundlessly through the trees above them. Far away the lion roared again—and again—and again. The night air was soft and warm.

In his mind's eye, Nainoa saw the spirit stone scowling at him with its fierce gaze, and a whispered word abruptly appeared in his mind, a soft yet definite command in Old Hawaiian: "*Ho'alahia!*—awaken!" He felt curiously light-headed, as though he were sitting at the edge of a cliff. Below, he sensed a vast chasm, a deep rift in the earth, from whose shadowy depths strange thoughts and images began to emerge and slip through his mind. Part of him seemed to be listening to William as if from a vast distance. Nainoa sensed this part as separate somehow, and he wondered if this part were the American.

The thought did not alarm him anymore. He accepted his visions and contact as part of the pattern. He was thinking about this when William put a hand on his arm and said, "I sense the presence of another. Is it him?"

Nainoa was startled by the older man's awareness and replied, "Perhaps —I do not know. William, I wish to deepen my connection with him. I want to meet him. There is much we need to discuss. Is it possible?"

The older man shrugged his broad shoulders. "Who can say what is possible? Your intentions and your abilities will provide the shape of what is possible for you. In the spirit world, time goes in both directions. Once you successfully shift into that level of awareness, you can go anywhere you choose. Tell me about him, Nainoapak. What is he like? What is his world like?"

Nainoa considered the question. "He is tall, but not as tall as I. He is older, a scholar, and his mind is filled with words. His house is filled with wonders." He described the visionary encounters in as much detail as he could recall and ended by observing, "He seems very familiar in a strange way, like an old friend or acquaintance. I feel as though I know him well— but of course, that is not possible."

Nainoa became very still as an odd thought emerged. "Something else is interesting: His wife reminds me of Kenojelak. They resemble each other physically—but more important, they resemble each other in spirit, at the level of *dorniok*. I do not know how I know this. It is just a feeling I have."

William drank some water, then passed the gourd to Nainoa. Both were still. Then the older man said, "These are things we sense as true but have no way of verifying. But—perhaps there is a way. We should visit the spirit hills. Perhaps you will be able to meet with him there. It is a strange place. The wind blows and the spirits speak. Perhaps the beings that reside there will help you achieve the meeting that you seek."

"Where are the spirit hills?" Nainoa asked.

William pointed with his lips to the east. "Out that way—some days' journey near the lake. We can leave the people here and take what we need. I will take you to meet the *dorajuadiok* at the spirit hills." His teeth flashed in the darkness. "I can assist you in meeting them, Nainoapak, but once you do, you will be on your own. Your intentions will determine the nature of your experience. You will have to build your questions carefully, and you must always be in control, both of yourself and also of them."

Nainoa felt an edge of unease. "What are *dorajuaks*?" he asked.

"*Dorajuadioks*," William corrected, "are spirits. They are immensely powerful and are able to control other spirits at the request of an *ungagok*. They can even summon and dominate the spirits of the elements. For example, we might wish to call on the *enerzuak*, the spirits of the water. By going through a *dorajuadiok*, a spiritwalker can request the *enerzuak* to help bring the fish up from the deep water into the waiting nets of the people. This is a very useful thing to be able to do if your people are hungry.

"The *dorajuadiok* can assist in many things. They can recover the lost soul part of one who is sick or injured. But one must be careful—they are also known to steal souls. This is why the *ungagok* must always be in control. Perhaps they can help you make contact with your ancestor—"

William suddenly broke off and looked intently into the eyes of the younger man for long moments. Then he said, "And if the other, the one you call the American, is here with you, I, William the hunter, say to him, *Kujonamek!*—Warm greetings to the visitor from the past!"

21
The *Sesshin*

THE SHOCK OF BEING SO DIRECTLY ADDRESSED across
the millennia broke through my concentration
and the contact, and I emerged from the altered
state at dawn, exhilarated and exhausted.

I had been able to understand the long conversation
between William and Nainoa. In the days that followed, I
excavated various fragments, recalling the conversation in
chunks, until I had reconstructed the whole on paper.
This took time, but I eventually was satisfied with what I
had written. The conceptual content of the long conversation between the two men is entirely theirs. The gram-
matical choice of words, syntax, and morphology is, of
course, entirely mine.

The implications of the Ennu's ideas about the spirit
and the universe and other transcendental truths amazed
me. The continuity of the shamanic experience from millennia before the Common Era to millennia in the future
was staggering, but it was also, in a way, comforting,

holding out the promise of some continuity of the human psyche as well as our emotional and spiritual nature.

I was struck, too, by the individualist, democratic nature of the ancient mystical method. There are no limits set by ethnicity, cultural background, or station in life. Everyone can have his or her own transcendent experience and gain access to the realm of the sacred, without need of an intermediary. The role of the spiritual teacher in this tradition is initiatory, functioning primarily to reveal what is possible and to help individuals expand their awareness. Once students have been set on their way, they are essentially on their own. As many spiritual teachers have said, "All real power and knowledge come from within," a statement echoed by Michael Harner and mystics from all world traditions.

My intentions had actually brought me into contact with an authentic tribal shaman across five thousand years of time, and it had happened through the awareness of someone who was in the process of becoming a shaman himself. I felt increasingly certain that I was involved in some form of mystical education, guided or influenced by the intercession of spiritual entities. William's comments about earth and water spirits particularly fascinated me, since I knew of the Celtic traditions about the "little people" and the elemental nature spirits of wild places. The spirit stone in the rock garden might be one such "elemental" that had taken me on. Had I been "enchanted" by the nature spirits in the trees and rocks on this active volcano where I lived? Had I been given this information about the future because of my contact with the spiritual essence of the land? Did some sort of energetic "informational field" exist around and within the wild natural places—one on which I had been able to pick up, once my ability to see and hear had been amplified?

On a Friday afternoon, a week after my greeting from William, I was driving south from my home in Honaunau along the Mamalahoa Highway. My destination lay on the other side of the island—a place called Wood Valley Temple, where I intended to participate in a *sesshin*, a three-day

Buddhist retreat, over which a visiting Zen master from Honolulu, Robert Aitken Rōshi, one of the deans of American Zen, would preside.

More than a decade had passed since I had first picked up Shunryu Suzuki Rōshi's slim volume, *Zen Mind, Beginner's Mind,* a book that had had a profound effect on me. Over the intervening years, I had read a modest number of writings and commentaries of various Buddhist and Taoist worthies who had lived and practiced during the past few thousand years. Among them was a book on ethics called *The Mind of Clover,* written by Aitken.[1]

As I negotiated the rural highway south of Honaunau, memories of my walks with Nainoa besieged me, to the detriment of my driving. Much of the highway is narrow, winding, and hazardous, and huge tour buses frequently appear around blind curves, taking up most of the two-lane road. As I passed a recent lava flow near the ninety-six-mile marker, I saw a cotton tree at the entrance to someone's property. The owners had nailed a *"kapu*—no trespassing" sign to its buttressed trunk. It looked very much the guardian towering over the macadamia nut and mango trees around it.

Blinding rain overtook me as I drove through Na'alehu. The main road beneath the craggy banyans and monkeypods was quickly transformed into a red river, and I drove at a snail's pace, barely able to make out the route until I reached the squall's edge, north of the town. The gleaming road snaked down toward the ocean, through open green fields filled with wet cows under a dramatic sky. Beyond lay the magnificent visual sweep of the island's southeast side, as it climbed steadily northward toward Kilauea, the active volcanic vent on Mauna Loa's eastern flank. A rainbow arched over the great swath of wrinkled sea to the east. I felt blessed to be seeing that intense moment of the land's and seascape's natural beauty.

I took the turnoff at Pahala and drove up the mountainside, through fields filled with green cane and wet red earth, toward the distant forest where the retreat center had been established. As I approached the dark treeline, the cloud cover parted, revealing the immensity of Mauna Loa soaring into the sky. I was struck to the core by the volcano's beauty and power and felt my *ku* become energized and active, grateful for such a vision. The moment passed as the road entered the trees and promptly forked. I took the left branch and soon drove into the large cleared area that served as the parking lot for the temple grounds.

Late afternoon sunlight again broke through the clouds, streaming down at a low angle through the tall eucalyptus forest that surrounded the temple grounds on all sides. As I stepped from my car, I was struck by the total silence of the place, in contrast to the drone of the engine, the whining and hammering of the tires on the road, and the roaring of wind and the rain. I listened to the silence and felt something shift within me—perhaps my *ku.* The heavy sweet odor of flowering white ginger floated in the air.

The temple had been constructed and painted in the Tibetan style, and it glowed orange and yellow, purple and blue in the growing shadows below the trees. For several minutes I quietly took in the forest. Slender trunks rose straight up for eighty feet or more before throwing out delicate gray-green crowns. Among the undergrowth were immense, green elephant ear leaves of *taro* and sprays of flowering ginger pointed white fingers at the sky. The mountain could not be seen from this place. There were only the temple, its gardens, and several outbuildings surrounded by the dark wall of forest, the whole capped by the circle of open sky. The place appeared deserted, and I felt as though I had stepped through Alice's looking glass —backward into another place in time.

A slight sigh of wind whispered eerily through the trees. I glanced around as if to reconfirm the essential reality of my surroundings and saw several other cars parked on the grass. I went back to my van, removed my few belongings, and headed toward the smaller outbuilding, which had great flowering vines climbing up one side. There the *sesshin* was to be held.

Removing my sandals, I entered the doorway and passed the small library beneath the stairway that ascended to the *zendo.* Nobody was around, but the doorway of the men's dormitory was well marked. Within were a dozen or so double bunk beds, on which bedding was neatly folded. I selected one that was away from the door, took a bottom bunk, and swiftly made the bed. I laid out my toilet articles wrapped in a towel and took out my Japanese-style *hippari* jacket and square-cut meditation "fat pants." The clothes were noticeably unworn, even though I had bought them many years before. My intention to begin a formal Zen practice had been set aside day after day, week after week, until a decade had passed—and yet I was here. I would try to begin here and now. My readings in Zen Buddhism up to this point had helped me learn to value life's ordinary moments and focus my attention upon what I was doing, no matter how humble or mundane. Whenever I was washing dishes or chopping vegetables or changing diapers, I tried to pay attention to the project at hand. I had gotten better at this practice with time and hoped to learn more about disciplining my mind at the *sesshin.*

I checked out the men's bathroom. It was spotless. A jar of water under the long mirror held a languid spray of white flowering ginger, which exuded the same thick sweet scent that had drifted out of the forest. I went down the hall to the kitchen, where I finally encountered other people, all of whom were involved in various tasks of preparing the evening meal. All were strangers.

Like the rest of the building, the kitchen cabinets and fixtures were of ordinary construction and materials, and the varnished plywood gleamed in the half-light. Beyond the kitchen was a long screened porch surrounding a linear series of tables, on which several people were setting places for the two dozen or so participants. A list of names was tacked to a bulletin board: I was to work in the kitchen during the retreat. I wondered what I should do. Nobody was talking. They were just doing, silently, what needed to be done.

Through the screens I saw the forest in the fading light. In between the pale uprights of the tree trunks, I suddenly felt a strong presence, and the hair on my neck rose a bit. Could it be that I was feeling the trees' collective awareness or was it something else?

The sound of a knife chopping vegetables pulled my attention abruptly back to the now, and the contact, if that was what it was, slipped away.

Turning, I saw a tall Asian woman with a thick mane of black hair erupting from the crown of her head. Her strong hands were wielding the knife with deft precision. A shock wave passed through me—

Kenojelak.

Someone approached her to ask for instructions in a barely audible tone. She paused and replied with a brief word and an equally brief gesture. The resemblance was uncanny. She was strikingly attractive, in the same strong angular way. Her simply cut dark *hippari* and pants concealed her lean figure. Her movements were restrained and elegant.

She turned and met my gaze. Her beautiful eyes were set in a smooth calm face dominated by high cheekbones and a wide mouth. She did indeed resemble Kenojelak, but her eyes were dark. The close likeness momentarily unsettled me. The woman gestured to the cabinet filled with stacked plates and glassware and glanced at the long tables behind me, indicating that I was to join the others setting places. She was obviously in charge of the kitchen.

Suddenly aware that I had been staring, I looked quickly away, but not before I saw the flash of amusement in her eyes, an expression so like Kenojelak's that I was again nonplussed. She came up to me and leaned forward to whisper in my ear, "During the *sesshin* we speak as little as possible." Once again she glanced at the tables beyond.

I started to move toward the cabinet of glassware, then paused and looked back at her, as if to reassure myself that she was not Kenojelak. She caught my look as she stood, knife in hand, observing me with Kenojelak's frankness. Again I was thrown by her resemblance, and impulsively I moved to the list and indicated my name to her. She responded by indicating hers—

Akiko.

Reassured, I turned and began to set the tables. Fellow participants continued to arrive and drift in. Some were young, some were midlifers like myself, and some were elders. More than half were women. All were plainly dressed, without ornaments or jewelry except for the odd wedding ring. I noted that all seemed somewhat withdrawn and that personal contact was minimal, limited to what was necessary to accomplish the task at hand.

Akiko was chopping vegetables once again, her back ramrod straight as she worked. As she reached up to take a large wok down from its hook, the wide sleeve of her *hippari* opened, revealing her arm to the shoulder. A shaft of late sunlight from the forest suddenly and clearly illuminated her armpit and breast for one long moment—then she placed the wok on the stove, and the instant passed. I glanced out into the forest wondering if a mischievous nature spirit out there was trying to disrupt the inner calm I was trying to achieve, because if so, it was succeeding.

Aitken Rōshi arrived shortly before dinner, wearing Western clothes. He greeted Akiko with an elegant bow, which she returned with equal grace. She returned to her work, and the Rōshi began to confer in low tones with a thin bearded young man with whitening hair who was wearing the habit of a Catholic priest. The same economy of movement, speech, and gesture prevailed during their brief discussion. The Rōshi looked older than I had expected and appeared somewhat frail.

My task complete, I approached the Rōshi and bowed to him in silence, receiving a warm bow in return, before I left the kitchen to explore more of the building. Beyond the narrow lanai, the forest stood silent and watchful as though waiting for the day to end and night's activities to begin. The beautiful call of a rainbird floated down—answered by another from deeper in the trees. The cleared acreage of the grounds still had a decidedly unworldly appearance. A peacock shrieked from behind the temple.

On the door of the *zendo* was another list of names for seat assignments. I entered and bowed according to Buddhist custom. The room was empty, the altar dimly lit, and an old bronze Buddha was seated squarely in its center. Before it a bronze incense burner filled with clean white sand squatted on a low table, flanked by flower arrangements in the Japanese style. I raised my hands in *gasshō* and bowed to the image and to my own inner Buddha mind, establishing intention.

The Rōshi's cushion was placed in the center of the room before the

Buddha. Around the room's perimeter twenty more cushions had been arranged, at each place a round *zafu* centered on a square *zabuton*. I knew that participants would sit facing the wall in silence and in correct posture for the next several days. We would attempt to empty our minds of thoughts, stilling the inner chatter, allowing the luminous emptiness of no-mind to appear within.

I found my assigned place and discovered that I would be facing a window rather than a wall, looking out into the darkening forest beyond the mown grass. I smiled, wondering if it would be easier or more difficult that way.

A bell announced the evening meal. When all were present, the Rōshi took an unoccupied place and made a brief speech of welcome in a soft muted voice. Then all bowed and sat. Bowls of food were passed in silence —rice, vegetables, tofu, and fruit—each person taking a small portion of each. Akiko approached bearing a large platter of sliced avocados, which the Rōshi graciously accepted, taking a small piece. She then took an unoccupied space, and when all had been served, we ate the meal in silence, with lowered eyes and economy of movement.

The typically boisterous Ennu communal meal flashed in my mind's eye, where everyone laughed and ate and talked all at once. I recalled Kenojelak tearing rare meat from a horse rib with her fingers and teeth. Finishing the morsel, she tossed the bone to a dog and wiped the grease into the skin of her arms. I glanced at Akiko across the table wielding her chopsticks, but she did not look up. The *sesshin* had begun.

Platters of food were passed again. A few took second helpings, but the Rōshi did not, nor did the majority of the group, so I declined as well, reflecting that I might lose a few unwanted pounds during the next few days. Akiko brought several pots of rice tea. The Rōshi stood and described the schedule we would follow for the duration of the retreat. Then all rose and bowed, and the meal was over.

We on kitchen duty cleaned up the food and dishes, placed the chairs on the tables, and swept and washed the floors. The kitchen and dining areas were returned to spotless order.

As I left the kitchen, I encountered Akiko again. She bowed to me, disrupting my inner calm again by that incredible resemblance.

The bell from the lanai summoned us to the *zendo*. I changed quickly into my *hippari* and fat pants, and holding my hands before my stomach with one fist inside the other, inner thumb tucked in, I entered the meditation hall, executed the required bows both to my cushion and the room, then sat and arranged my legs in the half-lotus position, assuming correct posture. Shortly after, the bell announced the beginning of the first session of *zazen*. I took three deep breaths, dropped my gaze, and let it slowly unfocus in the darkness beyond the window, consciously relaxing my body one segment at a time. Just as I was achieving a state of inner calm, I felt something just at the edge of awareness vying for my attention.

I refocused my attention on my breathing, counting each breath, practicing one-pointed concentration, but the presence remained. Thoughts and impressions appeared one after another in my mind—images of Akiko, Kenojelak, and Jill. Like phantoms, the three women merged as one and became three again. I groaned inwardly. This was going to be more difficult than I had anticipated.

After a time the Rōshi's soft voice invited all to face into the room and assume a relaxed posture. The venerable teacher wore traditional black Japanese robes and was seated in the full lotus. He had a curiously shaped wooden staff, about as long as his forearm, on the floor before him. All vestiges of frailty had vanished. Robert Aitken had taken on his aspect of power in a striking transition.

The Zen master then delivered a lecture focused on a koan, a Zen riddle or problem that cannot be solved by the intellect alone. He talked about Chao-chou's dog and the *koan Mu*, a traditional starting point for those entering Zen practice. At the talk's end we were all sent to bed.

Each day began before dawn at four and ended after dusk. The routine included ongoing forty-five-minute periods of sitting meditation, punctuated by brief walking meditations around the room's perimeter. All day we sat motionless in silence facing the wall. We had lectures by the Rōshi, and *dokusan*, a one-to-one interview with the Zen master.

I had my first *dokusan* with the Rōshi the next morning. Toward the end of the second period of *zazen*, I waited my turn, sitting on my legs in the *seiza* position out on the lanai. The dawn had just broken. It was the time before shadows.

Going eye to eye with a Zen master was not something I did every day, and I was nervous. Remembering Nainoa's centering technique, I imagined myself filling with *mana*. I breathed it in and visualized it entering my body and coming to rest at my navel. Almost immediately, I felt it flow, infusing me with warmth, raising goose bumps on my arms and legs, empowering me—and attracting mosquitoes.

At that moment, I abruptly felt something again. The presence I had felt the day before had returned. At that moment the bell sounded, summoning me to the interview.

On entering the small door to the Rōshi's room, I kneeled and offered the customary three deep bows, touching my forehead to the floor. Then I sat back on my heels, facing Aitken Rōshi, where he sat in full lotus, backlit by a small window. As I met the Zen master's eyes, a jolt of power surged through me, causing my entire body to give a strong reflexive jerk. It startled me, to say the least. The Rōshi smiled, his pale eyes and face luminous with energy and goodwill. The sense of power emanating from the teacher within the small space was palpable. I was amazed that I could feel it so strongly.

The exchange that followed was spare. Aitken Rōshi asked me to say something about myself, my practice, and my intentions. At the end, I was given a koan to work on, which, when I returned to my cushion, helped me succeed in entering the deep state at last. The rest of the long day of sitting proceeded well.

The third day of the retreat began like the others, at four in the morning. My right knee was aching from the unaccustomed "long-distance" sitting. The sound of the bell floated in the silence like a punctuation mark, separating what was past from what was now. Assuming correct posture, I prepared myself for the first session of *zazen.* I began to observe my breathing, composing myself to settle into the altered state of deep meditation.

I emptied my mind and observed my breathing, counting each breath and paying close attention to the inflow—the outflow. I had just reached the ninth breath when suddenly I felt the presence again. I remained utterly still. Whatever it was, it felt needful, as though it were trying to get my attention. This was more than just another invasive thought. I asked my *ku* for information, and the answer was immediate. The presence was coming in through the *ku* from outside my self. At this moment, the sensations of power also appeared, heralding the beginning of an altered state. The inner window was opening. I was being summoned—urgently.

I remained completely still, balanced on my cushion, feeling the power sweep into me, trying not to gasp for air as the invisible fist seized me in its awesome grip. Behind my closed eyes the curious crescent of light formed and began to expand. It had never looked quite this way before. The now-familiar phosphenes streamed from it, and as usual, there were discrete flashes, like heat lightning, followed by strange patterns—zigzags and lines, rows of spots that left ghostly trails as my eyes tracked them this way and that. My sense of inner illumination increased steadily as the forces grew stronger and stronger. The grid appeared, coalescing among the phosphenes. A jolt of power made my body as rigid as a stick of wood, as the inner window opened still further. My ears filled with the hissing sound, and light filled me, blinding me as I tried to limit my movements. I was in the *zendo* and had to remain still and silent. My *ku* took control of my body. All would be well. I was safe. . . . I was safe. . . . I let go and surrendered to the feelings of ecstasy that surged through me as I answered the summons.

The presence was waiting for me out in the forest—out in the trees in the dark. I greeted it with good intentions, reciprocating its invitation. The feelings of power increased even more. Spots of light flowed through the trees, toward the *zendo.* They grew in number, multiplying and taking form until they coalesced at the forest's edge into a sparkling, swirling, shimmering form I knew well.

The leopard man had come for me.

The pressure eased, and I felt as if I were floating. The leopard man stared straight at the window, waiting for me. Despite the *sesshin*, I had to go.

Carefully and slowly, I uncoiled from the *seiza* posture and stood up, glancing over at the student who was in charge of the *zendo*. He did not look at me. I bowed to the altar and headed silently toward the exit. The sensations of power were still there but were manageable. I felt almost normal once again, although somewhat light-headed. I paused at the door to glance at my place by the window and felt mild shock when I saw myself still sitting in correct posture, balanced on my cushion.

I was not alarmed, however. I bowed once more and went out onto the lanai. The golden light of predawn filled the sky and the forest, illuminating the temple grounds, where it had been pitch-dark only moments before. There were no shadows. I descended the stairs and emerged from the building, pausing to admire the flowering vines climbing up the wall before drifting around the building and heading toward the trees.

Tok!

A hollow, percussive sound rang out from the depths of the dark wall before me. The leopard man had disappeared. Drawn by the sound, I moved across the grass and into the forest. The smell of the white flowering ginger was very strong. A rainbird called. Mist and shafts of the golden light penetrated among the dark tree trunks. Something big was moving through the trees off to my left, keeping step with my progress.

Tok!

Wood struck wood, the trees flickered. Up ahead was a light area, a clearing among the trees. I paused to admire some mushrooms, their little conical caps on long spindly stalks glowing in the purple darkness below the trees.

Tok!

The closer I got to the clearing, the stronger I felt the power. When I arrived, an odd wrinkle of light materialized in the fabric of the air in the clearing's center. Irregular at first, it suddenly shifted into a definite symmetrical form, as though the brilliant sliver of the new moon had appeared in the air directly before me. It was the shape of the horseshoe-shaped pendant, the *nazha*, at the center of the Navajo squash-blossom necklace. The crescent of light was tiny at first, but it lengthened and opened until it formed a large circle about as high as I was tall. As it grew to its six feet, the sensations of power also expanded.

The center gradually became opaque, obscuring the trees on the other side of the clearing. The circle looked somewhat like a cloudy mirror, but it flickered in the same way as the trees, the shimmering preventing me from seeing what was within. It could only be the doorway, the *nierika*. Its interior cleared momentarily to reveal a glittering whirlpool of sparkling lights, swirling clockwise. Initially the whirlpool appeared flat, but then it changed into a three-dimensional vortex, streaming into some vast unimaginable distance. It was the old shamanic tunnel into and through the nonordinary levels of reality.

Then the *nierika* abruptly became opaque again. I looked away to see the leopard man staring at me from the trees at the clearing's edge, looking remarkably human, standing upright. As I sent it my affection, the strange being closed its eyes in a distinctly catlike squint, then opened them slightly, then closed them again, in friendly greeting. Its benevolence gave me a sense of calm and well-being, and I went right up to it, reached out with both hands, and ran my fingers through its beautiful spotted coat, feeling its fur, scratching its head between and behind the ears, and under the chin and along the jawline. I felt the power of the *akua* transmitted through the touch and said softly, "Warm greetings to the leopard man."

The therianthrope began to purr-roar softly in its throat in response. Its roar deepened—deepened into a rich, continuous, melodious, vibrating tone. As the sound intensified, the spirit shapeshifted slightly, its spotted coat becoming brilliant and reflective as its emotions heightened. It opened its green eyes wide and looked deeply into mine, increasing my own sensations of power. It squinted again with pleasure and slowly dropped onto all

fours, turned, and gracefully bounded into the vortex in the center of the clearing—and disappeared.

I vacillated for only a moment, then approached the doorway, raised my hands in *gasshō*, and bowed before stepping through.

I felt a slight resistance, not unlike pushing into an inflated balloon. Then I was through and immediately had a strong sense of falling—of falling quickly, as if I were on a swing. I looked behind me but could not see the entrance. I was surrounded by the sparkling darkness, and the power sensations were roaring through me. The lights blended into a single sheet of brilliance that momentarily blinded me. Even after I closed my eyes, the brilliance remained, coalescing into lavender dots. I was flying . . . flying . . . rushing through the tunnel. I had never seen it as vividly before. I could still hear the leopard man's roaring. My spirit helper was there with me, and I felt safe.

I wondered where we were going, and from somewhere deep inside myself, the answer arrived. I was going to Nainoa. He wanted to meet with me. We were finally going to meet.

The leopard man's deep, resonant roaring became a droning, buzzing sound that surrounded me. Then I felt a slowing, a settling, as the power sensations abruptly decreased to manageable levels.

I cracked open my eyes in a strange, roaring darkness. Had the shift occurred? Or was I lost forever in some hostile and unknown level of reality beyond human experience?

22
Eleventh Journey
The Spirit Hills

AINOA FELT THE ARRIVAL OF THE FAMILIAR PRESence and surrendered once again to the strange sound that filled the windy darkness all around him. For long moments before, he had been aware only of the sounds of the spirit hills. Then he remembered his and William's journey to this place.

They had come alone. They had gathered supplies for a trek of several days' duration and had left the band, following the lake to the east, crossing and recrossing it several times at numerous shallow fords. As they traveled, the older man pointed out various places where the Ennu had camped, telling stories of past events connected with each. Here a child had been born . . . there, a woman had miscarried . . . over there, a man had been killed in a hunting accident.

Late one afternoon, William pointed out a massif gleaming whitely in the distance, indicating it to be the spirit hills. The old hunter said little more about it, deflecting Nainoa's inquiries with monosyllabic replies.

William became increasingly uncommunicative and withdrawn, preparing himself in some way for what was to occur. They made camp that evening in a cave that had many bones embedded in the rocks.

Instead of going directly to the spirit hills, William insisted they remain near the cave for several days, fishing from the lake and eating lightly. Nainoa was often hungry, but William gently rejected his offer to hunt, saying, "It is better to approach the spirits with an empty stomach. It improves the contact. Perhaps they can sense our hunger, our suffering, and regard it as making sacrifice." The older man smiled and added, "You have also been able to store up your vital power—that which my daughter finds so irresistible—and that is also very good. We will wait until conditions are favorable for approaching and making contact with the spirits."

Each day at twilight, Nainoa watched the stars. When the Pleiades rose low in the eastern sky after sunset, he knew, it would be time for him to cross the mountains back to his own world. The long dry season was beginning, the days becoming hot and windy. Dust-devils danced over the arid plains. As he waited for William to decide when the time was right, he wrestled with his inner conflict over leaving the Ennu and Kenojelak.

At dusk the wind usually died, and the world became still. On this particular night, the wind did not die. Instead, the gusts continued to rise. The evening meal was minimal, and Nainoa had drifted off to sleep hungry and somewhat irritable. Shortly thereafter, the older man gently woke him, saying that the time had finally come.

Nainoa was groggy as they set off in the dark for the spirit hills, dimly discernible in the starlit distance. As they walked, Nainoa concentrated on his intention, as William had instructed him, focusing on his desire to meet with the American and on his faith in the power of the spirits.

After a fatiguing walk against the wind, they arrived at a single vast sand dune of considerable elevation and many peaks, not far from the lake's edge. William found a level place somewhat sheltered from the wind, where he spread a hide he had brought, pinning down its edges with stones. He gestured for Nainoa to lie down next to him on his back and wait for the spirits to approach them.

Nainoa did so, and the wind continued to intensify, blowing the sand down the slopes of the dunes. Covering his face with the hide's edge to protect his eyes and nose, Nainoa listened to the wind. He had almost drifted off to sleep when a strange noise brought him to full wakefulness.

A droning, buzzing sound was rising on the wind. It sounded as if a huge deep voice were coming directly out of the ground all around them. He lay still in the dark and abruptly felt the beginning of the sensations of power. His eyes snapped open, and he sat up, looking around wildly. Nothing was there but the wind, sand, and the ghostly, throaty hum. William lay immobile as though asleep, a flap of the hide across his face and shoulders. Nainoa lay down again.

He remained this way for some time, allowing himself to be lulled by the sound. The image of the tiger man emerged in his mind, and he asked the spirit to facilitate contact with his ancestor. The power feelings suddenly rushed into him, and the familiar paralysis gripped him as he gasped for breath. The sound rose to a booming roar, varying very slightly as the wind shifted. Suddenly he felt the other's arrival.

He fastened his attention upon it, feeling the familiar shape of it. His conscious mind formed a thought-phrase in Old English:

"Greetings, ancestor!"

Much to his amazement, the response was immediate. It was also expressed in Old English:

"Warm greetings, descendant!"

Then he heard the phrase repeated in Classic Hawaiian:

"Aloha pumehana mo'opuna!"

Nainoa felt as if this encounter had been agreed upon long ago. A question formed in Old English within his mind. It was not his thought.

"What of the *dorajuaks?*"

"Dorajuadioks," Nainoa corrected automatically—and as he did so, the visionary experience changed. The sensations of power increased once again, squeezing him breathless, and the deep tone assumed a steady, beautiful resonance. Struggling to open his eyes, Nainoa gasped as he saw a tall monolithic form in the dark windy night. It was completely black,

329

reminding him of the shadowy being of the *siti,* but this one resembled a long arrow point, with straight edges and a broken blunt tip. It was completely featureless—a towering, dark form backlit by the starlit dunes beyond. Was this a *dorajuadiok?*

The form made Nainoa uneasy, until he once again became aware of the American's presence within, which provided a sense of companionship. He was not alone. They were facing this awesome spirit together.

He felt the American's curiosity surface, requesting information about the relationship between spirits and power, and within both their minds appeared a clear understanding that the spirits were not the source of the power surging through them but rather were the activators and conductors of it. Only Io, the universal void itself, could be the source of such power.

As if in affirmation, the feelings of force increased to a level that stunned them both into a thoughtless emptiness. Then they felt themselves lifted up and being drawn into the dark form, as though it were a doorway of some kind—or could function as such.

The *dorajuadiok* transported them both, although each experienced the encounter in his own way. Amazingly, each was simultaneously aware of the other's cognitive perceptions and interpretations, as though they were really one being, as though they were different aspects of a singularity, and yet were also two. . . .

As two halves of a whole, their merged-yet-separate awarenesses were drawn through a blinding flash of exquisite fiery sensation and projected outward into the total blackness of the void. As they floated in the immensity of the silent darkness, there was no focus at all, only the vast, awesome, and total silence. They existed as though they themselves were the primordial emptiness from which all phenomenal forms had originated and to which all would eventually return. After a while, the empty, silent darkness was overwhelming, and they felt little twisted tendrils of fear. These were gradually replaced by a sense of tranquillity, and a whisper of vibrational tone.

Now there was a feeling of ease, a sense that all was as it should be, as it always had been and always would be. With this realization a state of complete and utter bliss engulfed them, carrying them, secure in their knowing, in their understanding that their knowing existed—that it existed within the void, and that it was the void's knowing as well.

In this way a knowing-feeling existed within the great emptiness, and because it is in the nature of all things to increase, the thought-feeling began to grow, slowly at first and then faster.

In this manner, a dream-seed took form in the empty darkness. It was the void's dream, infinitely small at first, a single point of solitary thought-feeling that began to form in two distinct directions, one as thought, the other as feeling—different aspects of the same dream-seed. It began to diversify, to become more—and the ancestral, germinal bud of the great pattern began within the dream. Within it, everything was contained—every thing.

The pattern grew with purpose, with intention, the third part of the dream—the primordial directive. Threads of connection between the different parts of the dream grew as well. In this way the grid came into being. At first just three tiny, infinitely primitive points of ism, of being, were joined by threads of connection—three minute bits of thought, feeling, and will. These were the primal, existential part of Io, the great void.

As the dream expanded, another kind of separateness manifested itself, and the subjective division of thought, feeling, and will was reflected in an identical and simultaneous division at the objective level—the partitioning of matter, energy, and awareness.

This separation was accompanied by an explosion of unimaginable magnitude as the physical level of reality came into being. The darkness of the great void was filled with a brilliant, blinding flash of light, as matter and energy expanded outward into the emptiness and the new universe flowed away into the darkness in immense rings, as great circular waves expanding outward, outward into the darkness, in every direction—forever. . . .

For an indeterminable period the Hawaiian historian and the American scientist existed only as the expanding matter, as the movement of the power flowing through the universal void and as the awareness of the process taking place. For uncountable aeons they perceived that their awareness was part of the initial awareness. They understood that the power they felt was the life-essence that pervades the universe. They watched primordial matter become physical reality in an infinite number of forms. They saw the universe as a vast entity charged with life-force, an immense being composed of matter, power, and ever-increasing awareness; they saw its purpose—the creation of intelligent life through the diversification of matter, life-essence, and awareness. They observed these three aspects of the universe changing, manifesting into countless forms and aspects. They watched the universe follow its own directive, creating more of itself, transforming the flow of power into form, process, and awareness. . . . The great pattern grew.

In their minds their humanity resurfaced, and with it their wish to know how they had come into being within the pattern.

Imagery began to flow within their consciousness in response. It began as raw, undifferentiated process in the void, where the directive brought into being a spark of light, a small fire in the darkness, a concentration of subatomic particles organized into atomic levels of integration and set alight as an atomic furnace. It was a star. It was their sun.

Hank felt its skin of warmth extending outward into the cold void, and he understood that the assemblage of matter into a planetary body at the correct orbit within that warmth would allow water to be liquid on its surface. Then the flow of power could be manifested into life-forms within the water—within the water of life.

"*Kawaiola,*" offered Nainoa.

Hank remembered that clouds of matter exist out there in deep space between the stars, clouds of large molecules that produce interstellar spectral rays perceivable with radio telescopes, clouds that contain porphyrins.

Nainoa followed this thought with great interest and wondered, "What are these molecules, and what are these porphyrins?"

The darkness of the void was the perfect blackboard. Information began to flow between their separate awarenesses, pulses of meaning filled with colorful imagery. Hank taught Nainoa about atoms and molecules, about the nature of living things, about respiration, oxidation, and the cycle of Krebs. He showed him the infinitely small coiled structures called porphyrins that occur universally in space and in the protoplasm within living things—molecules that become life-enhancing within the simplest organized forms in the medium of water on a water planet's surface—forming the foundation for the oxygen-carrying pigments, hemoglobin in the red blood cells of animals and chlorophyll in the green chloroplasts of plants.

As the last of the myriad red lozenges and emerald green orbs evaporated in the darkness, a certainty appeared within their minds. They understood that the deep emptiness of Io's void was pregnant everywhere with these precursors to life. The two men's consciousnesses shifted to take in the now-starry universe spread out in every direction forever, and they realized that it was alive—that there was life everywhere within its endless extent and that the creation of life was its purpose.

Their awareness refocused on the water and on the infinitely small. They saw tiny water beings shapeshift and change to produce an endless variety of primitive protozoans, coelenterates, and soft wormlike morphs that eventually segmented and hardened to produce a diversity of crustaceanlike beings. Still others were both soft and hard—the mollusks and fish.

The great diversification continued as "slimy things that crawled with legs out of the slimy sea" made the transition to land-living. The great reptiles rose up, and Nainoa gasped at the wondrous beasts nature had produced, which passed on, to be replaced by more active furry animals. Within the next group, the progression of creatures included hairy, shambling bipeds that inhabited the scattered mosaic of woodlands and grasslands along the edges of rivers and lakes. Among these unlikely candidates, the next stage then began—the evolution of consciousness.

Abruptly, the grid appeared against the dark field, disrupting the imagery. It was vast now, the lines of light stretching away into the distance, each knot in the web a glowing orb. A red jewel attracted them, and moving along its fiber of connection, they found themselves looking down on the cloud-swept surface of their own planet. Both wondered why it appeared red instead of blue. As they sensed the vast composite consciousness formed of the collective awarenesses of every living thing associated with it, they understood that the planet was the mother, within whose salty watery womb life had originated in their sector of the pattern. It was the mother.

And the father?

Their consciousness shifted to rest upon their sun blazing away in Io's great darkness, its light the flow of the universe manifested into a form of immense power. It was the provider of the generative life-energy, the source of the *mana* that was highly concentrated in all the living things associated with their world. It was their creator, whose power was transformed into living things within the life-sustaining medium of water. It was the sky father, the provider of the life-force, the source of life itself in their part of the universe.

A profound sense of the interconnectedness of everything pervaded them. They saw themselves as combinations of matter, energy, and consciousness interconnected through their *aumakua*, in turn part of the greater collective human spirit, and in turn, part of the larger collective planetary consciousness.

And what of the creator? What about that immense concentration of universal power burning away out there in Io's void?

In response to this query, they perceived that the sun also possessed awareness. They understood that the star's consciousness was in the process of being brought into existence through the evolution of the consciousnesses of its life-forms on the water planet. The solar mind was forming, becoming more, through the growing, evolving collective awareness of every living thing within its system. The inescapable conclusion was that all the myriad forms of conscious awareness on earth *were* and *are* the consciousness of the sun.

The scientist's mind trembled with this realization. The sun was blindingly bright, and yet at dawn and at dusk, all the living beings on the water planet were able to look at their creator directly. The eyes with which all creatures could perceive their creator were the same eyes through which their creator was able to perceive them. . . . It was through the evolution of their conscious minds that the solar being was now able to observe and know itself.

"Our father which exists in the heavens, sacred is your symbol."

As the merged-yet-separate awarenesses of the two men continued to expand into the great vision, they perceived the starry void as an immense collective of countless solar creator-beings whose purpose was to provide the foundation of life everywhere within the universe. This was the supreme accomplishment of the universe—the flow of power transformed into mind. It had always been this way, and it always would be—everywhere— forever.

The image shifted again, and there in the dark, transected by brilliant lines and dots of light, they saw the great matrix within which each universe formed its own vast collective mind, composed of all the minds of all its stars—the universal mind in the process of growing and becoming more in response to its own original directive . . . to grow and diversify and become more. . . .

Nainoa and Hank perceived the enormity and the simplicity of the great pattern, and their humanness emerged once again, accompanied by their distinctly human curiosity. Within both a query took form:

"What are human beings destined to become?"

Imagery and impressions began to flow across the dark field once again. The thought-line began in the past, when the ancestral protohominids known to science as the Australopithecines appeared out in Africa. By chance, these tropical bipedal primates had been on the scene when the planetary weather machine shifted gears, producing changing climatic extremes that tested the emerging sentient ancestors, selecting for behavioral plasticity, for ingenuity, accelerating the process of the evolution of consciousness.

During the initial stages of the late Pliocene climatic deterioration, around 2.5 million years ago, ice formed in the polar regions, and the sea level dropped. As the planet cooled, arid conditions spread across the formerly humid tropics, causing the great forests to shrink and the dry grasslands to expand. Shortages of fruiting forest trees necessitated a dietary shift within the evolving human populations, one toward a more readily available food source on the expanding African savannas. The great seas of grass were covered with grazing animals, and their carcasses were easy to find by watching the vultures. There the ancestors found food in a highly concentrated form—meat.

The ancestors cooperated in scavenging the kills of large carnivores. Their scavenging improved when they discovered that sharp flakes of stone could dismember even the largest carcass in a very short time, especially important when lions or hyenas were approaching through the grass. Eventually cooperative scavenging developed into cooperative hunting, a highly successful way of life during times of environmental uncertainty.

The weather continued to shift, alternating between periods of climatic stability and instability. The evolving hominid hunter-gatherers survived in their unpredictable world, pursuing a rich protein diet, which favored an expanding brain. Their conscious abilities changed and diversified in response, and their initially crude stone technology progressed from the use of randomly struck stone flakes into the making of more complex tools of carefully preplanned design. These trends continued to develop over the next million years as the hunters left their African homeland and followed the endless herds of animals out into the rest of the world. When the *sapiens* level of awareness and ability was achieved, the next stage began, one characterized by different sets of extremes, and as always, change followed change.

The early, archaic forms of *Homo sapiens* continued to pursue the now-ancient strategy of hunting and gathering, and among them a new kind of human appeared, a slender-boned, round-headed, flat-faced nomad whose populations would diversify and increase, dispersing outward across the earth until only they remained. The newcomers became considerably more innovative, producing ever more cleverly designed tools and ideas in rapid succession. Among them symbolic language was first expressed as art.

Then, roughly ten thousand years ago, the world's weather patterns shifted, changing their lives again. At the end of the last ice age, the climate warmed and the sea level rose. A wave of mass extinctions occurred, and the megafauna on which the nomadic hunters preyed disappeared. The ancestors shifted their diets once again. The first domestication of animals and plants soon followed.

With the invention of agriculture, the ancient nomadic lifestyle gave way to permanent occupation sites, and the first settlements appeared. The population size expanded dramatically, enabled by food surpluses and the stability of a sedentary lifeway. Technology diversified and ceramics and low-grade metal ores were discovered. States with societal classes based on occupation and status came into being for the first time. The first full-time religious practitioners organized themselves into the first state religions. Cultivation of grain crops yielded greater surpluses and stability, and the population continued to grow—and grow.

Human behavior and social organization continued to diversify and change, becoming more complex politically and economically as awareness continued to expand. Empires came and went, wars were won and lost, populations expanded and contracted, art and architecture transcended previous levels of accomplishment, and always, human consciousness continued to grow. The brief but glorious burst of the Industrial Revolution occurred, a golden age of extremes that resulted in accelerated technologies and great knowledge. It was a period that lasted for perhaps two hundred years, not much more than the blink of an eye when measured against a galactic scale of billions. . . .

Nainoa was stunned by his vision of human history. He sensed the American monitoring his responses, and a question formed within him:

"Was it true—was everything that I have just witnessed true?"

The answer came gently in Old English. Many words were strange, and yet Nainoa understood what he meant:

"Truth is a working hypothesis. As human understanding grows and expands, the shape of truth shifts and changes, yet everything you have just seen is true."

The tone of the American's thoughts turned somber as he concluded, "From your mind and memories, I've learned that all of our civilization was lost—our knowledge, science and technology, inventions, literature, music, and art—all gone . . . passed away like the sand blowing in the dark around us."

A long period of silence followed—and in the minds of both men, the question formed:

"Could it have continued—could Western civilization have lasted indefinitely?"

The flickering image of the monolithic spirit-being appeared briefly before them again, reversing into a bright form against a dark field. It showed them the pattern greatly disrupted, apocalyptic images of catastrophic overpopulation, the exhaustion of resources, the progressive poisoning and depletion of the land, air, and water upon which all life depended. Famine, social chaos, disease—death.

The ultimate limiting factors would be those things that sustained life. From the progressive contamination of the land, water, and air, there would be no escape, no excuses, and no exceptions. Once again the lineage would be tested. The planet would warm as it had many times in the past, and the seas would rise, creating conditions that would result in the extinction of those life-forms that were out of balance with the pattern.

It had always happened this way, and it always would, throughout the universes, forever. . . .

The minds of both men were silent for some time, overwhelmed at the inevitability of life's patterns. And then they formed another question:

"And then?"

The towering image of the spirit appeared again in their merged consciousnesses like a great, blindingly bright candle flame slightly flickering. Their awareness expanded once again, and impressions, thoughts, and feelings appeared in their minds, offering the certainty that the answer was there within the great pattern—an answer that had been accomplished uncountable times everywhere throughout the universes. . . .

The evolution of spirit was always the culminating event of the evolution of body and mind on the physical plane of existence. This was the great goal of the evolutionary process—the transformation of raw matter, power, and awareness into spirit, into the great mind-spirit of the universal matrix spread out across space and time. Within the matrix, the human-solar mind complex already had its place. For evolution's final stage high technology and machines would no longer be required.

Both were comforted. The evolving human body-mind-spirit complex was already woven into the fabric, a knot in the pattern, a spot of light in the transcendent nerve-net of the great grid. For the final stage of the ascent, the mystics and spiritual teachers throughout history had already revealed the paths to follow. Diversity was part of the directive, and so all spiritual paths were valid if practiced with discipline, sincerity, persever-ance, kindness—and mindfulness.

The human species was destined to become something else, and this, too, was part of the pattern. The survivors of civilization's fall would go on growing, changing, and becoming more according to the directive, but in a decidedly Neolithic future in which there would be no more machines, no more high technology. Humanity would continue to thrive and diversify, to manifest all possible physical types and aspects of experience. The human body-mind-spirit would continue to evolve until it reached the threshold.

And then the physical level of reality would be transcended, and human-ity would make its final transformation to exist purely as *aumakua*, as spirit, as microcosm within the macrocosm. At that point the human species would become the light, rejoining the creator of which it had always been and would always be a part, the father who existed in the heavens, the light at the end of the tunnel—the star.

· · ·

Finally, within their minds, the last question formed:

"And beyond? Does an ultimate godlike creator-being exist somewhere out there beyond the edge of the known?"

The feelings of force within them increased enormously, disrupting their flow of thought-feeling. When it had stabilized once again, a conviction grew within their minds—this question was and would always be the great mystery, the *mysterium tremendum*, unanswerable even by the *dorajuadioks*, the most powerful spirits.

This was the great question.

The towering spirit appeared in the visual field, as if to emphasize with its presence all they had seen. Then for the first time its own alien intelligence touched theirs—and offered that the matrix itself could be the creator, that they might think of "the creator" as "the created," as "the already-manifested," as "the formed-experience of everything within it." The great mind of the universe was being co-created through the evolutionary process, through actions on the objective level of physical reality and through those within the subjective level of thoughts, feelings and dreams.

They felt a sudden sense of unity with the *dorajuadiok* as it included them in its company with the next thought:

"We are the creators of our part of the great pattern. All the various personal god-selves, deities, and spirits are formed in reflection of what we do and become on the levels of action. They did not create us. We created them. They come into being in response to us and what we become."

The scientist, aware that he was communicating directly with the spirit, asked, "What is the nature of the *dorajuadioks*?" The answer arrived immediately.

"*Dorajuadioks* exist as beings of vast intelligence composed of pure awareness in association with dense concentrations of energy or universal power. They serve as activators, as conductors of power, and are without material, physical form but can be seen by the shadows they cast in certain levels of perception. They seem dark on the physical level of objective reality because in the spirit world they are actually blindingly bright. Their shadow crosses the barrier in reverse as black."

They saw visual impressions illuminated by colors that shifted rapidly back and forth between their complements or opposites—black to white to black again, orange to green to orange, reddish to blue to red again. They saw vignettes of the spirit world expressed in color negative—in hues opposite to those in ordinary reality, as if they were looking at black and white photo negatives with intense color washed in.

The imagery shifted, and they found themselves staring down at their planet once more. They understood now why the earth seemed reddish instead of green or blue. They were observing its spiritual equivalent—its shadow-form as it existed in the spirit world, in the level of archetypes. The image shifted, and they again saw the *dorajuadiok* projected into the objective level of physical reality through the reversal phenomenon. Because of this the bright, flamelike spirit appeared to their human minds as an utterly dark monolithic shape.

Feelings of agreement flowed from the spirit, confirming their insight. The tall form shifted again, appearing against a dark field or sky as a white obelisk of blindingly bright light whose edges flickered almost imperceptibly. Then they beheld it as an utterly dark form against the pale sand dunes beyond. With this shift in awareness, they became acutely conscious of the deep booming sound that surrounded them once again. The sound drew them back to their own level of reality and to the spirit hills. Both sensed they were losing the contact and reached for the connection. As it re-formed briefly, they felt a strong sadness emanating from the tall spirit-being—and within themselves.

The anthropologist perceived that he had been given a glimpse of the evolution of the great spirit of which the human spirit is a part. He understood that we as human beings are functioning as the co-creators of its local aspect, here in our corner of the universe. This local aspect has evil in it, and the evil is humanity's creation, its great sin. Humanity is creating evil within the great mind through its ongoing preoccupation with and acceptance of the dark side of human nature. Then his understanding shifted shape, and the dark side was revealed as simply the other half of the light—one of the selective agents in the evolutionary process, an aspect of experience that tests evolving humanity, fine-tuning the strain, refining the lineage. William's words appeared in their minds:

"Through experiencing our darkness, we discover what it is that we are not. And in this way, we also discover what it is that we are."

The world's spiritual traditions had revealed the solution. Salvation lies in the creation of evil's opposite, in the manifestation of light, of compassion. This is the Christ of Christianity, Bodhisattva Avalokiteshvara of Indian Buddhism, and Kwan Yin of China. This is the great task that lies before us: to achieve great knowledge and transform it through compassionate thought, feeling, and action into wisdom. This is the Bodhisattva path—to enlighten ourselves and then others, to save ourselves and everything else . . . and create Great Mind.

Within the minds of both men arose a certainty: that with the end of our evolution, with the completion and union of the human-solar mind complex, connection with the vast collective mind of the universe will occur, providing entirely new parameters of experience. Only in this manner will the human spirit "journey beyond the stars to go where no man had gone before."

Only then will the existence of an ultimate creator be known.

As if coming from a great distance, the high, clear sound of a bell disrupted the flow of imagery and thought. The meditation was over, and I felt my level of awareness shift. The strange deep tone of sound that had been carrying me decreased abruptly, and the vision began to fade. I felt myself begin to withdraw—to slip back . . . back. . . .

As the connection with Nainoa faded, I tapped my limited knowledge of Hawaiian, composing a message of farewell which was then repeated in English:

"*Aloha nui loa—a hui hou.* Aloha with magnitude—until we meet again."

No question was forthcoming from the now-dark *dorajuadiok,* yet I felt its watchfulness upon me. I sent it deep gratitude and requested further contact and discussion in the future. I heard and felt a distinct *pop* as its withdrawal released me from the forces that had held me.

Then I was plummeting back through the tunnel, through the light-filled whirlwind. I traced my way following the bell, tracking along its sound like a downhill skier tucked into a schuss. The lights merged into long lines that coalesced briefly into the grid. I crossed the zone of silence in an instant. A flash of ecstatic force was followed by a sudden sense of slowing. The feelings of power abruptly diminished as the bell's pure tone of sound evaporated into the silence of the *zendo*. A sense of settling accompanied my return, and the phosphenes dissolved, leaving me in darkness.

My right knee was buzzing.

My face was wet with tears.

23
Spirit Locals

D AWN WAS BREAKING THROUGH THE WINDOW OF the *zendo*. The leopard man was gone, but as the last of the sensations of power departed, I heard a noise from deep within the trees, a brief sawing of wood. From my Africa days I knew it to be the grating cough of a leopard.

I uncoiled slowly and rose from my cushion, wiping my wet face on the wide sleeve of my *hippari*. My body felt rubbery, my knees shaky, my mind staggered by what it had just been through. I managed to stand and bring my hands up, placing one fist inside the other before my stomach, inner thumb tucked in. Slowly, I walked in line with the other participants as we left the *zendo* and descended the stairs for breakfast. Feelings of wonder and enormous gratitude welled up within me as I ate the minimal repast of rice, tea, and pickled vegetables in silence.

· · ·

Later in the morning I had my last interview with the Zen master. He asked me how my practice was going, and I wondered how I could possibly explain what I had just seen. Deciding on the direct approach, I looked into Aitken Rōshi's eyes and asked him if Zen students ever had visions. The venerable teacher smiled and replied,

"In *zazen* there are several different kinds of distraction that most students encounter sooner or later. Fantasies or random thoughts are the most common, but there is also a class of distraction called *makyo*, mysterious visions. They can be much like deep dreams, spontaneous ones that may be very vivid and richly detailed and that are sometimes accompanied by bodily sensations. Some students hear voices, and some even experience astral travel. The Buddha himself had visions while seated under the *bodhi* tree. I also have had them, but some very advanced students never do."

The Rōshi paused for a moment and then continued. "While some religions consider visions of great importance, in Zen they are not felt to be the purpose of practice. They reveal little of the student's own true nature, yet some students talk about their *makyo* as something ultimate. While this may be true in one sense, one must be cautious because *makyo* are self-limited.

"In Zen experiencing *makyo* is a sign that you are making progress in your practice. It indicates that you have progressed beyond the initial stages of thinking randomly. Have you experienced a *makyo* during the *sesshin*?"

Where could I begin? Aitken Rōshi's pale eyes regarded me keenly as I replied, "I experienced a vision just this morning. It was part of a series of spontaneous visionary experiences that I have been having over the last four years. I would very much like to discuss them with you and in some detail, but the brevity of the *dokusan* precludes being able to do justice to what is a rather unusual story." I raised my empty hands and smiled.

Aitken Rōshi raised his hands in *gasshō*. "Perhaps you will travel over to Honolulu sometime," he said. "Please feel free to come and talk to me whenever you do." He smiled again. I bowed. The interview was over.

·   ·   ·

The formal *sesshin* concluded shortly thereafter, followed by a robust lunch created by Akiko. In contrast to the silent spare meals of the retreat, the long row of tables was now covered with delicacies, and conversation was lively, although my attention was still directed inward.

A phrase kept appearing in my mind: "the Father, Son, and Holy Spirit." The concept was an artifact of my Episcopal upbringing, and yet it was also broadly applicable to what had just happened. The word *holy* was originally derived from the Old English word *halig* or *hal,* meaning "whole" or "more." Through time, the term has come to mean "sacred," "character-ized by perfection and transcendence," "spiritually pure or godly," "evoking veneration or awe," "being awesome, frightening, or beyond belief," and finally "filled with superhuman and potentially fatal power." In this case, I was the ancestral "father," Nainoa the descendant "son," and the *dorajuadiok* was the spirit, an awesome "holy" being.

I expressed gratitude and said farewell to the Rōshi as I left, then sought out Akiko. She was alone in the kitchen finishing up her chores. I bowed to her, thanking her for feeding us all so well during the retreat. She responded with a wide smile that made my *ku* lurch. I asked her to tell me something about herself and learned that she was a dancer who occasion-ally lived on the temple compound as caretaker when its owners were absent. As she talked, I marveled at her resemblance to someone far into the future. The friendly conversation came to a natural end, and I bowed to Akiko once more and left.

As I put my bag in the car, I paused and looked back at the temple surrounded by the forest. Its sense of mystery still prevailed in the silence, broken only by the click of a falling leaf—the same sound that had initiated my very first contact with Nainoa. Then, once again, the call of the rainbird drifted through the forest, accompanied by the same melan-choly sigh of wind.

As I drove away, I heard Aitken Rōshi's words in my inner ear.

"Our practice is not to clear up the mystery. It is to make the mystery clear."

·   ·   ·

On my return from the *sesshin*, I read up on western Nevada's natural history. The expansive saline lake of Nainoa's time does not exist in the arid deserts of the Great Basin today, but during the Pleistocene a large inland sea called Lake Lahontan covered much of the Great Basin, remnants of which exist today as Pyramid Lake and Walker Lake. A future climatic shift toward warmer conditions could conceivably refill some of the former great lake, giving rise to the body of water I had seen in Nainoa's company.

What about the spirit hills? Some mountainous sand dunes do exist out east of Carson City, and a place southeast of there is called Sand Mountain. Nearby is a cave with fish fossils embedded in the rocks.

In several remote desert areas around the world—in certain desert mountains in China, for example, and in the Sinai Peninsula in the Middle East—there are so-called "booming dunes" that produce droning sounds like music or thunder that have been likened to a deep voice coming directly out of the ground. The booming sound is produced during dry conditions when the wind sets the sand into motion, and the grains hit against each other. Similar sonic occurrences have been reported from Sand Mountain in western Nevada.

I thought about Moses' encounter on the Sinai Peninsula with the powerful spirit that resembled a "burning bush" (the *dorajuadiok* could very easily be described in this way) and wondered if the sounds produced by the blowing sand had helped him achieve the expanded state of awareness in which he had made his visionary contact more than three thousand years ago. It certainly seemed that William had known about the power of this sound, utilizing it to assist Nainoa in making his connection with the spirit. And with me.

A pair of mystical encounters followed my return from the *sesshin*. The first was during a night of fitful sleep. It began when Jill heard something tapping on the outside of the house around midnight.

I had just fallen asleep when she woke me with some urgency. I listened, half-conscious. *Tap, tap, tap* . . . then silence. After a moment or so, the sound was repeated: *tap, tap, tap*—then silence.

This continued for several minutes and then stopped. It was not the barking of a gecko. I became progressively more awake and finally sat up in bed, waiting for the tapping to continue. I looked out the window but saw nothing. The night was completely still, and there was no wind. It was hard to discern which side of the house had been tapped.

I waited, but the tapping did not resume. I was not inclined to get up since I had only just succeeded in falling asleep, so I slipped back under the covers. Then I began to toss and turn in that strange, shallow border-land between waking and sleeping. Thoughts, ideas, and feelings began to pass through my mind, and I was unable to relax. Around two o'clock I was still awake when I sensed a presence. I never locked my doors in Kona —with growing alarm I wondered if someone was in the house. Coming fully awake, I eased myself out of bed, picked up my knobbed Maasai cudgel, and drifted silently through the dark house, all senses on full alert. A careful search revealed that there was nobody there. Rea the cat was restless, however, and so I opened the door and let her out before returning to bed.

More tossing and turning followed—and then about a half hour later, the same sense of presence manifested itself once again. As I lay quietly in bed, feeling the shape of it, a crash from the kitchen woke everyone. I bolted out of bed, snatched up my stick, then paused and did something that was quite uncharacteristic of my former self. I sent a quick check to my *ku* as to the nature of the presence and was most surprised as to what came up.

My *ku* produced an impression of a definite "something." It was female, and it was big—*very* big. I stood in the dark, soothing Jill's tense whispers of inquiry with reassuring gestures as I scanned this impression and considered how much someone that size would weigh—a thousand pounds, maybe more. This was a tad outsize for the average human female. The impression it gave me was not unlike that of the *dorajuadiok*—a tall, monolithic verticality from which power emanated. But this one was not as big as that formidable spirit had been.

I stalked silently down the hall holding the *rungu* ready. In the kitchen, one of Jill's decorative metal baking pans had fallen from the wall for seemingly no reason. All else was in order. Nobody was there.

The children were now awake, and some time elapsed before everyone was reassured, tucked in, and back to sleep. For me, there was more tossing and turning. This was the time at which my altered states almost always occurred, and I began to anticipate one now. I focused on relaxing my body as fully as possible and formed the intention for contact. On this particular night, however, I concentrated on contacting the presence that I had felt earlier. I reached out for it and—

Wham!

The sensations of power roared into me, paralyzing my body in an instant. Phosphenes danced behind my closed eyelids as I struggled to breathe, and then it arrived. It was most definitely female and huge. It was neither hostile, nor benevolent. "She" felt neutral, and yet I perceived intention—positive intention. In the midst of the ecstatic, buzzing vibration that filled me, I opened my eyes and realized with astonishment that I could see out through the ceiling of the room. Simultaneously, I felt my consciousness suddenly detach from my physical body and float upward. I could see in all directions at once, and yet the directional focus of my attention was creating one primary field.

I moved up to the ceiling, which offered no resistance as I drifted right through it. I emerged from the roof, noting that the wooden shakes needed to be replaced, and began to fly up. As my awareness expanded outward, the powerful female presence was proximate, although I could not see her. The power sensations I always felt seemed this time to be funneling into me through "the other."

I abruptly found myself suspended very high in the air above the summit of Mauna Loa, although the mountain did not appear as it is today. It was considerably lower in altitude and surrounded by dense tropical foliage. The vegetation had an orange tint to it, and the sky was an odd peach-colored sunset verging through reddish into black at the zenith, all reflected by the sea. I was seeing the reversal effect, the spirit image of Mauna Loa.

A huge mountain capped by a thick glacier to the north so resembled

Mount Kilimanjaro in eastern Africa that it momentarily disoriented me. I tried to figure out exactly where I was. My gaze swept outward to find the ocean in all directions. I was definitely not in East Africa. I realized that the peak must be Mauna Kea, the other major volcano of the island, and that I must be seeing Hawai'i as it existed in the past, perhaps during a cold period in the earlier Pleistocene.

The crater directly below me was a jagged, violet rent in the earth's crust with a large breastlike cinder cone in its center. Dark steam was rising from many places within the caldera, and I heard muffled thunder below. I suddenly knew the identity of the presence—

Pele.

Over the past several years in Kona, my family and I had been making regular pilgrimages to the crater on the other side of the island called Halemaumau in which the volcano deity resided. This had become our favorite day trip around the island, and we had always taken flowers from the garden for the children to offer to the deity at the crater's edge. I had also created a series of small bronzes of Pele—and now here I was, hovering in space above her mountain in an expanded state of awareness.

As if in response to these ruminations, I began to descend, dropping down into the caldera to land near the base of the cinder cone. The lava under my feet vibrated with force, rippling with the *mana* contained in and below it. The sensations of power within me seemed to be oscillating at the same frequency as the vibrations, as if confirming the mountain's influence in my visionary experiences. As I gazed at the stark landscape, a gust of hot wind smelling of sulfur caused finely grained pumice to blow hissing and tinkling along the rocky substrate.

Then the ground below me shuddered as the vent at the cone's summit started to erupt. I was much too close to the cone and the two-thousand-degree temperature of a volcanic eruption. The ground shook again as molten magma shot up in the air with a deafening roar. I started to run—and then realized that it would not matter. I was simply too close, and there was no time to get away. I understood at some deep level that I would simply have to trust that I would be all right.

I stood as calmly as possible as the volcano awakened and brilliant flows of molten lava emerged from the summit of the cone. Gases exploded in brilliant orange-red and greenish clouds above me, coalescing with the extruded magma into a great pillar of fire that roared into the heavens. Spatters of molten rock fell all around as huge lava bombs whistled by, but nothing harmed me. The tremendous heat generated by this awesome display hit me as only a mild warmth. I felt more at ease.

Throughout, the strong female presence remained. The pillar of fire reached a great height, forming a blindingly bright bar of light a thousand feet into the air.

Then—the focus of my awareness suddenly shifted, and I was back in my body in bed next to Jill. The night was still dark. I was still shuddering with the power surging through me, but saw I was safe, and I knew that Jill and the children were also safe. It was as though I had voluntarily withdrawn from the vision to check on my family and my physical self. Upon discovering that all was well, I closed my eyes, and my level of awareness shifted again.

I opened my eyes in a strangely altered, dreamlike version of my house. Jill was beside me in bed, and I tried to explain to her that "it" was happening, but she didn't seem to hear me. As I tried to make contact with her again, the female presence reached out and "touched" me, and as the power roared through me, paralyzing me, I fell in slow motion to the floor.

I suddenly wished that I'd had the opportunity to spend some time with somebody who knew a bit more about interacting with spirits than I did, and the imagery shifted in response.

I sensed myself moving outward and the visual field darkened. I crossed a boundary and when the light came up again, I was in a dimly lit room among a group of people I didn't know. Where was I and why was I there? I had never been in this place before. I looked again at the people, and then shock rolled through me as I recognized a bearded man with dark intense eyes wearing jeans. It was Michael Harner. I hadn't seen him in years. His beard was now almost entirely white.

In that instant the older man's penetrating gaze fastened on me with surprise. I decided an explanation was in order and tried to reintroduce myself. I got as far as "it's definitely female and huge" when the power seized me again, squeezing me almost breathless. Harner made a reassuring gesture, and I clearly heard his deep voice say, "Don't try to explain this, just experience it."

Then the older man's glance shifted to something behind and above me, and I saw his eyes widen behind his reflective glasses. He smiled somewhat uneasily and gestured in that direction as he said, "She obviously likes you."

I turned then and saw her in her human aspect. There before me was a woman in late middle age with strong Polynesian features. She was impossibly tall and dressed in a curious *pa'u* of plain black *tapa*, which descended in graded folds all the way to her feet, concealing them. I stared at the folds of dark cloth, which created a similar effect to that of the classic Greek statues of Athena.

Her long black hair had reddish undertones and cascaded down across her back and shoulders all the way to the ground, creating a monolithic effect. A thick *lei* of orange and red flowers was wrapped around her head, while a similar one around her neck covered much of her broad chest. She seemed ageless and yet ancient, but her face and breasts were remarkably youthful, and her physique signified immense strength. Her strong arms were crossed, and her eyes were luminous with light as she looked me over appraisingly. Her broad mouth expressed the hint of a smile, but just a hint.

I stared up at the *akua* towering over me, speechless with awe. She was easily twice my height, and her forearms were the size of my thighs. My scattered wits regathered slowly, and realizing that she might be waiting for me to react, I managed to summon courage. Raising my hands in *gasshō*, I bowed to her and whispered, *"Tutu Pele."*

I sensed rather than saw her smile as the power sensations increased, surging through me, crackling with energy. As I raised my eyes, she seemed to stretch upward, becoming even taller and more monolithic than before.

A word appeared in my consciousness, arriving as an even tone of vibrational "sound" that was incredibly soft. I stopped thinking and listened and the word came again—"*makalahia.*" It was a Hawaiian word breathed into my ears by a "voice" that was not unlike the wind sighing through the trees at Wood Valley Temple. Each syllable extended into a long malleable continuum of song—"*maaa-kaaa-laaa-heee-aaa.*" The effect was chantlike and was repeated several times. I had no idea what the word meant. Its eerie, etheric beauty caused a strong response in my physical body, however, and distracted my focused attention. I was suddenly returned to my bed in the dark in Kona.

I lay stunned, still feeling Pele's presence as the energy swirled around and through me, withdrawing into the distance like an echo fading. The cat called from outside, and Jill got up to let her back into the house. Anna awoke. Jill changed her diaper, gave her a bottle, and came back to bed. I was still in the last grip of the force but managed to pat her reassuringly. The cat appeared in the bedroom and became motionless, staring up at something that only she could see in the center of the room. Then the presence and the sensations of power were gone, and I immediately fell asleep.

The next morning, I looked up the word and discovered that *makala* means "to open" or "to awaken," and *-hia* is a suffix conveying an imperative command. *Makalahia* was thus a directive that stated flatly what was expected of me:

"Wake up!"

This is the Buddha's call. The term *Buddha* itself means "the awakened one."

The next visionary experience followed on the heels of the first as if to underscore the point that Pele had made. The following night was again fitful, and I tossed and turned for most of it until the cat got me up to let her out at four. Returning to bed, I relaxed as fully as possible and finally whispered, "All right, let's have it."

The sensations of power appeared immediately, rushing up my back and exploding into my brain. Once again I felt a presence and, reaching inward to my *ku*, learned that the presence this time was the large buttress-rooted *wi*-apple tree beside the carport near the house.

Abruptly, I was standing below the tree, staring upward at the moon through its dark branches. These trees, also known as Otahiti apples, had been brought from the South Seas long ago by Polynesian voyagers. From them, hulls of great oceangoing voyaging canoes had often been made. With that thought, I began to have impressions of floating above vast oceanic expanses dotted with mountainous islands under huge white clouds. A fleet of long double-hulled canoes with high sterns and great scoop sails catching the wind planed at great speed across the blue water tipped with whitecaps. I was so high up I could barely make out the human beings on board.

The scene shifted abruptly, and I was once again below the tree in my front yard. The myriad pinnate leaves above seemed to be shining with their own inner light. I felt the tree touch me with its *mana*. Then a strange rhythmic sound came from higher up the mountain. It was eerie, and as it came closer, it sounded like people singing or chanting. The words sounded Hawaiian, but I did not know for sure. I moved into cover behind the tree as I looked around in the darkness for the source. As the sound grew louder, shadowy forms moved among my trees: Many people were walking in procession through my land toward the ocean. . . .

A tall individual detached from the group and approached the place where I was standing beneath the tree. It was a Hawaiian man of robust stature dressed in a long cloak of black *tapa* that appeared to cover him from his broad shoulders to his heels. The sides of his head seemed shaved, and his thick white hair formed a crest along the crown of his head. He seemed at least a foot taller than I and carried a long dark wooden lance.

My immediate thought was that some local cultural event must be in progress. I could feel *mana* emanating from the Hawaiian as he approached. His mouth was broad, his face heavily lined, his presence so compelling that, on impulse, I made a deep bow, touching my forehead to the ground. When I stood again, he had turned and was looking curiously at my car.

Although he seemed very familiar, I could not remember ever meeting him before. I wondered if he lived higher up the mountain. Figures continued to walk past us in the darkness.

I suddenly felt the man's emotional state—a profound unhappiness emanated from him. I became anxious and he seemed to detect this, turning to reassure me. Resting his spear against the *wi*-apple tree, he put his warm brown hands on my shoulders and looked deeply into my eyes. Then, I finally recognized him. It was Kamehameha.

As this thought exploded in my mind, the king's face altered slightly and his broad mouth formed a smile, yet the sadness in his eyes remained. Something drew his attention, and he walked around my car to look at the *pohaku* in the rock garden. For long moments he stared at the stone in silence, then turned and looked directly into my eyes and said a single word in Hawaiian, *"Ike."* He repeated it a second time as though to make sure I had gotten it—*"Eee-kay."*

My body was still in the grip of the force, but I managed to bring my hands up in *gasshō*. I made another deep bow and whispered, *"Kamehameha nui."*

The king smiled again. His presence was so strong that the children felt it and woke up, their calls of inquiry disrupting the altered state. As my awareness shifted back into ordinary reality, my last vision of the king was of his huge cloak-covered frame filling the doorway of my house. Kamehameha was smiling down at the stone in the rock garden and was making a gesture with both hands in the air above and around it. His lips were moving, but I could not hear what he said.

Then I was back in my body, returning just as Jill rose to check on our daughters. I lay quietly, sensing the king's presence, seeing the sadness in his eyes, feeling the warm impressions of his hands on my shoulders until I abruptly fell into a dead sleep like the night before.

Upon awakening, I recalled the vision in all its details. I ran through it several times to make sure I had it all. Then I rose from bed and looked up the word that the king had uttered. As a noun, *ike* meant "knowledge," but it was also used traditionally to mean "spiritual power" or "vision." As a verb, *ike* signified "to show," "to know," "to feel," "to greet," "to recognize," and "to understand."

I regained contact with Nainoa about a month later, my last before departing the islands.

I was awake early one morning in the dark before dawn. The strong sweet scent of night-blooming jasmine was again flowing through the house, reminding me of a previous contact. I had been doing some work with a hypnotherapist, learning techniques of self-hypnosis to help me gain the altered state more easily. I glanced at the clock—it was that time of the night when my visionary experiences usually occurred. I decided to try the method.

I turned onto my back and formed the intention within. I invoked my helping spirits, forming images of the leopard man and the spirit stone within my mind. I focused on my intention with one-pointed concentration, inviting the two spirits to assist me. Then I used self-hypnosis and reached for the power. I waited, relaxing my body fully, my awareness expanding outward, inward, searching for the altered state. I waited.

I had almost decided to cancel the attempt when the doorway opened, and the energy was suddenly there. I held my destination firmly in mind as the grid appeared. The buzzing, hissing noise increased—and then ceased as I zoomed across the interface and through the zone of silence. As the shift was accomplished, the pressure of the force suddenly lessened, and my sensory perceptions returned.

The sense of smell reestablished itself first. The fragrance of the jasmine was gone, replaced by the smells of woodsmoke, furs, and the scent of a woman I had come to know very well.

24
Twelfth Journey
Kenojelak's Dream

I
T WAS CLOSE TO DAWN. NAINOA WAS DRIFTING IN AND
out of sleep in the hut of marsh rushes that he
shared with the sleeping Kenojelak. As she moved in
her dreaming on their bed of furs, his arm encompassed
her, holding her close. He was semi-awake when the
strong sweet smell of some fragrant flowering plant appeared briefly in his awareness. The scent was familiar,
but he was still drifting in the shallows of sleep, and he
couldn't recall where or when he had encountered it
before.

He awoke quickly as he abruptly remembered. It had
been that morning in the forest near the onset of his
journey. At that time, he now understood, some inner
connection had been established, and he had become
aware of the presence for the first time—the presence that
must have been the American.

He came fully awake, his nose seeking the fragrance,
but it was gone. Seven days had passed since his extraordi-

nary experience at the spirit hills. Perhaps the American had returned. He waited, but within his mind there was only silence.

Kenojelak moved against him again, and he smiled in the semidarkness of his hut. It was a definite pelvic thrust. Perhaps the American was embarrassed to have arrived at such an intimate moment. But did it matter? The American could very well be himself living a former life, far away in the past. Was his ancestor now visiting within him to discuss what they had both learned from their extraordinary trip with the *dorajuadiok*?

Nainoa extended a warm welcome to him—and thought over the aftermath of the cosmic vision at the spirit hills. The extraordinary vision had terminated as the awesome sound that had carried and sustained them ceased with the dying of the wind at dawn. Nainoa had sat up and looked around. The spirit was gone and the world was ordinary once again. He felt a deep serenity.

William had emerged from his own trance and glanced at Nainoa with a thin smile and made the hunter's gesture for silence. For a long time they sat on the hide and watched the growing light of dawn. When they rose, William rolled up the hide without a word. His eyes were vacant as the two of them retraced their steps back to the cave.

On reaching the cave they broke camp in silence and began their return journey across the open arid flats and sparsely wooded hills along the lake. They walked without speaking for much of that day, each absorbed in his own inner process. Nainoa ran the entirety of the vision through his mind again and again. His grasp of history had been extraordinarily enlarged. The American's reactions and interpretations of what they saw had expanded his own understanding beyond measure.

That evening, over a dinner of broiled fish, Nainoa finally broke the silence. "It was so lonely out there in the void," he observed. "It must have been so lonely for so long."

William simply smiled. "You may find it difficult to talk about what you have experienced," he said. "Just keep it to yourself for a while so that you can digest it. You have been given knowledge by the spirits. They have

decided that you are worthy and ready for instruction. Now it is up to them and to you."

"William, what was that incredible sound? Was it the spirit?"

The old hunter looked around carefully in the dying light, then nodded and said in a conspiratorial whisper, "No one knows for sure, but it is thought that the sound is the voice of Zilatu, the spirit of the air, a powerful entity. It is thought that Zilatu comes at the request of the *dorajuadioks* who have the power to control the spirits of nature."

The older man then paused thoughtfully and asked, "Did you make contact with your ancestor?" Nainoa nodded. William's long eyes widened as he smiled. Then he made the gesture for silence and did not press him further.

When the two men returned to the Ennu camp above the lake, the large gathering was preparing to break up. William's relatives were about to depart for a distant area in the south where the black glassy stone from which they made their tools was abundant. Another smaller group was heading toward their seasonal hunting grounds along the lake to the northeast. It was time to disperse and follow the game according to the ancient pattern.

A new sense of respectful formality now pervaded Nainoa's formerly easygoing friendships among the Ennu. They were hesitant and fearful when it came to dealings with the spiritual realm, and they now were deferential to him because of his ability. No one in camp asked him what happened at the spirit hills.

Even Kenojelak asked him very little. The evening of his return, she looked at him for a long time after they made love, then smiled, running her fingers over his lips affectionately. "So now you know what it is to be *ungagok*," she observed.

The way she said it made him wonder if she too was able to make contact with the spirits. Kenojelak glanced at him with her serious look and simply nodded as though reading his thoughts. She said nothing

further before curling up in his arms and going to sleep like a contented child.

Just before the camp broke up, one of the men of the neighboring band became ill and asked William to cure him. He agreed to conduct a healing ceremony.

In preparation for the occasion, a circle of stones was laid out on the hilltop, and William constructed a large shallow drum. Using a freshly flaked stone scraper, he transformed a supple tree branch into a long flexible wooden frame. He shaped and soaked it in water before bending it into a wide oval. Then he attached a handle and stretched a prepared goat skin over the frame. As the completed drum dried over a fire, William tested it from time to time, striking it with a wooden beater. He retied and restretched the drumhead on the frame a number of times until it gave a deep booming sound. When he had finished, William informed the camp that he would perform the healing that evening after dark.

The sufferer's name was Onarg, and he looked very ill as he entered the circle. He lay down on a deerskin in the center while the entire community gathered to witness the event.

All waited in watchful silence until William appeared carrying the drum. The old hunter's eyes were vacant, and he had intricate designs on his body and face, dots and lines painted with red earth and white ash from his fire-pit. A woven basketry cap, to which was attached a set of small deer antlers, was tied onto his head. A gourd rattle painted with designs hung from his waistband. An odd whistle hung around his neck.

William conferred with his patient in low tones for some time. Then he stood and began to beat the drum in a monotonous rhythmic fashion, striking it on the frame and on the drumhead with the wooden beater. After some time passed, he began to sing a high, nasal, repetitive song while dancing in a curious shuffling step around his prostrate kinsman. The assembled Ennu followed his lead, chiming in on the end of the chantlike refrain and striking short sticks together in time with the drum. Once the rhythm was well established, William blew into the whistle. Periodically, from a stylized birdlike stance, he blew shrill, piercing sounds into the darkness. He then resumed his dance, looking up into the night sky.

The old hunter continued to drum, sing, dance, and blow the whistle long into the evening. Nainoa thought that nothing much was going to happen. Finally, the older man began to stagger, and the drumbeat faltered. Kenojelak, who was standing closest, took the drum from her father and began to strike it in the same monotonous booming beat. The whistle dropped from William's lips as his eyes closed and he slowly lay down on the hide beside his kinsman.

He remained motionless for some time while the assembled Ennu waited watchfully and his daughter continued to drum. Suddenly William rose to his knees and made the hunter's signal for silence. All eyes were on him as he took the rattle into his hand and shook it, concentrating his efforts above his kinsman's prostrate form. The rattle seemed to be drawn to a point above the man's torso, and as William, eyes closed, continued to shake it, he gently felt Onarg's belly with his other hand.

Abruptly the old hunter dropped the rattle, clamped both hands to his relative's abdomen, then pulled as though he were trying to extract something from the man's body. His eyes remained closed, and he grunted and growled like an animal, continually tugging at something indistinct. Nainoa looked closely at William's hands but could see nothing—nothing at all.

With a crow of triumph, William finally wrenched his hands away, holding the "something" up so that all could see it. Although Nainoa still couldn't see anything, all the Ennu pointed to it, commenting on its hostile nature to each other in hushed tones. William threw "it" toward the lake with an explosive shout and a gesture of disgust. He repeated the sequence of motions several times, pulling, extracting, shouting, and throwing—pulling, extracting, shouting, and throwing—until he appeared satisfied that no more of the substance remained. Then he washed his hands and forearms thoroughly in a gourd of water held by Kovak and blew on his hands and fingers as though to dry them. Finally he lay down next to his patient once more and closed his eyes.

Kenojelak resumed her drumming. After another long interval, her father rose up on his knees again, holding something in his hands. This time, Nainoa saw what it was. It looked like a short section of hollow leg bone from some animal. It was shiny and stained reddish-brown with age. The moonlight glinted off its surface as William placed one end gently against Onarg's skin under his ribs and blew through it sharply. The older man repeated this action several times, then tucked the tube into his breechcloth.

Then he again shook the rattle over and around his kinsman at some length until he seemed satisfied. William sat his patient up and conferred with him at some length in a low monotone. When Onarg was helped to his feet, he looked considerably better. The healing was done.

Nainoa approached William the day after the healing and asked him about the ritual. At the older man's invitation, they withdrew to the same hilltop where William had previously talked with him about spiritual matters.

"Spirit helpers assist me in doing healing work," the Ennu said. "I appeal to them to determine the nature of the problem and to decide what is to be done. They tell me only what is necessary for me to know. I do not really do this work myself. The spirits do it at my request.

"The drum helps me to make contact with them. I listen to the drum, and my awareness shifts into their level of being. I fly on the sound of the drum in the same way that we traveled on the voice of Zilatu at the spirit hills. I ride on the drum to where the spirits are, then I call my special spirit allies to me with the whistle. When they approach, I appeal to them, asking for their assistance in the task at hand. They usually agree to help, although sometimes I have to convince them, especially if I am trying to help someone the spirits feel is unworthy.

"Long ago, my father's mother's brother lost part of his soul in a hunting accident. He was struck by a bull, as you were, and his soul left his body for a while. It was as though he were asleep, and we could not wake him. When his soul returned, part of it had gotten lost. An empty place appeared within him as a result. It was in this place that an illness took up residence.

"Sometimes when someone has lost part of their soul, illness simply enters the undefended empty place. Different kinds of sickness may be manifested, and so the illness-causing element must be removed in order for the person to recover. My kinsman Onarg had such an element residing within him. I simply shifted my level of awareness until I was able to perceive the spiritual aspect of his illness. Then I appealed to one of my spirit helpers to help me pull it out.

"The helping spirit and I succeeded in extracting the illness, but this left the empty space within Onarg's soul that needed to be refilled, so I appealed once again to another spirit, who helps me find lost souls. Together we journeyed to the place where it had gone."

The older man's voice drifted off, and his eyes unfocused as though he were looking into some vast distance. He continued speaking but in a noticeably flat tone. "I have never been to that place before, but there was no mistaking it. It was part of Onarg's *odiok*, his personal name soul. It had gotten lost during an encounter with something malevolent during Onarg's dreaming, and I had to convince it to return. The lost soul part was frightened, but in the end, with my spirit helper's aid, I prevailed and was able to bring it back and restore it to my kinsman."

William grinned widely. "He is much better now, and the illness-causing element is gone. It cannot return now that Onarg's soul is complete and his personal power restored." Then he paused and added, "His wife will be happier too."

Nainoa asked if he too could use the drum to help him see spirits more easily. William nodded. "As you become accustomed to the sound of the drum," he said, "it becomes easier and easier. Thereafter your awareness will shift into that level where you can meet the spirits whenever you hear it. The drum is indeed useful. Others do it in different ways, but all *ungagok* have special methods of altering their inner thinking and feeling so that they can perceive the spirits and the places where they reside.

"One does not do this for play or simply out of curiosity," William went on. "One has to have a strong reason to engage the spirits. It has to be a worthy one, or the spirits might become displeased. One does not simply beat the drum and shift into their realm and then have nothing to say or do. The spirits do not take kindly to this."

William concluded the discussion by observing, "You obviously have the ability to do this. You have been given a glimpse of them and their world. Now you must become familiar with the spirit realms, both those of the lower world and those of the upper regions. Your spirit helper, the one you call the tiger man, will be your guide and will protect you. You must meet and acquire more spirit helpers. Their assistance is essential in whatever you need to accomplish. You must now deepen your vision so that experiencing the spirits becomes natural for you. When that time comes, you will no longer need the drum or the voice of Zilatu. Then you will be able to do it easily and naturally whenever there is need."

According to the stars, a year had almost passed and it was time for Nainoa to return to the Hawaiian settlements. He was more conflicted than ever at the thought of leaving, especially since his spiritual training had become terribly important to him, overriding almost all other concerns. He wanted to be able to merge with his ancestor in the past. He would have to use these last days with William well.

But what was he to do about Kenojelak? He imagined her at the governor's court with her weapons and dogs. What should he do?

In the growing light of dawn, Kenojelak emerged from her dreams and whispered, "Nainoapak?"

He kissed her and began to caress her. She laughed, pushed his hands away, and sat up. "Nainoapak, I have had a dream, a very important one. I was sitting by the stream where we bathe, and a woman came out of the water. She was blue—her skin and hair and eyes were blue, and she had beautiful blue clothing floating around her like the water eddies. She told me her name is Riverwoman and that she had some important information for me.

"Riverwoman told me that I am to be *ungagok* for my people, that she will become my *dordok*, my spirit helper, and will teach me about plant medicines. She told me that I am not yet *zakray*, but the plants are and they will tell me what I need to know. I will learn to cure sickness and become a medicine woman for my people. The spirits have intended this for me, she said, since I was a child. They have been watching me, and the time has come for me to begin my training.

"Riverwoman said that the spirits have plans for you too. You are becoming a spiritwalker, and William has been chosen to help you. You will return to your chief and William will go with you, to continue your training and to meet your people. William has something of great importance to do among them, and he will then return to us when it is finished.

"Riverwoman said you have an important part to play in the history of your people and will be a powerful *ungagok* for them. She also told me something I don't understand but she said you would—that you have an important relationship, a connection through the spirit world, with one who lives far away, and that you will gain much knowledge from this person. You will help your people. . . ." Kenojelak's words trailed off as she struggled to express the idea. "Riverwoman said you will help refill the bowl with what has been lost."

Kenojelak's face brightened. "She also told me that I will have a child with you, a daughter, and that she will become a powerful *ungagok* for the Ennu. I have been chosen by the spirit of my grandmother to be her mother in her forthcoming life. My grandmother was a great healer for the people, and she has chosen to return. She has also selected you to be her father." Kenojelak twinkled at him and ran her fingers down his chest with a laugh. "Riverwoman told me that when our daughter is grown, she will be a spiritwalker like her father and will have something of great value for you, for your people, and for the Ennu.

"The water spirit told me that you will be a powerful man of wide influence among your people—that you will travel widely and that you will return to visit with your Ennu wife often. She said our lives will be different because of what the spirits have planned for us and what we will be for our people. We will have more children."

Kenojelak stopped. Nainoa stared at her in the dim light as his mind filled with thoughts. Kenojelak watched him for long moments, then leaned forward and placed her mouth next to his ear and whispered, "Riverwoman told me that I would become with child this morning." She giggled and twirled her tongue within the convolutions of his ear, then pushed him over on his back.

Nainoa laughed and gathered her into his arms . . . and within him the future settled into place.

25
Transition

IDID NOT COMMUNICATE DIRECTLY WITH NAINOA DUR-
ing this contact of very short duration. As he guessed,
I felt some ambivalence about trespassing into this
moment of intimacy and did not respond to his thoughts
of inquiry. His subconscious *ku*, however, perceived my
desire for information and began to scan his memories.
As Nainoa and I watched the selective flow of reminis-
cences appear, he was immediately aware of what was
happening and wondered if he, too, might be able to
extract information from my memories when he is "here."

A week later, in the middle of June 1989, I was at
Kealakekua Bay with my young daughters, mulling it all
over among the boulders half-buried in the grayish-black
sand below the *heiau.*

This was our last morning, but as we had done every
morning, we swam, dug holes in the sand, built castles
with towers and moats, and walked through the woods to
visit the water spirit in the pond. I smiled at how open my
children were to the nonordinary levels of reality. Their

belief in spirits came quite naturally because they spontaneously experienced them in their "daydreams" on an ongoing basis. They would continue to do so until their teachers and their peers taught them that spirits were imaginary—that they didn't really exist.

Like me, they had been touched by the spirits of this place.

Jill, too, had changed profoundly in the four years in Hawai'i. There was a quietness about her now, a new openness and a deepened awareness. She had previously had a successful physical therapy practice in the San Francisco Bay Area that had incorporated traditional Western medicine with bodywork and personal awareness training. She had left behind that success and recognition to raise her children in rural Hawai'i, a complete flip-flop. In the process she had learned how to be all right by living moment to moment. One day she shared a phrase she'd read: We had been living our life in Kona simply, she said, "without any alibis or self-promoting schemes."

Our daughters had become rather wild. Their hair was long and sunbleached, their skin deeply tanned. Jill and I could barely keep clothes on them, and they almost never wore shoes. My Eastern establishment parents (and grandparents) would think them unmanageable. My lineage had definitely taken a new tack.

The time had come to return to my profession. I had thoroughly enjoyed my teaching and students in Kona, but the job was part-time and Jill and I had reluctantly decided to return to the mainland at the end of the 1989 academic year. Our "Hawai'i project" was completed. The house was restored, our land was cleared, and money issues had become real once again.

I felt numb at the thought of leaving Kona. I had become so deeply connected to the island that I had no wish to leave, but like Nainoa, I had to return to my former life in order to finish what I had begun.

On this last morning with my family at the bay, a melody emerged in my mind—one I had never heard before. It began as short recurring phrases. As I walked among the rocks above the ocean and kept an eye on the children, I hummed the tune fragments over and over, until finally they came together as a whole. Words appeared and formed themselves into verses, and I suddenly realized that I had been given a song.

I sat on a flat rock among the boulders and trees above the sea and sang my song, repeating and engraving it into my *ku*. I continued to hum as I walked along the beach with my children, looking out for artifacts out of habit. I had never found that stone adze blade. Now time was running out, and I felt a twinge of regret at not having found it—but I had found a song. I'd also "found" my altered-state experiences and what a "find" those had been! I hoped my contact with Nainoa would continue once I left the islands.

We returned to the house from the beach, and it was very still as I sat alone on my lanai, waiting for the men who would pack up the remainder of the household and ship it all back to the mainland. The raucous call of a mynah shattered the silence. A neighbor's chickens stalked through my coffee trees, waiting in vain for my daughters to offer them stale bread crusts. A blur of movement revealed a mongoose watching them from the green mosaic of the garden. The first lychees were ripening on my tree, but I would not eat them this year.

I stared out at the horizon and thought of Nainoa. As in myths and legends, both of us had experienced the call to adventure. Both had accepted the quest and left behind our known worlds to search for answers to the mystery of existence. We had passed through an inner doorway, met spirits face-to-face, and received spiritual initiation. Our understanding of the nature of reality and ourselves had been immeasurably expanded as we discovered that our consciousnesses could journey across time and space, by being what William called spiritwalkers. We now knew with certainty that we would survive the death of our physical bodies. We knew the truth of reincarnation.

As I looked down into Kealakekua Bay, I thought about the transition that was about to occur for both Nainoa and me. Both of us had to return to our own worlds, bearing our experiences as offerings to others so that they might take courage and embark on journeys of their own.

I sighed and got up to weed the rock garden one last time. I pulled the invading grasses—with apologies—as I looked affectionately over the stones that I had collected. I was on my way to a new appointment as a visiting lecturer at one of the branches of the University of California. It was an opportunity to rejoin the world I had left behind four years ago and would hopefully be a step toward a full-time teaching position.

Time was short. I decided to burn some cardboard boxes that had been stored under the house instead of driving them all the way down to the dump on the coast. After shaking out the omnipresent cockroaches and cane spiders, I carried them all over to the isolated place on my land where I burned paper trash on windless days.

As I fed the boxes to the fire in a large pit encircled with stones, keeping the fire just high enough so as not to singe the trees or set the land ablaze, a rhythm and a mood developed. My song returned to me, and I hummed it softly, over and over. There was no wind, yet the fire danced.

Suddenly I felt her presence. There was no mistaking it. She was there in the pillar of fire dancing before me. I could feel her attention on me. My pulse quickened as I gathered my wits. I bowed to the column of fire respectfully and whispered, "Pele." I thanked her for blessing me with her presence at this time of sadness and things coming apart. In response, the fire immediately danced and roared in the still air.

I explained to her what was occurring in my life and why. I told her of my quandary over taking my sculptures. They had all been executed in stone—in her stone. I asked her permission to take them out into the world as objects of power—as art formed jointly by myself, by her, and by Kanaloa, the spirit of the ocean. The sculpted stones would give power to those who could perceive what they were, I said. Could the stones function as extensions of herself, through which others outside of Hawai'i might experience her own power? I asked.

I waited in silence for some response, staring into the fire for long moments in the strong sense of her watchful attention. Then I felt her assent come in through my *ku*. Gratitude and relief welled up within me. I asked for her blessing—for her stones, for myself, and for my family as we left the islands and went out into the world once more. Then as an afterthought, I invited her to make contact from time to time wherever I was—but especially when I was out in nature, in the wild places away from the distractions of Western civilization.

Once again I received strong impressions of assent mixed with affection.

Then I felt her go. One moment she was there, and the next, the intensity of the fire suddenly decreased by half, and she was gone. I emerged from the light trance state and noticed that the sky had darkened with an approaching storm. A memory of Chief Kaneohe emerged, and on impulse I raised my hands and blessed Pele and her land in the Old Hawaiian language:

"E ho'omaikai keia akua . . .

"E ho'omaikai keia aina."

The fire flared briefly, roared into the sky once more, then died as the first fat raindrops fell.

Ignoring the rain, I walked over to the spirit stone in the rock garden near my front door. I had become very, very fond of it, and the thought of leaving it behind brought me strong feelings of grief.

As the storm grew with tropical intensity, the water fell in torrents with a deafening roar. Impulsively, I took off all my clothes and stood naked in the tumultuous downpour, staring at the stone. I focused my attention upon it—and my skin suddenly raised into goosebumps as the sensations of power invaded me. I stood rigid in the roaring rain, shuddering and gasping with the combined effort of breathing and maintaining my stance. As though in response, the sensations decreased just enough for me to be able to control my body.

I raised my hands in *gassho* and bowed to the spirit stone, formally addressing it by name. I asked if it would like to accompany me out into the world for a while as my companion. I invited it to function as one of my spirit helpers, providing me with friendship, protection, and power, as well as access to my esteemed descendant.

I felt the stone's agreement.

Kapohaku'ki'ihele, the stone that travels, wished to take its first journey to the distant shores of America.

I smiled, then squatted and placed both hands on the stone. There was no doubt. Power flowed out of the boulder, numbing my arms and hands with vibrational force not unlike an electric current. In that moment of physical contact, my personal destiny locked firmly into a new place within the great pattern. I gripped the stone and made a solemn oath—that I, or one of my descendants, would someday bring it back to the island.

The power slammed into me as the stone's spirit affirmed that which had now been set into motion. So strong was the force that I was propelled backward to land on my behind on the wet driveway. I gasped with shock as I sat stunned, rubbing my hands and forearms in the rain. Then abruptly, feelings of joy appeared—great fluorescent surges of joy.

I managed to get up and stand there in the rain with the power hissing in my ears. Then slowly . . . slowly . . . I began to dance.

I moved carefully at first, finding my way. My blood sparkled with light as I danced with more confidence and with more speed. I had no choice—I had to move or go mad with the surging power that permeated me. Faster and faster I danced, filled with happiness, until I was jumping up and down with Maasai-like leaps in the tumultuous, drumming water-sound of the storm.

In the midst of my frenzy, I thought I heard somebody say something as if from a great distance. Higher and higher I leaped as tiny crackles of lightning seemed to flash out of my shoulders and feet and fingertips. I heard a laugh and glanced up to see Jill watching me through the screen door of the house. She turned and said something to someone over her shoulder, and this time I heard her.

"Come and take a look at your father."

Two pale little faces appeared at the screen. My enthusiasm dimmed somewhat—did they think I had gone crazy? Then the children threw open the door and dashed naked into the pouring darkness to dance with me in the rain, crowing with delight. The three of us leaped up and down, my daughters laughing with unfettered abandon as they stomped and splashed and hopped about. Flashes of light revealed Jill trying to record the event on film.

Then the screen door banged again, and Jill joined us, her teeth and long legs flashing in the growing darkness as she absorbed the mood, whirling and leaping with the grace of a trained dancer. She too threw off all her clothes, dancing like a madwoman with sheets of water sluicing down her long shimmering body.

Magic was in the air—great draughts of raw wildness flowed through me as I rain-danced with my women. Abruptly the sensations seemed to switch on an inner light, a radiance that continued until the sensations suddenly ceased, leaving me standing exhilarated and exhausted in the roaring darkness.

Here I was with three howling females dancing naked before a spirit stone in the height of a tropical storm on an active volcano in the middle of the Pacific.

Were California and my fellow anthropologists ready for us?

The next evening, at a resort hotel up at Anaeho'omalu Bay, Jill and I strolled the beach at sunset as the children played in the shallows. The long curving white-sand beach and grove of coconut palms had made this place a favorite day trip over the years, and we chose it as a refuge to nurture us in those final hours, as a place to unwind from the chaos of moving the household. The blazing sun hung over the dark ocean, dazzling me with brilliance. Memories of the future moved through my mind.

At the very instant that the sun touched the sea, I looked down at the ridge of coral rubble and broken shells along the tideline. And there it was —a small black wedge of stone. As the next wave washed over it, threatening to rebury it in the sand, I reached down and picked it up. It was an old adze blade, its features softened by years of abrasion as the ocean endlessly reworked the beach over and over. Viewed from above, it looked like a wide, flat foot, as long as the end joint of my thumb. Remains of the striking platform on its heel and the bulb of percussion on its underside were both features formed when its maker had struck the small flake off a larger core of stone. There was no doubt—it was man-made, fashioned by some long-gone Hawaiian craftsman to do the fine finish work on a carved wooden object.

My thumb tested its edge. Nainoa would have recognized it instantly, but most of the island's contemporary population would not. I wondered about its maker and when it had been made as my fingers continued to study the small stone tool. I had been looking for it for years, and the fact that I had finally found it in my last hours on the island seemed more than just coincidental. The sun dipped below the horizon, and the warm waves washed my feet. I touched the blade to my tongue to taste the salt.

I felt it was a gift from the spirits of the place. And in that moment I knew with certainty that magic is real.

Behind the magnificent white beach, a long grove of palms rattled in the warm wind. Far in the distance, the moon was rising between the dark massifs of Mauna Kea and Mauna Loa. I mentally replaced the hulking hotel behind the beach with a fishing village for those who would survive civilization's collapse—it would be a fine place for a village until the ocean rose.

As I turned the worked flake of stone over in my fingers, a fragment of an old Chinese proverb surfaced in my mind:

> Unless we change direction,
> we are likely to end up
> where we are headed.

Postscript

M Y FAMILY AND I TOOK UP RESIDENCE IN A SUBURB of San Diego for the next academic year while I taught anthropology at the local branch of the University of California. During this time, I wrote a year's worth of new lectures on human evolution, prehistoric archaeology, magic, shamanism, and the origins of religion.

When our household arrived from Hawai'i, the first thing I did was find and unpack the crate containing the spirit stone. The dark boulder looked rather dry, and I wondered uneasily if it was still "alive" after its trip in the hold of a ship. Since it had always been outdoors in Kona, it seemed quite natural to put it in our backyard, a postage-stamp-size piece of sunbaked clay with a few unhealthy-looking trees and an extinct lawn that had been neglected by the former tenants. It was a far cry from our wild, jungly *kuleana* in Kona.

We decided to place the stone under a scraggly fig tree that was badly in need of water. Shortly thereafter, the whole yard seemed to come to life. The grass made a comeback, some untended clumps of Cape honeysuckle erupted into clouds of orange-red flowers, and a large *Dracaena* burst into fragrant bloom. A stand of sickly-looking banana trees actually began to produce bananas.

The fig tree exhibited the greatest change, however. The day after we placed the stone beneath it, the tree started to throw out fruit and leaves at a truly impressive rate. It produced figs, even through the coldest part of the next winter, when the tree had dropped all of its leaves and frost had killed some of my bonsai. During the year and a half that the stone remained under the tree, the flow of figs never ceased.

I had no more altered-state experiences for almost a year, perhaps because I was so busy reading, writing, and teaching. Although I was somewhat worried that I had lost my contact with Nainoa, in the spring of 1990 my teaching came to an end. I considered what to do with all my "field notes" from Hawai'i. I took to sitting with the stone under the fig whenever I paused for a cup of tea, and one morning I felt an inner shift of attention. That same day, I sat down at the computer and began formally to write up my full-fledged version of this account.

That night, at the usual time, the sensations of power appeared once again. I began a new journal.

Notes

Chapter 1

1. Michael Harner, *The Way of the Shaman* (San Francisco: Harper and Row, 1990).
2. Joan Halifax, *Shamanic Voices: A Survey of Visionary Narratives* (New York: E. P. Dutton, 1979).

Chapter 5

1. Joseph Campbell, *Hero of a Thousand Faces.* Bollingen Series 22 (Princeton, NJ: Princeton University Press, 1968; original, 1949), pp. 77–78.
2. Ibid., p. 82.
3. Gary Smith and Michael E. Long, "Utah's Rock Art, Wilderness Louvre," *National Geographic* 157:1 (1980), pp. 97–117.
4. See, for example, Marija Gimbutas, *The Goddesses and Gods of Old Europe, 6500–3500 B.C.: Myths and Cult Images* (London: Thames and Hudson, 1982); and the same author's *The Language of the Goddess* (San Francisco: Harper and Row, 1989).
5. David Lewis-Williams, "The Thin Red Line: San Notions and Rock Paintings of Supernatural Potency," *South African Archaeological Bulletin* 36 (1981), pp. 5–13; "The Economic and Social Context of Southern San Rock Art," *Current Anthropology* 23:4 (1982), pp. 429–49; *The Imprint of Man: The Rock Art of Southern Africa* (London: Cambridge University Press, 1983); "The San Artistic Achievement," *African Arts* 18 (1985), pp. 54–59; "Cognitive and Optical Illusions in San Rock Art Research," *Current Anthropology* 27:2 (1986), pp. 171–78; "South-

ern Africa's Place in the Archaeology of Human Understanding," *South African Journal of Science* 85:1 (1989), pp. 47–52; and with T. A. Dowson, "The Signs of All Times: Entopic Phenomena in Upper Paleolithic Art," *Current Anthropology* 29 (1988), pp. 201–45.

6. See, for example, Richard Katz, *Boiling Energy: Community Healing among the Kalahari Kung* (Cambridge and London: Harvard University Press, 1982), and Richard Lee, "The Sociology of !Kung Bushman Trance Performance," in *Trance and Possession States*, R. Prince, ed. (Montreal: R. M. Bucke Memorial Society, 1968).

7. R. K. Siegel, "Hallucinations," *Scientific American* 237 (1977), pp. 132–40; R. K. Siegel and L. J. West, eds., *Hallucinations, Behavior, Experience and Theory* (New York: John Wiley, 1975); and H. Kluver, *Mescal and the Mechanisms of Hallucinations* (University of Chicago Press, 1966).

8. Joan Halifax, *Shaman: The Wounded Healer* (New York: Crossroad Books, 1982), p. 69.

9. Sandra Ingerman has since become a powerful shaman and medicine woman and is the author of *Soul Retrieval: Mending the Fragmented Self* (Harper San Francisco, 1991) and *Welcome Home: Following Your Soul's Journey Home* (Harper San Francisco, 1994).

10. David Lewis-Williams, "Seeing and Construing: A Neurological Constant in San Rock Art," paper given at a conference in honor of J. Desmond Clark, Berkeley, CA, 1986.

Chapter 9

1. See P. D. Ward, *The End of Evolution: On Mass Extinctions and the Preservation of Biodiversity* (New York: Bantam Books, 1994).

2. Tenth International Conference on AIDS, Yokohama, Japan, August 1994.

Chapter 11

1. See, for example, I. P. Couliano, *Out of This World: Otherworldly Journeys from Gilgamesh to Albert Einstein* (Boston and London: Shambala Press, 1991).

2. See William Anderson, *Green Man: Archetype of Our Oneness with the Earth* (San Francisco and London: HarperCollins, 1990).

3. Martha Beckwith, *Hawaiian Mythology* (Honolulu: University of Hawaii Press, 1940, 1985); David Kaonohiokala Bray, *The Kahuna Religion of Hawaii*, 2nd ed. (Kailua-Kona, HI: David M. Bray and Marian E. Charlton, 1987); Serge Kahili King, *Kahuna Healing* (Wheaton, IL: Quest Books, Theosophical Publishing House, 1983); Serge Kahili King, *Mastering Your Hidden Self: A Guide to the Huna Way* (Wheaton, IL: Quest Books, Theosophical Publishing House, 1985);

Serge Kahili King, *Urban Shaman* (New York: Simon and Schuster, 1990); Max Freedom Long, *The Huna Code in Religions* (Los Angeles: DeVorss, 1965); and L. R. McBride, *The Kahuna: Versatile Mystics of Old Hawaii* (Hilo, HI: Petroglyph Press, n.d.).

4. Witter Bynner, *The Way of Life According to Lao Tzu* (New York: Perigee Books, 1980).

5. Matthew Fox, *Meditations with Meister Eckhart* (Santa Fe, NM: Bear and Co., 1983).

Chapter 12

1. Nainoa uses the same term *Io* for both the universal void and for the hawk. I do not know why.

2. The fauna of Nainoa's time exhibits a mix of tropical New World and Old World animals. The New World forms are typical of those found in Central and South America today: iguanas, rattlesnakes, anacondas, bushmasters, boas, crocodiles, capybaras, agoutis, tapirs, peccaries, jaguars, marmosets and various cebid monkeys, parrots, harpy eagles, and so forth. The Old World elements include species from Asia, for example: elephants, tigers, sunbears, orangutans, gibbons, several macaques, blackbuck, chital, Burmese pythons, hornbills, and several parrot species. African elements seen (literally or through Nainoa's memories) include: lions, chimpanzees, gorillas, baboons and colobus monkeys, several guenons, possibly duikers, warthogs, gazelles, rock pythons, ball pythons, monitor lizards, and various parrots and other birds.

   I have given this curious faunal assemblage much thought and have concluded that these forms could be descended from animals released from zoos, circuses, and private collections when civilization collapsed.

Chapter 13

1. Ibid., Harner, 1990.

2. Charles Tart, *States of Consciousness* (El Cerrito, CA: Psychological Processes, 1983).

3. This shaman's costume is illustrated in William W. Fitzhugh and Aron Crowell, *Crossroads of Continents: Cultures of Siberia and Alaska* (Washington, DC: Smithsonian Institution Press, 1988), pp. 241 and 297. The embroidered crosses on the knees of this costume and their identification as birds are interesting when considered with relation to the recently discovered body of the Bronze Age "ice man" found frozen high in the Alps in the summer of 1991. This five-thousand-year-old individual sported crosses tattooed on his knees and a small rectangular grid on his back.

4. The small incised stone from Tata is illustrated in Bernard G. Campbell, *Humankind Emerging*, 5th ed. (Boston: Scott, Foresman and Co., 1988), p. 417. The same site also yielded a piece of ivory that was trimmed into an oval plaque, polished smooth, and stained with red ocher.

Chapter 15

1. This possibility seems to have been the case. I returned to California in 1989, to teach anthropology at a branch of the University of California for a year. During the late summer of 1989, I drove alone from southern California up to the Bay Area to do some work at UC–Berkeley's Laboratory for Human Evolutionary Studies. Nainoa's visit could very well have taken place during that drive. The freeway from which Nainoa saw so much collapsed during the earthquake that occurred in the fall of 1989 and has since been torn down. If Nainoa did make contact with my conscious awareness during that long all-day drive, I do not recall being aware of his presence.

2. For more information, see Serge Kahili King, *Kahuna Healing* (Wheaton, IL: Quest Books, Theosophical Publishing House, 1983).

Chapter 18

1. I do not have the gift of perfect recall of dialogue. Upon emerging from these visionary experiences, I always made notes as soon as possible and attempted to write down as many Ennu words as I could remember phonetically for later analysis. Upon my return to California, I passed through Berkeley and obtained an Eskimo dictionary through the kindness of one of my former professors. This document, Lucien Schneider's *Dictionnaire Alphabetico-syllabique du Langage Esquimau de L'Ungava* (1966) published by Les Presses de L'Université Laval, proved to be of help in deciphering some of the words, but most were not contained in that volume. Perhaps I misspelled or misheard (or misremembered) them. Additional assistance was provided by Schneider's companion volume, *Dictionnaire Français-Esquimau du Parler de L'Ungava* (1970).

Chapter 19

1. In the interval since the 1988 meetings, a new branch of the American Anthropological Association has come into being—the Society for the Anthropology of Consciousness.

Chapter 21

1. R. Aitken, *The Mind of Clover: Essays in Zen Buddhist Ethics* (San Francisco: North Point Press, 1984) and *Taking the Path of Zen* (San Francisco: North Point Press, 1982). See also Shunryu Suzuki, *Zen Mind, Beginner's Mind: Informal Talks on Zen Practice* (New York and Tokyo: Weatherhill Books, 1970).

Acknowledgments

MANY OF MY TEACHERS AND STUDENTS, family members and friends, contributed knowingly and unknowingly to this book. Included in this esteemed gathering are Robert Aitken Rōshi, Anne Amoral, Nelita Anderson, Francisco Arce, Jeanne Blackstone, Jeanne and Gus Bundy, Carroll and Jack Gardner, Michael Harner, Sandra Ingerman, Serge King, Tina Nappe, Carolyn Lee Precourt, Don and Molly Toral, Bill Tsuji, Chris Wesselman, Ron Young, and Marga Zack. A series of fortuitous connections through the Sacramento branch of the Institute of Noetic Sciences—Jill Kuykendall, Carolyn and Bob Blackstone, Sue Anne Foster, and Marilyn Starr—brought the manuscript to the attention of my literary agent, Candice Fuhrman. Homage and gratitude are also offered to Leslie Meredith, executive editor, and Brian Tart, assistant editor, at Bantam Books. . . .

To all of them—and to Nainoa, Kenojelak, and William—

E ho'omaikai keia po'e makamaka—a me ke aloha pumehana.

Blessings on this gathering of friends—with warmhearted affection.

About the Author

Dr. Hank Wesselman is a professional anthropologist who has conducted expeditionary fieldwork throughout the world independently and with an international group of scientists. He has taught courses in anthropology for the University of California at San Diego and the University of Hawaii at Hilo. He and his family divide their time between their farm in Hawai'i and northern California, where he currently teaches anthropology at American River College and Sierra College.

SHAMANIC TRAINING WORKSHOPS

Information and schedules of training workshops in classic shamanism and shamanic healing with Dr. Michael Harner, Sandra Ingerman, and their associates are available from:

The Foundation for Shamanic Studies
P.O. Box 1939
Mill Valley, California 94942
Telephone: (415) 380-8282
Fax: (415) 380-8416

For information and schedules of workshops in Hawaiian Huna shamanism with Dr. Serge King and his associates, please contact:

Aloha International
P.O. Box 665
Kilauea, Hawai'i 96754
Telephone: (808) 828-0302

Interest in Dr. Wesselman's presentations and experiential workshops can be directed to:

Dr. Hank Wesselman
P.O. Box 549
Fair Oaks, California 95628